THE BUSINESS BOOK THAT KNOWS HOW
BUSINESSES REALLY WORK, AND HOW
YOURS CAN TAKE FLIGHT TODAY.

FLIGHT OF
THE BUFFALO

"These are crazy times in the world's marketplace. They call for bold
efforts on the part of business and political leaders. No business leader
has been more bold, and few have been more successful,
than Ralph Stayer."
—Tom Peters, bestselling coauthor of *In Search of Excellence* and
Thriving on Chaos

"A book that has the potential to change American business and how it
perceives leadership."
— *Business Life*

"Extraordinarily articulate...an excellent job of offering specific suggestions about how management can better integrate its overall responsibilities with a more precise focus on the aspirations of colleagues and
the desires of customers. This book should help us all flap our wings!"
—Robert Crandall, chairman of American Airlines

"A hell of a book! Lots of great ideas, information, and examples
that will turn managers into leaders."
—Robert J. Kriegel, Ph.D., author of *If It Ain't Broke...Break It!*

"Whether you run a company or work for one, you'll find FLIGHT OF
THE BUFFALO a valuable addition to your business library."
— *West Coast Review of Books*

"The best of the new generation of proactive business books that
effectively teaches by example and empowers the reader to achieve
excellence in any organization."
—Lester Korn, chairman emeritus, Korn-Ferry International

"A masterful synthesis...compelling...the prescriptions are appropriate
to the times and trends, and they are practical."
—*Business Book Review*

JAMES A. BELASCO is the author of the bestselling *Teaching the Elephant to Dance: Empowering Change in Your Organization* and a professor of management at San Diego State University. He has consulted and done research with such organizations as IBM, AT&T, Royal Dutch Shell, Ralston Purina, and Merck.

RALPH C. STAYER is the former CEO of Johnsonville Foods, where his courageous, pioneering innovations made it one of the most progressive and successful employee-run companies in the country—and made Stayer the hero of Tom Peters's management video, *The Leadership Alliance*. Today, Stayer consults with such organizations as AT&T, Frito-Lay, BMW, and McDonnell Douglas.

FLIGHT OF THE BUFFALO

SOARING TO EXCELLENCE, LEARNING TO LET EMPLOYEES LEAD

JAMES A. BELASCO & RALPH C. STAYER

A DOVE BOOK

WARNER BOOKS

A Time Warner Company

Warner Books, Inc., 1271 Avenue of the Americas,
New York, NY 10020

 A Time Warner Company

Printed in the United States of America
First Trade Printing: August 1994
10 9 8 7 6 5 4 3 2

Originally published in hardcover by Warner Books.

Library of Congress Cataloging-in-Publication Data
Belasco, James A.
   Flight of the buffalo : soaring to excellence, learning to let employees
lead / James A. Belasco, Ralph C. Stayer.
    p. cm.
   ISBN 0-446-67008-1
   1. Leadership. 2. Managment—Employee participation. I. Title.
HD57.7.B447 1993
658.4'092—dc20   92-50527
                                                      CIP

Book design by Giorgetta Bell McRee
Cover design by Bernadette Anthony

CONTENTS

ACKNOWLEDGMENTS

I am blessed with the many great teachers who graced the classroom of my life. They taught what they could, learned what they needed, and enriched us both in the exchange.

There is first and foremost my wife, Candy, from whom I've learned the invaluable lesson of *caring*. She taught me the truth in the statement, "They don't care how much you know, until they know how much you care about them." In addition, she invested her considerable intellect and wordsmithing ability in converting some of my turgid prose into a readable format. I am blessed to have her as my life partner/best friend in family and personal matters as well as my trusted and valued colleague in business and consulting matters.

Then there is Meredith Kunsa, the director of my consulting office from whom I've learned the lesson of *partnership* and *support*. I could not do what I do without her doing what she does, so very well. Everywhere I go I receive grateful acknowledgments like, "Meredith is the best person to work with. She's terrific." I usually smile and say, "I know." Meredith is a world-class person.

My academic colleagues at San Diego State University taught me the lesson of *discipline*. They continuously encourage me to use rigorous academic tools to enhance the learning for myself and my students. I am blessed with their willingness to find ways where together we can build a very fine institution.

Peggy Covert is a marvel. She constantly teaches me about *entrepreneurialism*. As the Director of Professional Development Activities for San Diego State University, she creatively looks for ways to bring new and valuable educational experiences to the San Diego business community. We all learn because of her efforts.

Michael Viner taught me the value of *quiet creativity*. Michael is a genius in creating innovative ways to accomplish what needs to be done. More important, Michael does his inventing calmly and quietly. While I am still spewing anxiety into the air about "What can we do?" he has invented a great new solution. If only I could learn his secret for calmness under pressure.

Ann Sturgis taught me the important lesson of *gentleness*. She used her genteel southern-lady approach to smooth out my sharp edges, and her substantial editorial talents to bring the manuscript into the literary mainstream. I learned from her that how you say things is often as important as what you say.

From the many people with whom I've worked in my consulting and teaching I have learned different things in different ways, but most of all I've learned the value of *diversity*. Salads are more interesting and healthful than melting pots.

I am blessed with the employees/partners with whom I work, from whom I've learned the lesson of *focus*. Their urging has helped me focus on those few things I do best, and then to empower others to do what they do best. Together we are saving the planet—and helping each other continually learn.

I learned the value of *commitment* from my children: Michael, Leslie, Hugh, Marianne, Laura, Melissa, David, and my grandchildren: Eric, Michael, Scooter, Brandon, Dustin, Joshua, Mason, Candy—and especially Shaun. Business situations come and go, but the moral imperative/commitment to family is forever.

With all my heart I wish my parents could be here to share this with me. The strong foundation they gave me in *social equity* indelibly shaped my view of right and wrong, and my sense of personal responsibility. Wherever they are, they must know that they were my first and most powerful teachers.

It's been an incredible journey for me—and, as the Carpenters sang, "It's only just begun." I stand in awe of not what has been, but of what is yet to be: of not what I have learned, but of all that there is yet for me to learn. The insights shared in these pages are the direct result of the learnings from my great teachers. The errors are the products of the hubris and ignorance of the writer.

—JAMES A. BELASCO

If life is learning, then teachers are the key to living. I would like to acknowledge a few of the teachers who have unlocked so many doors for me.

My wife, Cathy, who taught me early in my career to ask myself, "Why does it have to be like this?" She has always been willing to question and challenge my "sacred cows." Her understanding of what is important in life has kept me from missing what is most important in my life—our family and friends.

My children, Michael, Ralph, Laura, and Patrick, who have taught me to accept people for what they are. Their ability to love me despite my faults and mistakes has made it much easier for me to work with others.

My parents, Ralph and Alice Stayer, who taught me that I was responsible for my own life and then allowed me to practice that philosophy. They actually allowed me to make important decisions in their business shortly out of college and then held me accountable for them. Their example provided the road map for my journey. Their trust in me taught me to trust others.

My father-in-law, F. K. Bemis, who I wish was here to share this with. He taught me that business has a purpose beyond profit and life has a purpose beyond business.

Elaine Crawford, my colleague at Leadership Dynamics, who makes me look far more organized than I really am. She has taught me what dedication to learning how to become a great performer looks like. I continually receive compliments about Elaine from the people she works with. People say, "Elaine lives what you talk about."

Professor Lee Thayer, who taught me how to get started on my leadership journey. I wasn't ready for him until I had admitted to myself that I was the problem. Lee helped me understand just how big of a problem I was—and what I needed to do about it.

Russ Wiverstad, Bob Salzwedel, Mike Roller, and all the members of Johnsonville. They took the time and personal effort to teach me to become a better leader and coach. Much of what others give me credit for was really their doing. Their willingness to accept on faith that there is a better way made our journey possible.

My sister, Launa, is a deep well of empathy that all who know her draw from. She taught me that you can't help people if you don't care for them first. Much of my ability to understand people and learn from them came from her.

My friend Mike Muth, who has taught me about commitment. He gives definition to the word. Whenever it counts, whatever it takes, he is always there. With him as an example, how could anyone do less?

All the people I have worked with in consulting. The constant exposure to so many people more talented than I has taught me how little I know. Whatever I have been able to contribute to them is far more a consequence of their ability than mine. Slowly, and very painfully, I am learning humility from them.

Tom Peters, who reinforced my faith in people. His belief that people aspire to greatness and his tireless search for kindred spirits led him to my door. The example of continuous learning that he lives reminds me that my journey has only begun.

Ken Blanchard, who taught me to concentrate on making the pie bigger not on how to get the biggest slice. His willingness to share his talents and time to help others is an inspiration to everyone who knows him.

And finally, my partner Jim, from whom I have learned a new definition of integrity, discipline, and excellence. He is to teaching, consulting, writing, and business what Michael Jordan is to basketball. Jim plays a different game than the rest of us.

My sincere thanks to all of you and everyone else who there wasn't space here to mention. Without you none of this would have been possible. The value of one's life can only be measured by what it has meant to others. Thank you for giving me so much.

—Ralph C. Stayer

INTRODUCTION

HOW "WE" BECAME "I"

The Blending of Theory and Practice

This book is the product of a unique collaboration. It is written by two authors, reporting their personal leadership experiences. It's about how I (Jim) learned and how I (Ralph) learned, and how that learning led to significant changes in our own leadership style. Change and learning is a personal experience. It happens in the first person. That is one reason why we wrote this book as "I." This book is also written in the first person by two authors, speaking with one voice because we think and act as one. This introduction is about how "we" became "I."

This book is also about the coming together of theory and practice. From two different starting points, each of us traveled parallel paths: Jim from the university and consulting arenas and Ralph from the sausage factory floor. We each brought different talents to the table and blended them together to produce this unique book.

Here's the journey each of us has traveled to come to this point.

Jim Belasco's Journey

Working together is tough for me. For thirty of the forty years I've been in business I've done it My Way. I've always known how to do it best—whether it was teach in a classroom, consult with an executive, or run a company. While I was never so overtly blatant, in my mind at least it was "my way or the highway." That is, until I met Ralph Stayer.

A little background first: Business is in my blood. I've been in businesses for approximately forty years. These businesses included a commission bakery, a self-service dry-cleaning "village," house moving, residential construction, trailer manufacturing, private education, laboratory instrument manufacturing, a specialty chemical business, and a software and services business. In most of these businesses I was the founder, owner, and manager. The businesses ranged in size from more than $500 million to a few hundred thousand.

Judged by the typical financial criteria, I was successful in all of these businesses. After I learned how to be a different kind of leader, however, several of these businesses were big successes. For instance, using my new employee empowerment leadership paradigm, I grew a commodity specialty chemical business twenty times in seven years, with the highest margins and average employee earnings in the industry. Using a similar leadership system, I grew a software and services business into the largest most profitable company in its market niche.

Of course, I worked all of these businesses alone.

Business was a mystery. I spent a whole lifetime working in business, but until recently couldn't quite figure out how business basics work— or how to make them work for me.

I worked hard, and took my business responsibilities seriously, and worried a lot about why I often didn't get joy out of what I did. I devoted long hours to business—because I thought I had to in order to succeed—and then wondered why I was too tired to enjoy the fruits of my success. I believed that learning was the key to my success, but I couldn't figure out what I needed to learn or how to best learn it.

I learned about profits and Dow Jones averages, but didn't understand what the "bottom line" of business really was. I learned from my studies how to read financial statements, but not how to run a profitable business.

I worked for bosses—and later became one—but never understood what bosses really did, or how to do it better. I sold products, services, and—mostly—myself, but didn't understand what customers really bought, or why or how to get them to buy more at a better price.

I learned that it's possible to put an entire library on a single chip no bigger than your thumbnail, but not why people behaved the way they did in my organization. I watched people travel to the moon but couldn't figure out how to get others to do what I really wanted them to do.

I worked hard to learn the "secrets of success in business." I took courses, attended seminars, read books, and accumulated degrees. Yet I was hurt and surprised when raw-material prices rose, which sliced my margins, people didn't do what they promised to do, and someone else got the job, the order, or the respect I really wanted (and felt I deserved!). For most of the past forty years business was a mystery to me.

Some more background: I can't get the chalk off my sleeve. I've been a college professor for thirty years, first at Cornell University, then at the State University of New York at Buffalo, and for the past twenty years at San Diego State University. My dad was a high school teacher whose advanced degree work was interrupted by the Depression. I went back to get my Ph.D. and finish what he had started. I originally intended to return to the business world (I was on leave from Sylvania at the time), but, the chalk got on my sleeve and I just couldn't get it off.

I love teaching. Nothing turns me on more than standing in the classroom in the middle of a spirited discussion. I love challenging people to think; to examine new ideas; to question "the way things are."

I love doing research. It gives me the opportunity to ask questions and seek new answers. My academic training gives me disciplined tools to ask the questions and search systematically for the answers. Besides, at least part of my drive to research is driven by my need to unravel the mystery of business.

In some ways I'm a typical academic. I'm committed to questioning current "truths." I'm committed to finding new answers. I'm committed to educating people to use whatever I discover to improve their performance. So I love to write, even though it's hard for me, as writing gives me the opportunity to learn and teach. My many research articles and academic books are some of the products of my previous educational efforts.

In some other ways I'm a very atypical academic. I work to practice what I teach, and help others practice it as well. I test my theories in the crucible of real-time experience. My practice orientation is different from that of some of my colleagues.

Even more background: When you teach, speak, and write, as I do, it isn't long before someone comes up and asks you to help him or her do what you've suggested. That happened early in my career. My first consulting assignment was to write job procedures for the owners of a twist drill manufacturing plant. That led to representing the owners in contract negotiations with the Teamsters union. All this thirty-three years ago at the tender age of twenty-three!

Since then I've sat at the right hand of the leaders of such organizations as AT&T, IBM, McDonnell Douglas, Heineken Beer, Royal Dutch Shell, Kellogg's, Ralston Purina, City of San Diego, Daughters of Charity National Health Care Systems, Fokker Aircraft (Holland), Eli Lilly, Royal Dutch Government, San Diego Gas and Electric, Teledyne Ryan, and the Commonwealth of Independent States. I've worked with more than two hundred clients, evolving the performance philosophy and practice you'll read about in this book.

There were many big successes. In a large international computer organization, I helped the country managers and their small to midsize business partners improve the partners' business performance. The three countries that implemented my program consistently exceeded company growth and profitability levels. I worked with the CEO of a large international beverage company where we improved quality levels 72 percent in two years and raised profit margins 32 percent. I worked with the CEO of a large international service organization to instill a quality and service mentality throughout the 13,000-person work force. The organization was chosen by customers as the "Best in Class" within two years.

Consulting is fun. It's challenging. But most important of all, it's educational. I take what I learn in my consulting and weave it into my classroom activities. I take the best of what I learn working with my clients and teach it to the employee-partners in my business. It works the other way also. I take the best of what I learn in my business and in my research and teach it to my clients. Consulting is primarily an educational experience for both my clients and myself.

As a *professor* I studied what worked and didn't work. As *owner* and manager of my own businesses, I wrestled with what it took to succeed. And as a *consultant* I coached others to succeed as well. All of this I did on my own, until a shift in my journey twelve years ago, when I heard a story from the speakers' platform about a 108-year-old man who, having found the new love of his life, had to get married. That story caused me to think about why some organizations consistently perform well, while most shine for a brief time and then sink into mediocrity. In turn, that thinking led to a major research project, the fruits of which were published in my best-selling book, *Teaching the Elephant to Dance: Empowering Change in Your Organization*, which presented a simple five-step process for implementing major organizational change.

More important than the research and the subsequent book, the story triggered thinking about my own leadership style and behavior. That thinking led to several significant insights into what it takes to successfully lead an organization. I discovered that I as the leader had to change *first*, before I could get anyone else to change. In most situations, my mental picture of desirable leadership behavior often was the biggest obstacle to my company's success. Only when I learned to examine—and change—my own leadership picture did I really start learning how to be successful. This book reports my insights and struggles as I sought to convert from a traditional leader to letting my employees lead.

Throughout the early years I felt very much alone in my journey. Clients often looked at me with puzzled expressions, like I was talking a foreign language. Students assiduously took notes but had difficulty restating my propositions in words other than my own. "Oh well. That's the way it's supposed to be," I told myself. After all, teaching, researching, and consulting are solitary tasks; so is running a company.

The vice-president of human resources for one of my clients suggested that I talk to another of his consultants, a gentleman named Ralph Stayer. Ralph was the president of Johnsonville Foods and had been featured in a recent Tom Peters video. The vice-president also sent along a package of information about Ralph. I put the package on the shelf, finally taking it with me to read on an overseas trip after several calls from the vice-president asking for my reactions to the material. I was only marginally interested. My academic cynicism warned me, "What could a sausage maker know?"

But Ralph's material intrigued me. Ralph was doing some very innovative things. Many of his practices closely paralleled what I taught in my classes, advised my clients, and applied in my own business. I called him from England as soon as I got off the plane. After an hour's conversation, I was convinced that we had a great deal in common. We agreed to meet in a couple of weeks in Long Beach along with our common sponsor, the VP of HR.

I found a soulmate at that Long Beach meeting. Our two paths were amazingly parallel. We were both lone wolves. We struggled with many of the same issues. In another part of the world, far removed from sunny Southern California, Ralph Stayer was busy applying much of what I'd been talking and writing about for years. His was the case study to prove my theory.

But it's a long distance from being on a parallel path and being able to travel the same path together. Eagles don't flock. Lone wolves don't often run together.

After several additional meetings, we decided to work together on a consulting project. One project led to another, which led to another, which led to still others. We worked well together, complementing each other's strengths. Ralph was creative. I was systematic. Ralph could more easily use words to paint a picture. I could more easily write readable prose. Ralph had the practical examples. I had the conceptual framework into which we could fit those examples.

The working-together partnership blossomed. We grew into personal friends. We both had addicted sons, and agonized over how to handle them. I vividly recall walking with Ralph in the dunes in Holland talking about our common pain, wrestling with the question "Can you really fire a family member?" (The answer is in the book.)

Working together was not without its costs. Each of us lost consulting work because of the other. I because my potential client felt that Johnsonville might be competitive. Ralph because his potential client couldn't see a college professor adding any value. Working together also meant that both of us had to stop and think, "How will the other person react to this?" Partnerships require advance thought about the impact of any action on the other person. That's difficult, particularly if you guess wrong.

But working together provided me with a great learning opportunity. Ralph is a great teacher. He is also a great learner. His dedication to learning is a source of personal inspiration.

Because of the great benefits, I wanted very much to build a joint business. So we traveled together, consulted together, and gave seminars together. Our business is very successful today. I keep on learning. I keep on growing. Ralph is my close friend, my compatriot, my consultant, my partner, and my soulmate. We think, speak, and act as one.

Ralph Stayer's Journey

I have always been a dreamer. One of my dreams was to be a great success in business. Every success I achieved in business changed the size of the playing field, but it never changed the dream. I don't believe that it ever will. The success I've enjoyed is gratifying, but, as I look back, it is nothing compared to what it could have been if not for one thing.

I was always a loner. I had close friends in my personal life but never in business. I was able to give advice to my friends but was never able to take it. I always knew better. I tried to work with others on several businesses but it never worked. I either took control and did it my way or left if I couldn't get control. For years I never got involved in anything I couldn't control. Then I met Jim Belasco.

This introduction is the story of two lone wolves who learned how to form a partnership based on the same principles we espouse in this book—the ability to add value to each other. Jim has already told you his story. This is mine.

I always wanted to be in business, specifically my parents' business. I grew up in Johnsonville, Wisconsin—population sixty-five. My parents owned several retail stores in neighboring cities and a small sausage factory in Johnsonville that supplied those stores. I lived next to the factory and spent a lot of time there while growing up. I worked there every summer from the time I was fourteen through college. Joining my parents in business was the only career I ever considered.

The business was a retail operation when I joined it in 1965. After several years, it became apparent that we couldn't grow in that business. I decided to focus on running the factory and wholesaling to other retailers. This was the beginning of Johnsonville Foods.

Through the seventies and eighties, Johnsonville grew from a local manufacturer of sausages to a food company with national distribution. Most of this growth was fueled by the same new leadership principles that Jim learned to use in his businesses. They form the subject matter for this book. Just like Jim, I had to relearn most of what I believed to be true about business in order to lead my company. My journey is described throughout this book, so I won't elaborate here.

My journey is about learning. Actually, it's about learning how to learn. This is a skill I didn't acquire in school. I was never a very good student. I didn't see the importance of getting good grades. I learned enough to get into Notre Dame and graduate (another childhood dream), but I certainly didn't set the academic world on fire. I just didn't see the importance.

It was the same in business. I learned what I had to in order to succeed, but I never thought that learning was all that important. My willingness to do whatever it takes to succeed is what fueled Johnsonville's growth. In 1980 I hit the wall. I realized that if I kept doing what I had always done, I was going to keep getting what I was getting. And I didn't like what I was getting. I would never achieve my dream. I could see the rest of my business life being a never-ending stream of crises, problems, and dropped balls. We could keep growing and have decent profits, but it wasn't the success I was looking for.

I had to change to realize my dream. Understanding that things weren't working was the easy part. The hard part was understanding that I was the problem. It was much easier to blame others, the industry, fate—anything but me. Coming to grips with this was a very emotional journey. Seeing myself as the problem required stripping away the veneer of my excuses and rationalizations and getting down to the very core of my existence.

At first, it was a painful process, but I am convinced it was the prerequisite for my learning how to be an effective leader. This kind of learning is also very personal. There are no cookbooks. That is why we wrote this book in the first person. This book isn't about *Them*. It is about me, it is about Jim, and it is about you.

This learning helped me lead Johnsonville into national prominence in the 1980s. Please don't think that I am taking credit for Johnsonville's success in the last ten years. The people at Johnsonville did that—but it wouldn't have been possible if I hadn't changed.

I had to learn how to listen and really hear.

I had to learn to work with others and trust them.

I had to learn to appreciate their contributions as much as or more than my own.

I had to learn the value of learning and how to systematically accomplish it.

Without this learning, Jim and I would never have become partners. At that first meeting, I would have smiled, talked to Jim, told him what I thought he ought to do, and gone my separate way.

My dream of business success then expanded in the mid-eighties. As I was learning a new way of doing business at Johnsonville, I created a new picture of my future—getting good enough at leadership to be able to coach leaders in other companies. I really enjoyed working with others at Johnsonville and helping them learn. It became far more rewarding for me than managing the business day-to-day. I wanted to work with leaders of large companies where the problems were complex. The odds, however, were not in my favor. For a sausage maker from a small town in Wisconsin, it just didn't seem possible.

My friend Tom Peters changed all that when his book, *Thriving on Chaos*, and his television special, *The Leadership Alliance*, brought Johnsonville Sausage to national prominence. People started calling for information. This gave me the opportunity to pursue a consulting career—as an independent, of course.

I have consulted with many companies since then in fields that range from small flower-growing companies to high-tech multibillion-dollar multinational companies. I've worked with military and government leaders. The experience has been invaluable. Like Jim, I translate the lessons learned in my consulting into more effective ways of doing business in my own company.

More important, consulting gave me the opportunity to meet Jim. Jim is a great businessman. He is a great teacher. He is also a vacuum cleaner. He sucks up learning like no one I have ever seen. My nickname for him is "Hoover." But much more than that, Jim is a soulmate. We traveled parallel paths to our first meeting. We each wrestled with the same issues.

We quickly became each other's sounding board. But talking together isn't enough. Learning comes from doing, not talking. Learning together comes from doing together. We knew we had to work together. Working together deepened and broadened the relationship. When we started working together, we were both on the same page of music, but we were singing harmony. We now hit the same note at the same time. Our clients can't tell whose voice is singing.

The "We" Becomes "I"

"When I close my eyes I can't tell which one of you is talking," one of our clients said recently. That comment underlines why we wrote this book in the first person "I," even though there are two authors. Each experience, insight, and learning happened to one of us, but a similar parallel experience also happened to the other. We've blended our different experiences together and produced a new synthesis. That's why "I" is the best representation of the author's perspective.

More of the words on the following pages are Jim's, the product no doubt of all those years of academic experience. More of the word pictures, like the buffalo and the geese, are Ralph's. All of the words, however, were discussed together first, drafted by one of us, and then revised—and revised—and revised again by both of us. Truly it is impossible to say where Ralph Stayer ends and Jim Belasco begins, both in our consulting and in this book.

Therefore, don't waste any effort trying to determine who did what. It isn't important if it was Jim or Ralph. What Jim or Ralph did isn't the point. What *you* do with what you read in the following pages is what counts. Take these personal experiences and put them to work for you. Let "I" be the dominant first-person voice in *your* book.

James A. Belasco

Ralph C. Stayer

PART I

OUR PERSONAL LEADERSHIP JOURNEY

CHAPTER 1

The Challenge of Leadership: Our Personal Journey

The Powerless President

The president shifted nervously in his big chair. His youngish face, belying his early fifties age, was creased with worry. His company was greatly admired and mentioned frequently in business magazines. His stock sold at healthy P/E multiples. With his Ivy League training, he was a leading spokesperson for American business. Yet, now his eloquence had deserted him.

He got up, strode to the window, and peered out at the bucolic setting. "Not on my watch," he said to the huge oak outside his window. "This can't happen on my watch." After an eternity of silent shuffling of feet and clasping and unclasping of hands, he whirled and faced me, steel flashing in his eyes. "I've got five years to retirement. What can I do to make these five years count?"

The challenge was daunting. The company, despite its favorable press, was failing badly. They had lost market share in every single phase of their business and were significantly late in several new product launches. Their cash cow was under attack by the Japanese. Despite their cash hoard and dominant market position, the company was in serious trouble. He saw with crystal clarity the potential danger if the business did not change radically now. The unthinkable could happen on his watch and he did not know what to do. Nothing in his previous experience or training had prepared him to deal with this situation.

This president's problem is all too familiar. Although he sat in the CEO's chair, he was powerless to accomplish the changes he knew had to be made. He saw clearly WHAT had to be done. The management mantra of the nineties was familiar: teamwork, better quality, improved service, faster time to market. He knew them well. He preached them to anyone who would listen. Yet, he was unable to produce any of these vital outcomes in his organization.

He had tried valiantly to effect changes. In the last six years he'd instituted programs designed to stimulate quality, customer service, and teamwork. He'd trimmed the organization, reorganized functional groups into product/customer focused units, and reduced the number of management layers. Yet, he continued to lose market share, competitors continued to beat him to the market, and he'd lost 50 percent of his market value. He just couldn't move his people to do what he knew had to be done.

I know how that president feels. I've sat in the same chair, felt my gut crawl, and felt like throwing chairs through windows in frustration. I know it is easy to talk about being different. It is a lot harder to be different. I also know many other presidents feel very much the same frustration and sense of helplessness.

All leaders face a challenge of leadership. The old models and paradigms no longer work. How leaders develop, and live a new model of leadership, is and will be the critical success factor for most every business. It is for mine.

The Old Leadership Paradigm: The Head Buffalo and the Herd

For a long time, I believed the old leadership paradigm that told me that my job was to plan, organize, command, coordinate, and control. I saw my organization functioning like a herd of buffalo. They looked

like the figure above. Buffalo are absolutely loyal followers of one leader. They do whatever the leader wants them to do, go wherever the leader wants them to go. In my company, I was head buffalo.

Originally, I liked that arrangement in my organization. After all, my brilliance built the organization. I wanted people to do exactly what I told them, to be loyal and committed. I loved being the center of power, and I believed that that was the leader's job.

I realized eventually that my organization didn't work as well as I'd like, because buffalo are loyal to one leader; they stand around and wait for the leader to show them what to do. When the leader isn't around, they wait for him to show up. That's why the early settlers could decimate the buffalo herds so easily by killing the lead buffalo. The rest of the herd stood around, waiting for their leader to lead them, and were slaughtered.

I found a lot of "waiting around" in my buffalo-like organization. Worse, people did only what I told them to do, nothing more, and then they "waited around" for my next set of instructions.

I also found it was hard work being the lead buffalo. Giving all the orders, doing all the "important" work took 12–14 hours a day. Meanwhile my company was getting slaughtered out there in the market place because I couldn't respond quickly enough to changes. All this frustrating work as the leader of the buffalo herd was growing old—and making me old before my time.

The New Leadership Paradigm: A Flock of Geese

Then one day I got it. What I really wanted in the organization was a group of responsible, interdependent workers, similar to a flock of geese, like in the figure above. I could see the geese flying in their "V" formation, the leadership changing frequently, with different geese taking the lead. I saw every goose being responsible for getting itself to wherever the gaggle was going, changing roles whenever necessary, alternating as a leader, a follower, or a scout. And when the task changed, the geese would be responsible for changing the structure of the group to accommodate, similar to the geese that fly in a "V" but land in waves. I could see each goose being a leader.

Then I saw clearly that the biggest obstacle to success was my picture of a loyal herd of buffalo waiting for me, the leader, to tell them what to do. I knew I had to change the pictures to become a different kind of leader, so everyone could become a leader.

Out with the Old, In with the New

Rather than the old head-buffalo leadership paradigm, I developed a new lead-goose leadership paradigm. Crafted in the crucible of real-time leadership experience, that paradigm is built around the following leadership principles:

- Leaders transfer ownership for work to those who execute the work.
- Leaders create the environment for ownership where each person wants to be responsible.
- Leaders coach the development of personal capabilities.
- Leaders learn fast themselves and encourage others also to learn quickly.

This book is about how I became a different kind of leader and many of the lessons I've learned on my journey. It's also about how I transformed every person in my company into a leader in his or her own situation.

It Isn't as Easy as It Looks: The Ved-up Herd

I'd like to tell you that I have achieved perfection: that my geese are off flying now, that every person is a fully functioning leader. Unfortunately, that's not true. While I've made great progress, there's still a long way to go. My own organization is successful. I help other leaders transform their buffalo into geese. With many false starts and stumbling through many bad decisions, I've traveled a rocky road to get where I am now. I am still learning my leadership lessons. So are my dependent buffalo. They are V-ed up as you can see in Figure 3, but they aren't flying yet.

Preview of Coming Attractions

What follows in the first chapter of Part One is a mid-course summary of the leadership journey. While every situation is different, I begin the book with this summary because I've learned the fundamental principle that every leadership journey is a personal, emotional one, like mine. Changing your leadership paradigm happens first in your gut.

Chapter 2 spells out the insight I realized early and return to often: "In most situations I am the problem." My mentalities, my pictures, my expectations, form the biggest obstacle to my company's success.

You'll notice that this book is written from a different perspective, and this second chapter spells out that difference. I used to see others as problems. They were the reason my business didn't perform as well as it should. They were the reason my plans never worked as well as I thought they would. My effectiveness as a manager and leader improved dramatically when I learned to see myself as the problem. I learned that when I see performance that is unsatisfactory, the first question to ask is "What is it that I did or didn't do that caused that to happen?" Understanding that I am the problem allowed me to learn how to become the solution. This became the fundamental perspective for my leadership journey and the foundation for everything in the book.

The third chapter lays out the problems I faced in coping with a world very different from that for which my academic and prior experience had prepared me. I was prepared to be the "leader," to lead the charge up the hill, as Teddy Roosevelt had done so many years ago; to rally the troops with stirring words, as Knute Rockne did with his halftime speeches to "win one for the Gipper"; and to lay out the brilliant strategies that would be extolled in the pages of *Fortune* and *BusinessWeek*. Those paradigms no longer worked when I showed up to be the leader. I was ill equipped to handle the realities of leadership in the last decade of the twentieth century. My difficulties in leading with an obsolete paradigm empowered me to see that I was the problem.

Part Two spells out the fundamental leadership principles I learned during my years of wrestling with the task of becoming a more effective leader in the age of intellectual capitalism. These principles became the framework for my journey into understanding and practicing a new paradigm of leadership.

The chapters that follow in Part Two will share the fundamental leadership principles:

- Transfer ownership.
- Create the environment for ownership where each person wants to be responsible.
- Coach the development of personal capabilities.
- Learn faster and encourage others to do the same.

How I learned these principles comprises the second part of the book. Use these principles to take charge of your leadership journey, rather than just letting it happen to you. You can be the skipper of your ship, rather than a storm-tossed victim. You can be the driver of this vehicle called life, rather than just a passenger.

The systematic method I developed for transforming buffalo into geese is the Leading the Journey (LTJ) leadership system. The following model shows the LTJ system. That system forms the framework for Parts Three, Four, Five, Six, and Seven, much as it formed the basis for my own leadership journey.

The journey is fun, and difficult. It is exciting, and tedious. It has moments of euphoria, and moments of deep despair. Perhaps my story will provide guideposts to make your journey a little easier. In this way everyone in your organization can become a leader.

You'll notice that there are persistent themes that appear over and over again throughout the book. These persistent themes sounded the clarion calls for me on my journey. They are the "red threads" that weave my story together. Again and again I came back to the following insights:

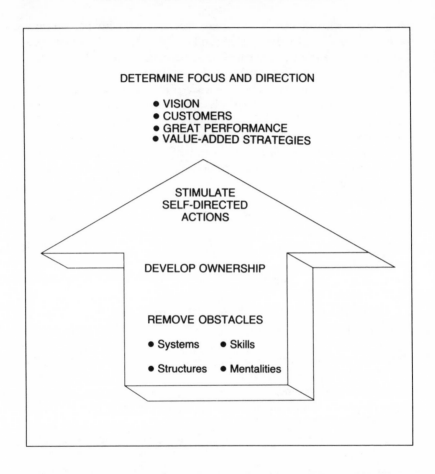

1. In most instances "I am the problem." My desire to be the head buffalo, my wanting to rescue people, my previous success, all got in the way of successfully handling the current situation. Nothing constructive happened until I recognized me as the obstacle and changed my behavior.
2. The customer is the boss, not the internal organizational boss. For too long I insisted that the person in the corner office had to be served first, with data, with deference, with swift response to requests. We didn't make the progress I knew we had to make until we started serving the customer first.
3. Think strategically. I used to begin with what we could be and

then manage forward. We struggled to make inches of progress and usually finished out of the money. It wasn't until I began with what we must be for customers and managed backward from that, that we won gold medals.

4. Practice the intellectual capitalism leadership style. Create the conditions where the intellectual capital holders assume responsibility for delighting their customers. Everyone must be a leader before there's effective leadership in the new organization.

5. Leading is learning. I languished until I realized that learning faster was the key to my survival. Maximizing everyone's learning is the key to my organization's success. My organization didn't soar until everyone became an avid learner.

Watch for these themes. They will reappear throughout the book. Let them become your guideposts as well.

If you're ready to begin the journey, so am I. It will be exciting. Welcome to the journey of the flying buffalo.

QUESTION:
What do I know that just isn't so?

LEADERSHIP SOLUTION:
Begin the journey now!

CHAPTER 2

Can the Head Buffalo Become the Lead Goose?

I've faced many difficult decisions in my business career—none more difficult than the one I faced in 1985, as reported in a Harvard Business School case, which began with the following words:

> . . . [he] hung up the phone and leaned back in his chair, deep in thought. One of Johnsonville's private label customers— Palmer Sausage—was considering increasing its purchases from Johnsonville by a huge amount . . . [he] wondered how he should react.

How I handled that decision showed how far I'd grown as a leader, and how much further I needed to grow.

Beginning in 1980, I completely recast my organization. In the next ten years, return on assets doubled, sales increased ninefold, and product and service quality levels significantly improved—all this in a mature, declining industry.

How? I embarked on my personal, emotional journey of changing my leadership behavior. I had loved being the head buffalo. Now, however, I needed to learn how to be a lead goose. Here's my story, told in my own words, written as I lived it. Then, in the *OBSERVATION* sections I reflect on lessons I've learned during my journey and broader leadership issues. If only I'd known then what I know now . . .

The Gap

First, some history: In the late 1970s, I was doing business in a traditional way. By conventional measures I was successful. Profits were above average for my industry. So was quality. We averaged 20 percent annual growth. The company was highly regarded.

The financial statements looked healthy. Yet I knew something was wrong, because I observed that my business was operating far below its potential. Every day I saw people being disinterested in their work. They just didn't care. They were careless. They made thoughtless mistakes. They dropped equipment, wasted time and materials, and didn't accept responsibility for much of what they did. They came to work, did what they were told, and went home. They just weren't committed.

> *OBSERVATION: Many leaders report similar perceptions. They see the huge gap between what they have now and what they know they must have if their business is to survive. They see clearly what needs to be done. They just don't know how to do it.*

I had been telling myself, "I can't expect them to be as committed to the company as I am. After all, I own the place. They don't." Many of my friends expressed a similar rationale. That answer didn't seem right, however. The knot in my stomach wouldn't go away. Neither would the voice in my head telling me, "There must be a better way."

Moreover, I was worried about competition. I headed a small regional producer. We were strong in Wisconsin, just making inroads into neighboring states, but we were small in comparison to several of our larger national competitors. These larger companies could "outmuscle" us virtually anytime. In any head-to-head competition they could outadvertise us, outprice us, and put us out of business.

In addition to the large national competitors, there were a host of local and regional producers who had the advantage of being small enough to provide superior service and quality to their own local markets. My company was too big to have the advantages of small companies and too small to have the advantages of big ones. I realized the business was vulnerable. If some competitor figured out how to close the huge gap between actual and potential performance before I did, my company could be history.

The Search for *the* Leadership Recipe

Beginning in the early 1980s, I searched for a recipe book on leadership. I wanted a book of instructions on how to lead people so that they cared about their jobs and their company.

> *OBSERVATION: The fruitlessness of my search for a leadership recipe was surprising. I discovered the awful truth about leadership—each person must write his or her own personal cookbook.*

I spent four years trying to get the people at my company to change. I had a team of consultants come in. After they left, I tried job descriptions; then "management by objectives." Next came new communications techniques, and then a forerunner of quality circles where I listened to problems and then tried to fix them. These meetings quickly turned into complaining sessions. Then I started changing managers, then compensation plans. You see the picture. If anything, the company's performance grew worse.

By 1982 I was very frustrated and considered selling the business. My business associates said, "Join the club. That's how life is. There isn't any work ethic anymore. People just don't care." I wasn't willing, however, to give up that easily. I continued pushing my managers and looking for The Answer.

I became an avid seminar attendant and reader. In one seminar, a professor turned on a light for me. He argued that performance was the key to organizational success. Management's job was to establish the conditions under which performance served both the company's and the individual's best interests. That made a lot of sense to me. I hired that professor to become my personal coach and sounding board.

> *OBSERVATION: Because I encounter many similarly searching executives in my seminar rooms, I know my story is not unusual.*

Others have come to a similar conclusion after many failed attempts to copy someone else's leadership recipe. Usually, this insight follows huge personal and human costs. An executive must be ready to hear the I-am-the-problem message in order to accept and make use of it.

I Needed a Guide to Make the Journey

The professor insisted that he wouldn't work with me unless I was willing to work with him. Specifically, he asked me whether I was willing to look at myself as the problem, instead of the other people in the company. Initially, this was very difficult for me to accept. After all of my previous frustrations, however, I was ready to consider anything. I agreed.

The professor gave several seminars for me and my management team. In addition, I called him several times a week to discuss specific issues. He helped me think through my new role. He coached me as I guided the senior management people to develop their new ways of thinking.

> *OBSERVATION: Without this outside help I probably would not have made the transition from head buffalo to lead goose. The day-to-day pressures of running the business continually distracted me from what I wanted to create. I needed someone whose specific job was to help me focus on learning my new leadership role. I needed a coach to continue reminding myself that I was the problem. It is all too easy to fall back into the "fix them" leadership mode because that message is reinforced in most readings and seminar presentations.*

I was learning to focus, but the knot in my stomach just wouldn't go away. The carelessness and disinterest I saw moved me to continue my search so I could fix it. I conducted an attitude survey. I was startled when the results showed that we had an employee motivation problem. Something was definitely wrong. I had a small entrepreneurial company with the potential to be above average. The company, however, was only average. We were performing no better than big impersonal companies like General Motors.

At first I didn't want to believe the survey. I looked for all kinds of excuses. The methodology must have been faulty. The questions were poorly worded. To admit that there was an employee motivation problem would mean it was up to me to do something. I had no idea of what to do.

> *OBSERVATION: It was easier to shrug off the mistakes and poor performance by saying, "That's how it is these days." What drove me crazy—and drives many other executives to intellectualize rather than actualize change—was the absence of a pat answer to fix the situation. I couldn't escape the unmistakable signs I saw. The carelessness and lack of commitment were too obvious to ignore. The buffalo, milling around, waiting for instructions, were too big to overlook.*

The "Fix Them" Mentality

"Why is there an employee motivation problem?" I asked myself at last. At this stage I was still blind to one of the biggest obstacles—me. Everything I had learned and done up to this point convinced me that if I didn't do it myself, it wouldn't get done right. I saw my leadership job to create the agenda, and then "motivate them" to carry it out. This became a self-fulfilling prophecy—the less I expected of my people, the less they delivered.

My major obstacle at this point was fear about my self-respect. I believed that most of my value as the leader of Johnsonville came from being a decision maker and problem solver: "the man in charge." I was afraid that I wouldn't have much to do without those aspects of my job. In spite of my belief, to move forward I had to accept on faith that there was far more rewarding and productive leadership work I could do once I freed up the time for it. I needed to learn to take pride in the collective results the company produced, not only in my singular accomplishments.

> *OBSERVATION: I see myself frequently in leaders with similar "fix them" attitudes. Leaders seek to fix problems—including people problems. Leaders do things to the organization, and the*

people in it. Much of their own self-worth comes from the actions they do to "fix" the organization.

The Realization: I Got What I Wanted, but I Need Something Different Now

One day it finally hit me: "I built this place. I set it up. If it isn't working right, it's my responsibility. I am the problem." As Pogo said, "I have seen the enemy, and he is me." I finally realized that my previous success as Johnsonville's leader was my biggest obstacle. The very leadership decisions that had brought me success sowed the seeds of my own failure. The way I designed the business, the way I acted, the organization structure I put in place, the business practices I used, were causing the effects that were now causing me to be unhappy. If I wanted to change the results, I would have to change the way I led the business.

> *OBSERVATION: My organization reflects my leadership behavior. My brilliant strategies, my innovative product ideas, my customer service mentalities, are all reflected in the organization's performance. So are my not-so-brilliant decisions and my "I am the boss so do as I say" attitude. My love for being head buffalo showed. My business reflects my leadership paradigm. Your business reflects yours, for better or for worse.*

I wanted a different outcome and made the decision to change. I wanted to create a new level of organizational performance. I believed I could order it to happen and it would.

From Authoritarianism to Abdication

With this new picture, I committed a grievous error. I reacted instinctively to my newfound learning and ordered my people to be different. I used my authoritarian style to abdicate. "From now on," I told my senior staff, "you're responsible to make your own decisions." From authoritarianism, I went to abdication. They hadn't asked for more responsibility; I forced it on them. They were good soldiers and worked hard to meet my new expectations, but they couldn't. I had trained them to expect me to solve their problems. I knew how to do their jobs because I had been making most of their decisions for them. Unfortunately, they didn't know their jobs nearly as well as *I* knew their jobs. I had developed their incapacity by expecting them to be incapable. They had met those expectations.

My vice-president of sales was a prime example. He was a close personal friend. He was dazed when I told him that he'd be responsible for all the sales decisions. He sincerely tried to make the same decisions I would have made. He knew that I liked my decisions better than his, so he spent a lot of time trying to decide what I would do in a situation.

I had trained him one way and now expected him to behave another way. He couldn't do it. Even though I worked with him extensively for over a year and a half, and hired personal consultants to work with him, I eventually had to replace him. I was devastated, for I had failed my friend.

> *OBSERVATION: I found that a new level of organizational performance is not a fast-food item to be delivered from room service in twenty minutes. In fact, you can't order it at all without running the risk of having it ignored by the people who have to make it work. Ordering the organization to perform differently is like standing in front of the buffalo herd and commanding them to fly. Now I know that I must empower people for the new level of performance—not order it. The best way to empower people is to ask: What am I doing or not doing, as a leader, that prevents them from assuming responsibility and performing at the new level?*

Emotional Short Circuits

All three top managers went eventually, unable to cope with the new reality I had forced upon them. In fact, everybody in the company short-circuited. Months of laborious work convinced me that what I was doing wasn't working. I couldn't just order people to be different.

They couldn't change their expectations of themselves, or of me, fast enough. The realization wrenched my gut.

> OBSERVATION: *In retrospect, I see clearly now that this over-load is all part of the journey to a new level of performance. Without it, different performance levels don't happen. Although I recognize the importance of the overload intellectually, it is difficult to live through emotionally.*

Retreat into Abstractions: The Vision

Initially, I responded to the emotional costs of change by retreating into abstractions. I met for over a year with my direct reports working on "the vision." After much struggle, we finally agreed upon four principal dimensions of the vision: job security, increasing compensation, rewarding jobs, and making everyone realize that their best interests are served by the success of the entire organization. We labored mightily and brought forth a mouse.

> OBSERVATION: *"Safe" discussions about the vision consume gobs of time and result in very little real difference. Intellectualizing about new performance levels doesn't produce them, but this phase may be an important "softening up" period, in which people hear the message "Things are going to be different around here." Key lesson: Don't stop with vision. Vision alone is no solution. Everything is execution.*

First Reactions Are Usually Wrong

My disastrous experience during the first years of the eighties helped me realize that my instinctive leadership reactions were wrong. I had learned a whole set of leadership behaviors and habits based upon one set of circumstances. Now that the circumstances were different, I had to be different. I began to work with all the people in our company to modify many of the systems and structures I had set in place. I also came to realize that my first reaction is usually wrong. It was too often a remnant of the old leadership paradigm.

> OBSERVATION: *"Instinctive" reactions, based on past learnings, can lead to disastrous current results. That which got me to where I am, and precipitates those "instinctive" reactions, will not get me to where I need to go. I had to learn to stop and ask, "What am I about to do that is probably wrong?"*

The Palmer Challenge—a New Learning Opportunity

By mid-1986 I was pleased with my progress. The people expected to take responsibility for their performance; they generally wanted to, and they generally did an excellent job. Return on assets was up significantly, as were margins and quality levels. Then Palmer Sausage came along and presented me with a golden opportunity, and a significant threat.

Palmer was a much larger sausage company which was consolidating plants. They offered to let us take over some of the production of a plant they were closing. This represented a huge increase in their current order. I was particularly pleased because Palmer had the reputation as the highest quality supplier in the field. The new philosophy was working.

The business was very attractive. It could be very profitable. It could also justify the costs of a new, more efficient plant. The upside was all extremely positive—if my company could do it well.

As Hamlet said, "Aye, there's the rub." To make our Palmer production work successfully, Johnsonville quickly would have to hire and train a large group of new people and teach current people new skills. They would need to keep the quality high on both the Palmer products and our own, working six and seven days a week for more than a year until the new plant could be ready. If Palmer canceled (which they could on thirty days' notice), Johnsonville would face a significant layoff and be saddled with new capacity we no longer needed. While it may not have been a "bet the company" decision, it was as close as I would like to come to one.

It was clear to me from what I had learned in becoming a different leader that the critical success factor in Palmer was the commitment of the people who make the sausage. They had to make it work. Therefore, they had to make this decision.

> *OBSERVATION: The current leadership paradigm stresses leaders making decisions and "motivating" employees to do the job. That paradigm robs leaders of effective power in their organization. By realizing that the people had to make the Palmer decision, I was able to transfer ownership of the actions to the people who needed to be responsible.*

My executives met with all the members in the plant and presented the problem to them. Almost immediately, the small groups met and discussed the decision. Two weeks later, the members decided almost unanimously to take the business. Left to traditional leadership paradigms, I would have wrestled with the Palmer decision myself and probably turned it down. The risks were just too great. The people, however, believing in themselves, rose to the challenge.

People Rise to the Challenge— When It Is *Their* Challenge

The results? Johnsonville beat their own projections. Learning occurred faster than anticipated. Quality actually rose throughout the plant, as well as for Palmer. The new plant came on stream in 1987. Palmer came back several times since then and asked Johnsonville to take on even more business.

> *OBSERVATION: Profoundly, Johnsonville people learned what they needed to do. They learned to be responsible for more of the strategic decisions at Johnsonville. They changed the career tracking system and set new team performance standards. Then they went to work on transforming themselves from buffalo into geese.*

The process is still going on. As you read this, teams are meeting at Johnsonville to discuss next year's capital budget, new product ideas, next week's recruitment plan, today's production schedule, and yesterday's quality, cost, and yield performance.

Success Is Always the Enemy

Success continues to be the greatest enemy. Johnsonville has made great strides: Sales, margins, quality, and productivity far exceed anything I could have imagined ten short years ago. At that time we had plateaued and competition had begun to gain on us. One of the people hit the mark when he said, "We've lost sight of our vision. We've been talking about *what we are* instead of talking about *what we want to become*."

That comment was as much about me as it was about Johnsonville. I had become comfortable with the new process. There hadn't been a knot in my stomach for months. I had stopped "pushing back the envelope." Johnsonville's performance was reflecting my performance. If the people weren't learning fast enough, that could only mean *I* wasn't learning fast enough.

> OBSERVATION: *It is all too easy to become focused on yesterday's success, rather than on today's challenge. The biggest obstacle to producing quality products in the future is winning the Baldrige Award this year.*

I have turned it around again, and am busy learning and growing as a leader again. I realize that I'll have to keep doing this forever, for being a leader requires continual learning.

QUESTION:
What am I doing or not doing as a leader that makes me the head buffalo instead of the lead goose?

LEADERSHIP SOLUTION:
See leadership as a personal, emotional journey. Understand it happens in your gut before it happens in your or anybody else's head.

CHAPTER 3

The Shocker:
"I Am the Problem"

Being the Lead Victim Is the Big Problem

I love being a victim. It's so easy. After all, why be responsible when I can blame someone else for all of my misfortune? I've often heard myself say, " 'They' won't let me do it. 'They' are the problem. If only 'They' would get out of the way, everything would be all right." I've also all too often heard other people in my company say the very same words.

I used to be a world-class victim. When I didn't get the order, I'd blame the "dumb customer" who couldn't see the benefits of my wonderful product. When someone didn't do what I wanted him/her to do, I'd blame the "dumb employee." I wondered why the world was inhabited by such "dumb people." I didn't realize that I was the creator of that "dumbness" in my company.

One day it happened. I discovered how my own victimitis created a whole company of underperforming "victims." I had a tough customer to please and we were behind on deliveries. The problem was a short shipment from a critical supplier. As usual in those days, I was right in the middle of the discussion. "Why haven't we leaned harder

35

on that dumb supplier?" I railed. "Why are we doing business with this jerk, anyway?" Later I found out that I had picked the supplier and stuck with him even though he was a poor performer. I thought we couldn't replace him. That's why, I rationalized, we had to put up with his late deliveries. Everyone else saw my willingness to tolerate the supplier's poor performance and didn't push him. Furthermore, the supplier believed he had a "friend at the top," and therefore he ignored everyone's demands. My willingness to play victim led everyone else to play victim and accept poor performance. Not only was my face red and my ego bruised, but, more important, it was the dawning of insight into how my willingness to play victim was encouraging others to use the supplier's nondelivery as an excuse for their own nonperformance. My victimitis attitude was the problem in my company.

Victimitis Is an Epidemic

I worked with the management of the premier company in its industry. They were very successful, particularly as a result of clever financial dealings. But then the market changed and they got saddled with a lot of inventory they couldn't sell. The interest costs drove profits down for the first time in a decade. The senior management said, "We were blindsided by the market. That's what caused our problems." What a great example of not taking personal responsibility. They were only responsible for being successful, not for failing.

The sad fact is that too many people see themselves as victims. In traditional organizations people aren't responsible for their own performance. The boss is responsible. The bank floor manager is in charge of seeing to it that the tellers are friendly and efficient. The QC person is responsible for the quality of the machine operator's output. The supervisor is responsible for the quantity. Executives become squirrel-cage managers. They work very hard going 'round and 'round—without much change in scenery.

People feel powerless when they experience no control over their work. All power seems to be outside their control. They feel disconnected from the organization's success or failure. They see themselves as victims. The common attitude is "we" would be great if only "they" would stop messing things up.

The same is true for the managers. They also feel powerless. They see *what* needs to be done, but can't figure out *how* to do it.

Leaders Add Value by Helping People Feel Powerful Rather than Helpless

The leader is powerful when he/she figures out *how* to achieve *what* needs to be done. People are very different in organizations led by leaders who feel they know how to do what needs to be done. They feel powerful in having the control and influence necessary to do whatever it takes to get the job done. They see themselves as the instruments of their own destiny. They are connected to the organization's success and failures because they know they are responsible for it. They are all working to achieve a common vision.

Redefine the Situation to Convert Powerlessness to Powerfulness

I encountered a severe case of victimitis with one of my clients. In the following synopsis, watch the conversion from powerlessness to powerfulness once the client was able to redefine the situation. Note also how focusing on things we can't control occupies our mind so that we are unable to focus creatively on what we can do to make real progress.

Mike was the general manager of a large division of a very large manufacturing company. His division was bleeding more than $1 billion in red ink annually.

When I asked Mike for the biggest obstacle to turning the division around, he replied quickly, "The rotten compensation system. Look, we lost more than a billion dollars last year. But all of my executives got big bonuses because their bonus is tied into overall company profits, not our division's performance. Same with the hourly employees. We make the poorest products in our industry. How can I convince anyone to change when they keep getting rewarded for doing more of the same?"

"Have you tried to change the plan?" I asked.

"I've spoken to the president. I've been to see the chairman. I've even pitched the board. Everyone believes that the company-wide bonus system is the best. I can't change the system."

Listen to rampant victimitis at work. As long as Mike believes that he can't change the biggest obstacle to his success, he is a victim. He might just as well polish up the résumé, because he's going to be looking for a job soon.

This anecdote has a happy ending, however. I was able to help Mike see that, while he couldn't influence the incentive compensation system, he could restate the problem to give him influence and control. He saw that there were many aspects of the reward system that he could influence. Merit increases, promotions, job assignments, and the whole range of nonmonetary rewards were well within his reach, and those could motivate a significant difference in the division's performance. He went from being a powerless to being a powerful executive by redefining the situation so he had influence and control.

The Magic Conversion Question

I learned to change from being a victim to being responsible by asking myself, "What am I doing or not doing that causes the situation I don't like?" Restating the problem into factors that I control helps me feel, and be, powerful.

I learned to use the magic conversion question in a situation at Johnsonville. We were the sole supplier to a major customer. They continually threatened to bring in a second supplier, primarily, we thought, to pressure us on price. They expressed concern over our potential nondelivery. "Don't worry," I reassured them, "we'll never short you."

One day it happened, though. We made a special batch for them, which they needed the next day. The plant completed their job, packed up the product, and called our independent trucking company to pick it up. The truck driver failed to show up, and the product was late. I got a call from the head meat buyer, who said, "I told you so." They cut our order and brought in a second supplier.

When I discussed the situation with the plant people, they responded in classic victim language. "We don't control the truck driver. He doesn't work for us. We did our job. There's nothing we can do."

"Are you willing to let someone else control your destiny, cost you your livelihood?" I responded.

"No," they said, "but there's nothing we can do."

"Perhaps you can't get total control. But what can we do that would help us reduce the chances of this happening again?" I asked.

Soon the plant people had a list of actions they could take to improve their control over the situation, ranging from finding alternative trucking firms to frequent calls between the trucker and the plant to track current location.

We learned two valuable lessons: Being a victim is dangerous to our success, and there's always something we can do to get better control over virtually any situation.

I Loved the Comfort of My Chains

"The way things are" seems comforting. We know exactly what to expect. We know precisely what's going to happen. We know just where we stand. And we know where everyone else stands also.

While it wasn't exactly what we want, and we can complain bitterly about how we "deserve" better, we defend staying just the way we are. In fact, it is easier to complain about what we don't have than to give up what we do have.

Some time ago I attempted to break into the textile coloring market. I saw a big opportunity. I had been successful in other markets by offering guaranteed delivery as a way to justify our higher prices. I made the rounds of the textile producers. They yawned at my offer of guaranteed delivery. Their nonresponse should have told me that I was on the wrong track, but I loved my solution. Who cares if "they" didn't recognize the great benefit I was offering them. I figured I just had to be louder, clearer, more aggressive. I put more money into advertising and spent more time selling. The results hardly justified the expenditures. Seven months and several bushel baskets of money later I withdrew. Licking my wounds, I cursed the "way things were" in that market which prevented the customers from recognizing the great benefit I could bring to the industry. I didn't realize until much later that the real difficulty was the way I was.

The Chains of "the Way I Am" Prevent Getting What I Want

Several years later I met the president of a large apparel manufacturer at a social function. He asked me to stop by and see what I might do to help his firm meet a particularly vexing problem. What he wanted was bright, color-fast dyes. My firm had the technology to provide that. We struck a very lucrative deal together. When I asked him why he hadn't mentioned his need to me several years earlier, his answer was classic. "You never asked what we *needed*. You were so busy selling your solution that you didn't hear what we wanted."

In one of those "light bulb" experiences, I recognized that I so loved the comfort of the mental chains imposed by my current solution that I couldn't break out of my mental jail to hear his problem. To listen and hear would have required doing something different. I was not about to do that.

I resisted changing my leadership behavior. I always sought first to get "them" to change. I was okay. "They" needed to be different. It was that way inside my company as well. It was easy to talk about what the employees needed to do differently. Most of my efforts in the early years were consumed with changing "them." I only came to realize later that "they" behaved the way "they" did because I behaved the way I did. If I wanted "them" to change their behavior, I had to change mine first.

It was only when I recognized that "I am the problem" that I was able to also become part of the solution. My journey was indelibly shaped by this insight.

QUESTION:
How must I be different to be an effective leader?

LEADERSHIP SOLUTION:
Understand that I am the problem. Accepting that enables me to be the solution.

CHAPTER 4

Leading in
an Upside-Down World

Things Don't Work the Way They Used to

The leader presumably sits at the pinnacle of power. At least, that's what I was led to believe. The corner office is the symbol of authority in America. Yet read the business press and feel the pain and anguish of so many executives as they are unable to get the people to produce the changes they know are essential to their organization's survival. Feel your own gut crawl as you worry about how to get "them" to do what you know needs to be done. I know how it feels. I've been there through the long sleepless nights. I've felt the helplessness.

One of my CEO clients said, "I work a whole lifetime to make it to the top. 'Now,' I say to myself, 'I can finally get things done the way I want them done.' Only now I discover that I have less ability to get things done than in any other position I've ever held. It's a cruel joke."

And it's dangerous. The sword of Damocles hangs heavy over the corporate head. The turnover in the corner office is at the highest level in history. Boards are saying clearly, "We want performance—or you're history!"

Every single executive with whom I speak wants to be different, and produce different results. Unfortunately, very few know how.

Current Leadership Thought Robs Leader Power

Why do these feelings of helplessness exist at the pinnacle of power? The single biggest reason is the obsolete leadership paradigm that robs leaders of their effectiveness. Under the current paradigm, leaders are responsible for the performance of their people. Under this paradigm, leaders fix problems—including people problems. Leaders answer questions. Leaders make decisions. Leaders do things *to* the organization, and the people in it.

You've probably read it and heard it a million times. Leaders plan, organize, command, coordinate, and control. That's the current command-and-control paradigm. It's found in every management textbook. It's taught in virtually every college classroom and seminar room. You see it practiced in virtually every organization. It is the "conventional wisdom."

Take "this vision thing," for instance. Leaders are responsible to craft a vision. Leaders are responsible to implement that vision. Leaders are responsible for empowering their people to use the vision. That paradigm of leader responsibility for other people's performance, given today's circumstances, guarantees organizational failure.

Rather, my experience in running my own company and in helping other people run theirs is that the leader's job is to get the people to be responsible for *their own* performance. This revised leadership paradigm significantly alters the behavior of everyone in the organization. I learned this lesson the very hard way. It cost millions of dollars. I wasted years of my life. This book is my effort to help you shorten your learning curve.

The Golden Rake Example of Obsolete Leadership Thought

I coach the president of a $6-billion company. As I walked with him out of his office one day, I passed a groundskeeper raking leaves. She was using a rake with only five teeth. It originally had thirty-one. I stopped and asked her, "What are you doing?"

"Raking the leaves," she replied.

"Why are you using that rake?" I asked. "You're not picking up many leaves."

"Because that's what they gave me to use," she replied.

"Why didn't you get a better rake?" I asked.

"That's not my job," she said.

As I walked away, the president was visibly angry. "We have a backlog big enough to choke a horse," he said, working hard to restrain the level of his voice, "and it's growing every day. We are way behind on two large development projects that are draining us of cash. We're behind in both production lines and bleeding cash there too. This incident is a perfect example of what is wrong. People are constantly complaining because they don't have the right tools, parts, drawings, and God knows what. This just caps it off for me. This shows the lack of a sense of urgency I talked to you about. How are we ever going to make it if we can't even give someone a decent rake? I've got to find that supervisor and be certain she gets a better rake."

"Are you certain the supervisor is responsible?" I asked.

"Absolutely!" he almost yelled. Gaining his composure, he continued, "His job is to make certain his people have the right tools."

"If he is responsible, how would you solve this problem?"

"More training for the supervisor, better selection, perhaps, or possibly replace him."

"Are those actions going to get you where you need to be?"

"What do you mean by that?" he asked with a puzzled look on his face.

"What is it going to take to turn this place around? What do you need to create?"

"Well, now," he replied hesitantly, "if I'm going to be a hands-on leader, if I'm going to demonstrate a personal sense of urgency, if I'm going to live the vision, I guess I'll go and get the rake." He turned to head in the direction of the storeroom.

"Whoa," I said. "Is your getting the rake really going to fix the problem?"

The president stopped to think for a moment. Finally, he said, "If every person in this company doesn't get a sense of urgency about meeting their commitments, we aren't going to make it."

"Okay," I said. "If everyone must be committed to doing their jobs no matter what it takes, then who must take responsibility in the case of the gardener and the rake?"

"The gardener has to be responsible. She's the only one who can be certain that she has the right rake. We have been making it too easy for people to be uncommitted by allowing them to blame others. Many of our problems will disappear if we can fix the commitment problem. Each person needs to be responsible for their own performance. But"—there was a hesitancy in his voice now—"isn't the supervisor also responsible?"

"Yes, but not for getting the groundskeeper a better rake. The supervisor is responsible for getting the groundskeeper committed to doing a good job. His job is to help her want to be committed and responsible. In the best of all worlds, who else needs to be committed to getting the right rake?"

He thought for a minute and said, "I'll bet I am not the first person who saw her using that rake. Ideally, anyone who saw her should have called her on it. So every person who sees her needs to feel a sense of responsibility for the gardener getting the right rake."

"And how about your role?" I asked.

He smiled and said, "Ultimately, I'm responsible because I've been focusing on the wrong problem. Rather than focusing on the real problem of lack of commitment, I've been working on the symptoms: no parts, wrong tools, inaccurate drawings."

Hear the old paradigm at work: "It's the supervisor's responsibility to get the right tools . . . I'll go and get the rake myself . . ." This president had been working fourteen hours a day, seven days a week, and getting further and further behind, all because he had defined his role according to the old paradigm. The president could chase rakes all day and not get his development projects back on time or get his production lines back on schedule. As long as he sees his role as solving problems, people will bring him problems to solve. They won't be responsible for solving their parts shortage or tool problems themselves, because he's there to solve them for them. In every organization there are dozens of rake examples waiting to be used as a prism to help people envision their roles differently.

Once the president saw his role in a different light, he began to turn it around. Rather than chasing missing parts, he and his team began to focus on building commitment and getting people to take responsibility.

The Old Paradigm Gets Lots of Reinforcement

Initially, it is very difficult to make the transition from problem solver to leader. The new perspective flies in the face of everything we have learned. As children we are taught to obey the person in authority. Our safety requires that we follow unquestioningly such orders as "Don't run in the street" and "Don't take candy from strangers."

That pattern of obeying the person in authority continues through school and into adult life. We learn early and it's reinforced often. Parents are responsible for their children's behavior. Teachers are responsible for their students' learning. The boss is responsible for the gardener's raking. That's why the gardener says, "They gave me the rake," and "It's not my job to get a better one." Now, in the face of all this learning, we want people to be responsible for their own performance. It's no wonder that it isn't easy to change leadership behavior.

Another example illustrates the differences. One CEO I know became excited about creating a vision. He saw it as the answer to his organization's quality problems, service deficiencies, and overall lackluster profit performance. He went off to the mountaintop, created his vision, and brought it back to the people. He announced it with appropriate flair at small-group, all-employee meetings. Then he sat back and waited for "them" to "buy it." He was disappointed when nothing happened after a year.

He called me and discussed changing the compensation system. "That'll do it, won't it?" he asked.

Note his emphasis on "doing things" to "fix" the situation. His vision was an effort to "fix" the problem of poor performance. Throughout, hear his responsibility to change others. He owns the vision. He owns its implementation. That's the old leadership paradigm.

"No," I answered, "changing the compensation system won't fix anything. You've got to change your paradigm first."

A little history puts the absolute necessity of this paradigm shift in perspective.

Why the Current Model Came to Be— and Now Must Go

FINANCIAL CAPITALISM

Karl Marx was right. The owners of the tools of production determine the economic structure. When Marx looked around in the middle of the nineteenth century, he saw that the capitalist owned the equipment and machinery, which were the tools of production. Therefore, the capitalist set up the economic system in which he wielded the power and made the decisions.

This system arose because in the mid-nineteenth century:

- Markets were local or national.
- Communication took days or weeks.
- Work was unskilled and manual.
- Workers were uneducated.
- Stability was the rule.

Capital was the critical scarce resource. People were plentiful, being driven in droves from the farms by the agricultural revolution. The Welsh businessman and early management writer-philosopher Robert Owen wrote in the early 1830s, "A good horse is worth five pounds a day. A good man is worth two pounds." Guess who got treated better. The man or the horse?

Early business owners accumulated capital and risked it to build factories, buy equipment, and produce goods in advance of payment for those goods. All of this required high risk, for which there was great return. Jobs, on the other hand, were rudimentary and mechanical. The Luddites were correct. Factory jobs demanded little of the craft skills typical of the time.

MANAGERIAL CAPITALISM

Times changed. One hundred years later, in the middle 1930s, another historian, James Burnham, looked around and saw that professional managers now effectively controlled the corporations, which were the tools of production. In his book *The Managerial Revolution* he argued that power had passed from the shareholder-owners of the major corporations to the professional managers. He saw the professional managers set up the system so they wielded power and made the decisions.

Adolph Berle and Gardiner Means came to the same conclusion in their book, *The Modern Corporation and Private Property*, published in 1932. They saw clearly the separation between managers, who effectively ran the corporation, and owners, who had little or nothing to say about the disposition of their "property."

Michael Jacobs in his recent (1991) book, *Short-term America: The Causes and Cures of Our Business Myopia*, updates and validates the Berle and Means and Burnham observations. He argues that the short-term myopia that plagues American business is the result of the separation of management from ownership and the ascendancy of management to the seat of power.

This transfer of power occurred because the brainpower capital supplied by the professional managers became more important than the financial capital supplied by the shareholders. Thus, the critical capital resource needed for survival changed from such tangible physical assets as plant, equipment, and money to the brainpower supplied by managers. Capital had been transformed from a physical to an intellectual form. The brainpower was limited to the executive suite because most jobs were still elementary and mechanical.

Karl Marx was right again. The owners of the tools of production become the dominant power in the economic landscape. Only, sitting in his apartment in Vienna, Karl Marx could not have envisioned the day that human brainpower would be more important than tangible assets.

INTELLECTUAL CAPITALISM

Today circumstances have changed again. The principal tools of production today are not machinery and equipment. Neither is it solely the brainpower of the managerial leadership. Rather, the tools of production are the ideas and talents (the intellectual capital) of the scientist, the machinist, and the programmer. Therefore, the possessors of the intellectual tools of production, the people, will come to exercise effective power.

The Organization Is the Last Feudal Vestige.
Park Your Brains, and Your Sweat, at the Door

It isn't happening fast enough, though. Sir James Egan, commenting on his tenure as managing director of Jaguar Cars company, said, "We lost because we gained their hands, but not their hearts and minds." Witness the recent spate of articles reporting the lack of commitment and loyalty on the part of employees, and the fear that cost cutting has gone too far and may be the precipitating cause of all sorts of corporate disasters, ranging from Exxon's string of spills and explosions to IBM's chronic underperformance. Even Tony O'Reilly, the CEO of highly successful Heinz, worries about reducing the "bile factor."

Unfortunately, leadership theory hasn't caught up with this new reality. The leadership systems currently in use are designed to control relatively uneducated, mostly untrustworthy people in an environment of very slow change. In our free and democratic society, employees park their rights (and usually their sweat)—along with their brains— at the door. Organizations today are the last remaining feudal enclave. Too many people in organizations are subjected to authoritarian, and what they believe to be unreasonable, treatment. This is why there is so little effort to achieve in authoritarian organizations.

A recent personal experience highlights this feudal thinking on the part of leaders. A midlevel supervisor in a large publicly traded company asked her secretary to get her car washed and detailed. Her instructions were not to get it done if they didn't take her credit card, because she didn't have enough money in her checking account. The secretary took the car down, during working hours, of course. When the car wash didn't take the credit card, she paid for the wash and detail herself, telling her boss, "Pay me back when you have the money, no problem." The boss was furious and fired the secretary on the spot.

Notice several assumptions. The boss thought nothing of asking the secretary to run a personal errand for her during working hours, or to terminate her at will when she was displeased with the performance. After all, the secretary "worked" for her. Notice the master-slave concept in action. Much of the early thinking about the employment relationship was based upon that concept. The vestiges of that thinking still exist. It didn't even occur to the boss that her request was inappropriate or her termination action likely illegal.

Notice also the boss's assumption that she could take care of her personal business during working hours and use company resources to do so. Hear the assumption that "I'm the boss and I'm in control of these resources to use as I see fit." This is managerial capitalism at its worst. Hear how the property rights of the boss take precedence over the civil rights of the employee. Furthermore, as a stockholder in this publicly traded company I am exceedingly angry that the boss breached her fiduciary responsibility to me—an owner of the resources she so freely uses for her own personal use.

But the payoff was the immediate dramatic fall in her department's productivity. She couldn't figure out why. It's clear to me. The people in the department, possessors of the real power in that organizational world, were withholding their intellectual capital. In many departments across the world this same soap opera is being played out, to the detriment of everyone.

Cadavers of Leadership Paradigms: 100 Years and Still Stinking

Our leadership paradigms are obsolete. How did they get that way? They evolved in the mid- to late-nineteenth century when that was the most effective way to manage in the conditions existing at that time. The best examples of this approach were the German army and the French coal mines of the mid-nineteenth century. Henri Fayol wrote his *Principles of Administration* almost one hundred years ago. Based upon his experience running the French coal mines, he outlined the functions of management as planning, organizing, commanding, coordinating, and controlling. Max Weber, studying the German army of approximately the same time, came to similar conclusions. Our present organizational methods are based on their model, even though our circumstances are far different. Today:

- Markets are global.
- Electronic highways enable instant communication and rapid competitive responses.
- Work involves the creation, transmission, and manipulation of information and knowledge.
- Workers are highly educated.

Circumstances have changed. The paradigm has not. The result: consistent organizational underperformance, as individuals withhold their intellectual capital. Management responses of cost cutting, restructuring, and leveraged buyouts reflect the old paradigm. They are actions that leaders do *to* the organization, and the people, to *fix problems*. We are treating the symptoms of high costs, inefficiencies, poor quality, lousy service, but not the root causes—inappropriate leadership paradigms.

I was thoroughly caught up in the old paradigm. I believed it, practiced it, even taught it. And I spent long sleepless nights wondering why it didn't work. It was so logical. It was "proven." And I loved being the driver of things in my organization. Because of my personality, the more difficult something is to accomplish, the more I want to accomplish it. So I worked harder and harder to get the old paradigm to be effective. No matter how hard I tried, though, I couldn't get the old planning-and-control paradigm to work. Out of my frustration came my search for a new, more effective model.

Leadership Mind-sets Must Change

I learned that I had to change my leadership paradigm in order to live these new responsibilities. I needed to change my mind-set so that others would invest their intellectual capital in helping the company become great. Changing my mind-set isn't easy. One of the executives I coach said, "You outsiders don't understand. We have a long history of failure. We have a long history of looking to headquarters to take care of us, to protect us, to provide for us. Getting people to be responsible for themselves flies in the face of a deeply ingrained cultural heritage. In addition, my entire experience has been protecting people, making their decisions, planning for others. How do I stop doing what I know and get others to do what they, and I, don't know?"

My own experience is that changing my own leadership mentalities was the hardest step, and the first. My struggles, insight, and mistakes are contained in the following pages. Read on and let us learn together how to lead in this world turned upside down.

QUESTION:
How must I change my leadership paradigm to utilize all the intellectual capital in my organization?

LEADERSHIP SOLUTION:
Become an effective leader by increasing the effectiveness of the people I lead.

PART II

THE INTELLECTUAL CAPITALISM LEADERSHIP PARADIGM

Introduction

We live in a new era: an era where the old rules no longer apply. We need to develop "new" rules. I probably don't have to tell you that the old rules don't work anymore. You wouldn't be reading this book if you didn't believe that your leadership behavior needs to be different. But what are the new rules?

The Principles of Leading in an Intellectual Capitalism World

This is not easy. We've all grown up learning to follow authority: first our parents, then our teachers, and then our bosses. The first and probably most often reinforced lesson we learn is "Do as you are told by the person in charge." Now, however, the "person in charge" is the person who formally reports to you. In this topsy-turvy world, as a leader you actually work for the people who work for you. In the past, as leaders we planned products, budgets, facilities—the concrete financial aspects of the business. The assumption was that the people would go along with the plan. I learned the hard way that assumption was no longer safe. In addition, I must plan for the mind-sets and mentalities of the people, if I want the financial plan to work.

Our leadership tools haven't changed significantly, but the focus of their use has. The primary purpose of strategic planning is not to strategically plan for the future, although that's an important purpose of the exercise. It is primarily to develop the strategic management mind-set in each and every individual in the organization. The purpose of the process is not only to produce a plan. It is to produce a plan that will be owned and understood by the people who have to execute it.

I discovered that the leader has a new set of responsibilities. The leader, at every level in the organization, must strive to implement these four principles:

1. Transfer ownership for work to those who execute the work.
2. Create the environment for ownership where each person wants to be responsible for his/her own performance.
    a. Paint a clear picture of great performance for the organization and each person.
    b. Focus individuals on the few factors that create great performance.
    c. Develop the desire for each person to own—be responsible for—his/her own great performance.
    d. Align organization systems and structures that send a clear message as to what is necessary for great performance for the individual and the organization.
    e. Engage individuals—their hearts and minds, as well as their hands—in the business of the business.
    f. Energize individuals around the focus of the business.
3. Coach the development of individual capability and competence.
4. Learn faster.
    a. Learn themselves.
    b. Create the conditions under which every person in the organization is challenged to continually learn faster.

These are the leadership principles I've learned that produce more effective organizations. I discovered these principles through the expensive process of trial and error. I've learned them at the great cost of both dollars and emotional wear. And they are constantly undergoing change. Not to ruin your dinner, but the only certainty on which we can count is that these "new" rules will likely fade someday, all too soon for most of us, and be replaced by a set of "newer" rules. I've learned that my job is to work hard to understand what it takes to (1) win today and (2) create the circumstances where I can win tomorrow. In today's world, these are the principles I've found that produce those two important outcomes. This part spells out these four principles.

QUESTION:
What do I have to learn to lead in this new age?

LEADERSHIP SOLUTION:
Learn the new paradigm today—and get ready to learn a new one tomorrow.

CHAPTER 5

Transfer Ownership

"Help me fix them" is the most frequent request I receive from leaders. "I know what's got to be done, but 'they' won't take responsibility for getting it done."

Not only have I frequently heard these words from others, I've heard myself say them many times.

I've learned as the leader of my organizations that my job is not to solve other people's problems, but to create the circumstances where they want to own the responsibility for their own performance. That mind-set switch from problem owner to problem conveyer was most difficult for me. Most likely it is difficult for you as well.

Upward Delegation Is the Curse

One of the biggest problems in transferring ownership is that "being responsible" runs counter to most of our training and education. Because we have been trained to look to someone in authority for direction throughout life, most of us are constantly looking to avoid responsibility. Furthermore, avoidance worked for most of us in the past. This trained response creates the victims I talked about in Chapter 3.

The biggest challenge we face as leaders in this intellectual capitalism world is to encourage people to unlearn what they've learned about avoiding responsibility, and learn a new "I am responsible" behavior. In practical terms, "I am responsible" translates into "I am able to respond effectively and appropriately." Helping people regain their own authority and power to respond appropriately in work and life is a leadership skill of the highest order.

Children Learn Early

Children learn early to be world-class avoiders. "Can't clean my room now, I've got homework to do." Or errands to run. Or a piano lesson to take. We parents teach them this avoidance response. After all, isn't homework more important than a clean room? Isn't learning the piano more important than a clean room? Children learn to cast the alternatives so that not doing the unpleasant task is in the authority figure's best interest, and get the authority figure to decide.

Who Makes the Tough Choices Anyway?

We unwittingly train our children to avoid responsibility by making the choices for them. After all, don't we want both a clean room *and* the homework done? Why are they mutually exclusive? Aren't both possible?

More important, who's responsible for making the difficult choices? Why are we, the parents, responsible for deciding which one to do? Shouldn't the child be responsible for figuring out how to do both?

This malady surfaces in the corner office as well. Most often we get to make the tough choices, and the choices are none too desirable. "Do you want better service or lower costs? Improving quality costs money. Do you want to spend that money? Will we get sufficient return on it?"

World-Class Rescuers Are World-Class Losers

Some time ago in one of my plants, I encountered a series of situations, all built around meeting budgets to earn bonuses and shipping not-up-to-snuff product. The plant had a quarterly bonus based upon meeting budgeted goals for shipments and margins. Situations often arose where, at the end of the quarter, decisions had to be made about shipping product to meet the schedule, even though it didn't meet standards.

The question inevitably landed on my desk. "Do you want to ship the product even though it's not up to quality standards, or not meet the budget this quarter and not make the bonus? The product exceeds what the customer needs, so we're not really shipping junk. It's just that it doesn't meet our own tougher standards."

As head buffalo I was a world-class rescuer, so I rushed in and made those choices. Guess what? No matter what I did, I was always wrong. If I shipped the lesser quality material, the customer problems overwhelmed us and people said, "See, it's your fault. We shouldn't have shipped the stuff." If I withheld the shipment, people said, "Now look what you've done. We didn't get a bonus this quarter all because of what you decided. It's not fair. What are you going to do to make this up to us?"

Playing world-class rescuer led to being a world-class loser. A lot involved with being the head buffalo is not fun.

The People Propose; the Manager Disposes: The Loss/Loss Game

Early in my leadership career I had the employee involvement bug. I read a lot about it, and it sounded good. So I began by holding employee meetings to get employee participation. I wanted them to share in a two-way exchange of information and, I hoped, some problem solving as well. It rapidly deteriorated, however, into a bitch session. The employees kept bringing up situations that needed "fixing." I made long lists of things to fix, and worked hard to fix everything before the next meeting. Fixing turned out to be a full-time job. I told myself, "You have to demonstrate good faith. It will take time. Eventually, they will run out of things to fix and you can get on with solving the plant's real problems." Besides, fixing their problems, after all, was part of my leadership task. Eighteen months later, I was still getting long lists to fix at every meeting. I ran out of patience before they ran out of things for me to fix.

In retrospect, the problem is clear to me. I was owning all the responsibility for fixing the problems. The employees' job was to identify what needed to be fixed, and they were truly dedicated to doing that job well. They worked hard to keep me working hard; and I worked hard solving their problems. And the plant continued to flounder. My "fix them" leadership paradigm was failing.

The People Propose; the People Dispose: The Win/Win Game

Some time later I encountered a quality problem in one of my plants. Vowing to avoid taking responsibility for the problem, I called a meeting of the employees involved and asked them for their input on fixing the problem. This time, however, I insisted that they had to be responsible for implementing any solution they suggested. The discussion took a very different tack.

The first suggestion was to change the equipment. When I revealed to the people that the cost of that change would be $1.5 million, they were shocked. Next, they suggested that I talk the customer into taking a lesser quality product. I arranged for a group of them to visit the customer and discuss it face-to-face with him. The group returned from the visit with *higher* quality standards, not lower ones. "Whew," one of the group told me, "this is hard work."

Avoidance at Work: This Is Management Work. We're Not Doing Your Job

As the group struggled with what to do, several members complained. "This is management work," they said. "We don't get paid to do this. This is your job. Stop imposing it on us."

I was stunned and hurt by the comment. After all, the writers had told me that everyone wants to be self-actualized. People really love to be responsible, they wrote. I asked myself, "Why is it that *my* people don't? What am I doing, or not doing, that causes my people not to want to assume responsibility?"

It was then that I realized that I had trained them to be dependent upon me. I liked their being a buffalo herd, doing whatever I told them to do. When I wanted them to be flexible like a gaggle of geese, they had no model or training in how to fly, or share leadership.

Restrain Yourself from Helping People out of Their Responsibilities

I asked them if they'd rather I made the decision. They mumbled something about "Well . . . no. But it isn't supposed to be so hard."

"Haven't I been making all the decisions?" I asked. "And do you really think it's working out better? What do you need to do to make the decision easier, and to make a better decision? How can I help you make the decision?" The stewing and shuffling of feet convinced me that I was on the right track.

I got dribs and drabs of requests, but it was clear that the people were wrestling with what to do. After what seemed like an eternity (but was only four days) the group came back with a plan to redo several of the procedures and learn a new process. Total cost: less than $10,000, and it solved the quality problem. The group tried one last time to hand me the problem. "Here it is," they proudly said. "Now you go get it fixed."

"Whoa," I said, "that wasn't the deal. How are you going to make it work?"

The sheepish grins told me I had successfully transferred the responsibility. "Here's the plan," they said. "We're ready to roll."

"Go for it," I said without looking at the papers thrust in front of me.

It took a lot of restraint on my part not to respond to my old leadership instincts and rush in to "help." Their answer was not as good as my own, or so I told myself. It took maximum control to keep from reading their proposal and "improving" it. My restraint paid big dividends. Their execution of their own plan was flawless. The problem was solved and never came back. It was a win/win outcome. Gradually, I learned to transfer responsibility for solving other, similar problems to the rightful owner.

The Person Doing the Work Must Own the Responsibility

I learned that the best person to be responsible for the job is the person doing the job. Since the person doing the job is the expert in that job, he or she should be the one who makes the decision about how the work can best be done. In the intellectual capitalism model, that's the person who has the ultimate power, anyway.

Performers Must *Want* to Own the Responsibility

Great performance is driven by the individual's passionate desire that he/she alone be responsible for his/her performance. Remember Eric Heyden? He won an unprecedented six gold medals in speed skating during the Winter Olympics several years ago. The key to his success? In his own words, "desire." It had to be his desire, a desire that welled up from deep inside himself. He practiced six hours a day. He bicycled twenty-five miles a day. He duck walked six miles a day. He worked until he ached, and then he worked some more. No amount of pressure from parents or coaches could have produced that level of dedication and practice. The gold medals Eric won were the result of his wanting to win and being responsible for his own performance. That desire for responsibility is the heart of success in the Olympic arena, in the boardroom, on the shop floor, and in the production control office.

Stop Acting like the Head Buffalo

For people to want to own the reponsibility, and stop being victims, I had to change my behavior. I loved rescuing people. I loved solving problems. The result? People were lined up waiting to be rescued. People kept bringing me problems to solve. My people did just what I wanted them to do. If I wanted to play head buffalo, they were more than willing to play buffalo herd member.

When I realized that rescuing people and solving problems is a permanent job, I understood the error of my thinking. People would never learn to take care of themselves because I was always there to take care of them. People would never learn to solve their own problems because I was there to solve them for them. I'd take this job with me to the grave. Suddenly, the overwhelming task didn't seem as attractive as it once had.

As Rosa Parks was too tired to move to the back of the Birmingham bus and thus started a revolution, so did my weariness start a revolution in my company. If I was going to have a gaggle of geese, I realized, then I'd have to stop playing head buffalo.

Old Habits Die Hard

I learned the hard way that old leadership habits die hard. It takes lots of practice to get rid of them. I frequently fall back into the rescuing/ solving problems trap. In future chapters I'll talk about ways to both avoid the traps and dig yourself out when you fall in (as you undoubt-edly will).

QUESTION:
How can I get people to do it right the first time?

LEADERSHIP SOLUTION:
The person who does the job must own the responsibility for doing it correctly.

CHAPTER 6

Create the
Ownership Environment

I Own It All

I was always in the middle of everything. My head-buffalo mentality led me to always want to be involved and in control. That meant that I wound up owning most of the responsibilities. That was just the way I wanted it, until I realized that I'd take those ever-increasing responsibilities to my early grave. As long as I owned it, no one else did.

I then became an expert at "delegating" work. I learned how to give assignments and follow up. That relieved my work load a little. But I was still stuck with making all the decisions. People soon learned that I preferred "my way." So they spent most of their time working to figure out "my way." They constantly asked me what I really wanted. They checked every little detail with me. They kept me constantly informed. Soon I was spending more time, not less. The delegation approach was not working.

Finally, one incident brought my foolishness home to me. We had a trade show to prepare. It was the big annual event. We showed off our new products and booked orders. We had to put on the best program possible. I hired a communications coordinator to handle these kinds of events. He was highly recommended and high-priced. He spent weeks preparing the booth, the handouts, the demonstrations. His mistake was to not keep me informed at every step. When I realized that the date was just two weeks away, I asked him to brief me on his plans. What he presented was dramatically different from what we'd done in the past. I didn't like it and told him so. I insisted that he redo the program.

But it was too late. The time was too short to make any changes. Several of my managers told me how much they liked the new approach. So although I was tempted to cancel the show, I reluctantly agreed to go forward. My "I told you so" speech was just waiting until the show closed. To my amazement, I was wrong. We had the best show ever. We increased our bookings by 41 percent. Our booth was the hit of the show. The next day the coordinator resigned, saying he couldn't work in such a restrictive environment.

My owning all the responsibility cost me a great person, and almost cost me a year's worth of orders. It was clear to me that I had to change. As the leader of my organization I am responsible for creating the environment that enables each person to assume responsibility for his or her own performance. The people own the responsibility for delivering great performance. I am responsible for creating the environment where this ownership takes place. (In Part Five I'll talk in greater detail about how to create the environment that fosters this transfer of ownership).

Shortly after my trade show experience I had an opportunity to learn how to transfer ownership to the people who do the work by creating the ownership environment. As usual, it was serendipitous.

The First Strategic Decision Is "Who Should Make the Decision?"

One unit was selling software to government units in our geographic region. Initially, the first team of employees sold, installed, and supported all the systems, since they were the only people in the company. Everyone assumed that that pattern would change as soon as the company grew sufficiently. It is standard in the industry to separate selling, installation, and support. There's an assumption that salespeople are not good programmers and good programmers are not good salespeople, and good support people are different from both. That assumption did not prove true.

The team quickly sold out their local market. In order to grow, the team either had to seek out smaller customers within their geographic area, which meant changing their product, or they had to move into new geographic areas. I sensed an opportunity for people to assume increased responsibility. So I posed the following question to the group: "What can you do to assure that each customer gets the best service?" Rather than my deciding what to do, I turned the decision over to the people who had to make the decision work.

The people decided to hire new people to sell smaller customers in their original geographic area and to move into new geographic areas. They set up a rotation system within the teams so that everyone learned all the skills. They set up an internal monitoring system to keep the skills current. They assumed ownership for the training and monitoring themselves, and for assuring superior service to their customers. One of the team members offered to start the new team for the smaller customers. Another offered to relocate temporarily to start up a new operation in a new geographic area.

Today, there are more than seven hundred people in the company, organized into thirty-seven semi-autonomous teams stretching from Singapore to Moscow. These team members are responsible for hiring, training, and maintaining superior levels of service to customers. The team members themselves assumed responsibility for delivering great performance to their customers when I created the environment which encouraged that to happen. That's leadership in the intellectual capitalism age.

Modify Systems to Enable Ownership

As the company grew, so did complaints about performance discrepancies among teams. We tried several different tactics to deal with the discrepancies, all to no avail. Finally, one day, I realized that this was another opportunity to transfer ownership. At the next all-employee meeting I asked, "How can we assure consistent high performance across all teams? What can we do to be certain that we are all equally proud of the work of each person in the company?"

The employees wrestled with the problem for a complete day. Finally, they decided that each team would meet each week and set individual and team goals. The goals would expect measurable, responsible action from each member. These goals would be entered on the E-mail system along with daily progress. Team members agreed to help other team members—both in their own team and in other teams—to set realistic and stretching goals and then support each other in attaining them.

Today, each team member inputs his/her individual and team goals every week, reviews and comments on others' goals, and reports daily progress. There is a lively E-mail exchange about goals and performance among most people in the company. And goal attainment averages 99 + percent every week. A system designed by the people helped create the environment wherein the people assumed ownership for their results.

People Need to Know the Results of Ownership Actions

We have an extensive full-cost, real-time cost accounting system. I heard a discussion some years back on "activity-based costing," and became a believer. I urged the design and installation of this system in the company. Everyone charges his/her time, expenses, and materials directly to a project, customer, or program. These costs are collected daily, where a real-cost thirty-day rolling average is computed for every product for every team.

This real-time, full-cost data bank gave the teams the opportunity to make such business decisions as pricing and delivery. It enabled them to own the responsibility for making profitable bids.

Initially, I reviewed and approved each bid. I was concerned that bid prices wouldn't be high enough, and they weren't. I found myself continually raising the bids. I realized that I had to change the situation or else I'd be there forever reviewing bids, and I didn't exactly see that as my preferred future. It was fun being the head buffalo, but it required too much work. So I looked to change another critical system which helps create the ownership environment: the reward system.

If You Want Ownership Behavior, Pay for It

In the first year, each person was paid a bonus based on a percentage of overall company profit. The executive committee determined that bonus. The first year's bonus was not very large, as start-up costs ate into the profits and we needed to conserve cash. This caused considerable discontent. Finally, after much fruitless discussion, I realized that I had another opportunity to transfer ownership. I was learning my new leadership behaviors.

At the next quarterly all-employee meeting I asked the question "What is a fair and equitable bonus system? What would make you feel like a winner, and still leave a return to our shareholders and enough capital to grow the business? What bonus system would reward people on the basis of their contribution?" As a trigger to the discussion I suggested a 50/50 split of net profits before tax to be allocated on the basis of team performance.

The group took some time to decide. Eventually, they chose to use the 50/50 split as a framework, but added certain provisions. They decided that the teams would allocate the bonus among team members, ensuring that everyone received a reward based upon his/her contribution. But eligibility for the bonus pool was initially restricted to those individuals who met their weekly individual and team goals 90 percent of the time and received a rating of 8 or better (out of a possible 10) on the monthly customer satisfaction survey. Interestingly, the group has continually raised the standard for admission into the bonus pool. Today, the group has established 100 percent goal achievement and a perfect score of 10 on the customer survey.

Almost immediately, bid prices and margins rose, as did the preoccupation with supplying superior products and services to create the additional value. Furthermore, after the initial excitement caused by the distribution of big monthly team bonus checks, the focus shifted to the weekly performance management reports. E-mail notes flew back and forth challenging, supporting, and sharing information relevant to the attainment of individual and team goals.

Over the period of a few months I withdrew from approving bids. The teams now had full responsibility to bid jobs and deliver a superior product, which delighted customers and earned the company a profit. I had created the ownership environment. They accepted the ownership for running their business. They had the intellectual capital. They were in control.

Managing External Chaos While Keeping Customer Focus

All the while we'd been changing so dramatically internally, the market was doing flip-flops. Our technology base changed four times in four years. Our programming language changed several times in the same four years. Our customer base shifted five times in the same four years.

All of my leadership efforts directed toward transferring the ownership paid off. Despite the external chaos, the people were able to keep focused on delivering great performance for their customers.

My job as a leader in the intellectual capitalism era is to create the environment wherein the people want to take ownership.

QUESTION:
Am I creating owners or dependents?

LEADERSHIP SOLUTION:
If you want them to act like it's their business, make it their business.

CHAPTER 7

Coaching
Personal Competence

Coach People, Not Scoreboards

Our view of coaches comes from watching television. We see them furiously pace the sidelines, yell at the referees, make stirring locker room speeches, lay out game plans, and give directions by poking their fingers into their players' chests. That picture makes great viewing, but it makes for very poor leadership performance.

Rather than that highly charged emotional picture, I've learned that coaching is about providing support and guidance. Coaching is very *person-centered*. Great coaches know that teams with the best skills and competencies have the highest winning percentages. The primary purpose of coaching is to develop the individual's skills and competencies. A coach helps you do what you know you must do!

I've played competitive sports and watched my children be coached playing competitive sports. The most effective coaches I've ever seen don't yell at the referees. They don't swear at their players. My football coach put it best. He told me, "You didn't come to this university to learn how to play football. You came here to learn how to be a better person. So this season you'll learn to be a better person by learning how to be a better football player."

He never yelled at me. He never poked his finger in my chest. He helped me learn how to block and tackle and catch a football, and be responsible and take pride in my actions. He coached me, not the scoreboard. In the process he helped me consistently play over my head, and win games.

Anyone's a Coach—Everyone's a Coach

Anybody can be a coach. In fact, in some settings, everyone *must* be a coach. The boss needs to be a coach. Teammates need to be coaches. Colleagues need to be coaches. Everyone needs to be a coach.

As a leader I coach my associates, partners, and members when they need help and support in delighting customers. I also coach my end-user customers when they need help and support in seeing what they need to do to be great performers. I even coach the people who coach me when they need help and support in being great performers.

I Know I'm Supposed to Be a Coach— but What Am I Supposed to *Do*?

This question comes up often. It resonates in my soul, as I've asked myself the same question in operating my own company.

Coaching is "in" these days. One of the politically correct things to say is that the executive's job is to be a coach. But what does that really mean? What does a world-class coach do? And how do I measure whether I am a world-class coach or not? These are not easy questions. It's particularly not easy because most of us have been raised in the old command-and-control leadership style. I've worked hard at learning my coaching role. It isn't easy.

Asking Questions and Not Giving Answers

Initially, I felt that great coaches helped other people find their own answers. So I concentrated on asking questions. I knew that good coaches didn't substitute their judgments for those of their players, so I worked hard at not giving answers. I became expert in the "grunt and pause" methodology.

That frustrated a lot of people. It was certainly not a style they had come to expect from me. I had led them to believe that I'd tell them what to do, not ask them what they felt should be done. It was a big surprise and shock. Many people never recovered. And since I'd been providing them with answers, they had difficulty finding their own. I had trained their incapacity.

There were lots of emotional casualties. We missed several significant business opportunities, as senior people didn't know what to do. I learned that great coaches did more than ask questions and not give answers. Great coaches had to provide guidance so people could find the "right" answer. So I sought to provide more guidance.

Create Certainty Through Focused Conversations on Great Performance

I engaged each person in continuing conversations about the identification and measurement of great performance for his or her job. I still used the question-asking technique and worked not to provide answers, but to focus conversations on great performance.

This improved performance, but still left many people feeling insecure. They were still unclear about what constituted great performance. And I couldn't/didn't want to provide the answers. I needed a better set of questions to provide more focus.

Involve Customers in the Continuing Conversation Stream

One day it finally hit me: The real expert in great performance is the customer. Everything begins with delighting the customer. That's why every one of our job descriptions begins with this statement: "The things I do to get and keep customers are . . ."

Things really improved when I modified my focus to ask, "From the customer's point of view, what is great performance?" The coachees finally had a way to get their questions answered from the true expert in what they had to do. They felt more focused and secure.

Coaches Raise Expectations

Don't get people too secure, however. Coaches help people see beyond where they are now. Coaches help people see what they *can* be, which is usually much more than what they are now. The view of the "tomorrow that *must* be" creates discomfort. But it's the discomfort that leads to learning and growth. Hear the discomfort and learning that happened in the following situation.

I was coaching a president in a very competitive distribution industry. They've had a particularly difficult time in recent years and have averaged less than 1 percent net profit margin on sales over the past three years. Last year they averaged 0.5 percent. The CEO had established the goal for this year as a 0.7 percent return on sales. I asked him if he was satisfied with this return.

"Well," he said, "that's not bad. Competition's tough. We've come back from a very bad period. I think that's all we can achieve."

"Are you willing to come to work every day and bust your tail for less than a penny on a dollar? Does that give you a warm and fuzzy feeling at the end of the day?" I asked. "Is that really great performance?"

"Well . . ." he replied hesitantly. "When you put it that way, maybe we could be a little better than that. Industry average is about 1.1

percent. We even did 1.2 once. So maybe 1.3 would be great performance."

"Maybe," I replied. "Tell me, what do the best locations in your industry make?"

"We've got locations in our company that make 2.26, 2.08, and several that make between 1.75 and 2. We know that one of our competitors has a location that makes a little better than 3 percent. When I think about it, I guess we can do better than 0.7."

"Are your competitors any smarter than you? Are the people who run those higher margin locations in the company any smarter than the rest of your location managers? If they can do that well, why can't everybody?"

"You're right," the CEO said. "One point one percent would be great performance for this year, and then 2-percent-plus next year would be fantastic."

"That will bring you closer to the best in your business, but is that *great* performance? Is that as much margin as you can make? Look, how much do credits cost?" I asked, referring to the returned merchandise almost always due to shipping or order packing errors.

After some time searching through papers he said, "They run about 4 percent."

"How would your margin look if you eliminated all the credits?" I asked.

After some calculation he responded, "Three point one percent."

"So, if you could have zero credits, you could be the best in your industry, right? Why can't you do that?" I asked.

"I don't know why we can't," he said. "In fact, I'm sure we can. We just never thought about it before. We've assumed that credits were a normal part of business."

Listen to how the CEO's low level of expectation yields a low level of return. "Point seven percent is the best we can achieve. One point one is great performance. Two percent is fantastic." Yet, achieving a zero defects level in his order packing and shipping departments alone could give multiples of that return. How much more money he could make by improving other areas of his operation is yet unknown. My coaching questions helped him raise his expectations so he could become more of what he could be, which was far greater than he ever imagined.

When you set the high-jump bar at five feet, you get average performance. When you set that bar at eight feet, you get gold-medal-winning performance. Moreover, you'd better be able to clear eight feet one inch, because that's where the record will probably be next year. As one athlete put it, "They keep raising the bar all the time." As a coach you help people raise their expectations high enough to encourage great performance today and even greater great performance tomorrow.

Coaching Questions

Great coaches help people examine their own performance objectively so they can see what they need to improve in order to reach their goals. So the first important question is:

1. In the best of all worlds, what is great performance for your customers?

The beginning point for any coaching is the definition of great performance in the person's present position. As usual, all definition of great performance begins with the customer. This question helps people see beyond what they are today and raises their expectations of what they must be tomorrow.

2. What do you want to achieve in the next two to three years?

Quite often people don't see the relationship between their current assignment and their personal longer term goals. This question helps to clarify that crucial linkage. People will be more committed to performing well when they see the work they are doing as serving their longer term best interest.

3. How will you measure your performance?

Measurement is the motivator for improvement. Resist the temptation to define the measurements for the person. Make certain that he or she owns that responsibility. Wrestling with the "How will I know when I do it?" question helps the individual learn about what he or she really wants to accomplish. It is not uncommon to find that clarifying measurements often changes the objective. The expert in answering this question is often not the individual alone, but the individual in conjunction with his/her customer. Again, this drives the individual back to discussions with the customer.

4. What things do you need to learn in order to reach your goals?

Growth always involves learning new skills. Get the individual involved in defining the skills he or she will need in order to obtain the goals. Open discussion about strengths and weaknesses is often very difficult, so avoid it. Focus on the new skills to learn (or the old ones to strengthen). That gives a positive cast to the discussion.

5. What work experiences do you need to help you learn what you need to achieve your goals?

Learning is something you do, not something you are told. People don't learn chess by watching. They need to begin playing in order to learn the game. As a coach you need to be able to see all the decisions, problems, and actions that need to be done as opportunities for yourself and others to learn and grow.

Vary the Role with the Needs of the People

I've learned that great coaching performance depends upon the needs of the players. Great coaching is more than just asking questions and listening for answers. Great coaches provide a structure within which the players can focus their energies. To provide that structure, great coaches may sometimes be very directive with people who really don't know what to do. Like when I told one of my executives, "We will have an information system that tracks and reports whether we have zero errors in our software." Sometimes a great coach is nondirective with people who really do know. Like when I told another executive who came to me with a problem, "What do you think is best? . . . Why don't you do that?" What you do as a coach depends upon the developmental level of the coachee.

Coaching is hard stuff. It doesn't come easily or naturally in our culture. As I constantly develop my coaching performance in my own company, I learn more and more about the many-faceted role called coach. I don't know what my next coaching role will be. I only know that it will be different from the last and require learning and growth, and that's the challenge and the fun of the journey.

QUESTION:
Is the person becoming more capable?

LEADERSHIP SOLUTION:
Focus on developing the person, not the scoreboard.

CHAPTER 8

Leadership
Is Learning

I learned the hard way that leaders learn fast—or they don't complete the journey. Leaders need to keep on learning. The world changes so fast that we need to keep learning new things so we can cope. The rapid pace of change drives the need for continual learning.

Change Is the Natural State

Change is a constant. The history of mankind is about change. History is a chronology of change. One set of beliefs is pushed aside by a new set. The old order is swept away by the new. If people become attached to the old order, they see their best interest in defending it. They become the losers. They become the old order and in turn are vulnerable. People who belong to the new order are the winners.

Geese Survive; Buffalo Perish

The pace of change used to be much slower than it is today. Generations could pass before things were perceptibly different. This is no longer the case. Things are changing far more quickly.

The increase in the rate of change has profound implications for us. It means that the changes we make now may only be useful for a few years or even only for a few months. We must see life as a journey, because even the things that change must subsequently change again. We never "get there." We just move another few miles down the road.

Speed is essential. The gold medal goes to the swiftest. Rapid change requires rapid learning. Success has always depended upon learning, but in the past the change was slower, so we could take longer to learn. As the pace of change quickens, the race belongs to the swiftest learner.

I've seen it in my own business. My rapidly changing software and services business changed itself seven times in five years. The nature of the market changed; the customer changed; the competition changed; the technology changed. If we hadn't changed, we'd have been one more corporate fatality.

Learn from Success Without Being Trapped by It

Success is a valuable teacher, providing you don't get lulled into complacency by her succulent fruits. I've learned that what got me to where I am will not get me to where I need to go. Circumstances change. I must change also or be left behind. The skills I learned to be a good supervisor will not help me be a good president. No one of us is born a great leader. One must learn, for learning is the key to success. Learn the "right" skills and ideas and you will be successful. Learn the "wrong" skills and ideas and you will fail. The skills that were "right" yesterday become today's "wrong" ones. Continued learning is crucial to continued success.

Johnsonville Foods experienced this "success malaise." I was a national hero lecturing around the world on how Johnsonville "did it." Sales grew, margins rose, and profit-sharing bonuses increased. Then it happened. People took a deep breath and started to "tweak." Sales continued to rise, but margins didn't, and bonuses actually fell. The roof fell in when Johnsonville sausage finished out of the running in a taste test. That experience was a cold shower that awakened members to start learning again.

The mentality of "If it ain't broke, don't fix it" focuses on the present, rather than on the future. The present becomes the past overnight, and the future becomes the present all too soon. Success is the greatest enemy. I've got to keep learning new leadership skills, new leadership techniques, new leadership approaches, new leadership paradigms.

Changing Leadership Behavior Doesn't Come Easy— It Requires Learning First

I discovered that the only way to change my leadership behavior was to learn how to lead differently. I thought I could just "turn on" the new behavior like you turn on a light bulb. If only it were that simple.

I hired a consultant to help me. His conclusion was devastating. "You are the problem," the consultant told me. "You prevent people from really doing their jobs. You dominate meetings. You give your own solutions—sometimes even before the problem is raised. You finish other people's sentences. You state your opinions first. Who's going to argue with you? You cut people off. You change agendas during the meeting, raising issues no one else is prepared to discuss. People leave meetings feeling discouraged rather than energized. You insist on making every decision. No wonder people don't take responsibility. You won't let them."

I was stunned, particularly after I listened to several tape recordings of my meetings. Damn it, if the consultant wasn't right! I saw that my leadership behavior was counterproductive. So I said, "I'll change."

The next meeting I tried to be quiet. That lasted about three minutes. I tried to stop providing answers. That lasted about as long. It was tough being different. It was too easy for me to slip back into old leadership patterns. The staff, as much as they complained about the old me, liked the comfort of knowing what I was going to do. That helped them figure out what they needed to do. All of us were trapped in this "death dance" of hating what we were doing but hating more the task of changing it.

To change my leadership behavior took lots of conscious work. First, I changed my mental picture of my leadership job. I stopped being the decision maker and micro-manager. I stopped deciding production schedules and fixing sales problems. Instead, I insisted that others handle those situations. I changed my leadership job to providing resources and developing people.

Then I needed new leadership skills to support this new leadership job definition. I inventoried what I needed to learn, and went to work to learn it. I worked on such people development skills as asking questions, rather than giving answers. I worked hard to be certain that the right person owned the right problem.

It wasn't easy for me to unlearn old leadership habits. I was afraid that I'd have no real function to perform. Consultants and writers can talk glibly about coaching and question-asking as the "new" leadership responsibilities. But I was afraid that people wouldn't respect me if I didn't have quick, good answers. Asking questions looks wimpish. I still catch myself making decisions, telling people how to solve their problems. After all these years I still keep learning that I need to keep learning.

I Don't Know How to Get There. I Just Know I Have to Go

When I decided that I absolutely had to change my management style, I didn't know in detail how it would work. I knew I had to change. "How to change?" and "What will the final change look like?" were questions to which I didn't have good answers. But I knew that if I didn't start I'd never finish. If I waited until I had all the answers, I'd be old and gray—and probably out of business.

When I first stopped tasting the sausage, I didn't have a clear picture of what would happen next. I didn't know that the people would jump in and ask for production and quality data. I didn't know that they'd seize the opportunity to get more control over their work lives. I just knew that I had to change my style. My ceasing to taste the sausage was an opportunity for me to learn how to manage in a different way.

I did something when I started changing myself and my company that made it easier. I told my customers and my people what I was trying to do and what it would mean for them. I told them that I didn't know how to get there, but doing something was so important, I was going to get started, anyway. I said this meant we would probably make lots of mistakes, but nothing would be etched in concrete. We would make them together, and the minute a mistake became apparent we would fix it together. I gave myself and everyone else permission not to be perfect.

Both the customers and the people saw my sense of urgency to improve. They knew it would no longer be business as usual.

QUESTION:
Am I learning fast enough?

LEADERSHIP SOLUTION:
It's never fast enough.

PART III

LEADING
THE JOURNEY

DETERMINE FOCUS AND DIRECTION

- VISION
- CUSTOMERS
- GREAT PERFORMANCE
- VALUE-ADDED STRATEGIES

STIMULATE
SELF-DIRECTED
ACTIONS

DEVELOP OWNERSHIP

REMOVE OBSTACLES

- Systems
- Skills
- Structures
- Mentalities

Introduction

Lead the Journey so Others Follow

The systematic method I developed for transforming buffalo into geese is the Leading the Journey (LTJ) leadership system. That system forms the framework for Parts Three through Seven, much as it formed the basis for my leadership journey.

The Four Leadership Tasks in Leading the Journey

The Leading the Journey model is based on four leadership activities:

1. Determining focus and direction
2. Removing the obstacles
3. Developing ownership
4. Stimulating self-directed action

My leadership journey begins in the only place a journey should ever begin: by defining the destination. You begin by deciding what it is that you really want to create. What do you really want to have? This is your end state. The unfortunate truth is that most people spend their whole lifetime waiting for their ship to come in—at the bus stop—and wondering why it never shows up! You need to know where you are going. That is the first step.

The second leadership activity is to look at where you are now in terms of the obstacles that prevent great performance. Then you can remove the biggest ones. There are two kinds of obstacles: those that are found in the systems, structures, and practices, and those that are found in the mind-sets of the people.

Mind-sets are powerful obstacles. I was drawn to the mind-set obstacles, like a moth is drawn to the flame. I worked on problems in communication, motivation, and getting the right people. I bemoaned the death of the work ethic. But I learned that system/structure factors produced these troubling mind-sets. I learned to focus my efforts on the context obstacles, so I can affect the powerful determinants of behavior.

The third leadership activity is to develop ownership, by the people, of the obstacles to great performance. The people are the ones who can remove them. Inevitably, the wrong people own the obstacle. Remember the story of the groundskeeper? The president felt he owned the problem of that person's performance. Wrong! The employee must own the responsibility for his or her performance, not the manager. Newton discovered the law of gravity. He was correct, except in one situation. Everything does flow downhill. Except in an organization, where ownership flows uphill. We call it upward delegation. The result? Managers own all the wrong problems.

The fourth leadership activity is to stimulate self-directed actions to achieve great performance. Leadership is not about what you know. Leadership is about what you *do* with what you know. So the emphasis in the Leading the Journey process is on action.

The LTJ process involves every individual in the organization. Leadership, in this intellectual capitalism age, is all about engaging people's minds, hearts, and hands in these leadership activities.

QUESTION:
What must I do to be ready to lead this journey?

LEADERSHIP SOLUTION:
Leadership is making it possible for others to follow by thinking strategically and focusing on the right directions, removing the obstacles, developing ownership, and taking self-directed actions.

CHAPTER 9

The Magic of Vision

Vision Is the Focus

Vision is the beginning point for leading the journey. Vision focuses. Vision inspires. Without a vision, the people perish. Vision is our alarm clock in the morning, our caffeine in the evening. Vision touches the heart. It becomes the criterion against which all behavior is measured. Vision becomes the glasses that tightly focus all of our sights and actions on that which we want to be tomorrow—not what we were yesterday or what we are today. The focus on vision disciplines us to think strategically. The vision is the framework for leading the journey.

Vision is the most sought-after executive characteristic. I recently sat next to an executive recruiter on an airplane. He told me, "More than half of the searches I'm engaged in now, ranging from presidents of Fortune 100 companies to leaders for major cultural centers, require people with vision." Whenever executives get together, vision is the topic of conversation. Most of them see that vision is the difference between the long-term success of any organization and a certain second-rate position.

Vision Sees What *Must Be* Tomorrow, Beyond What *Is* Today

Vision is not some mystical, mysterious insight. John Teets, chairman of Greyhound Corporation, puts vision in perspective. "The executive's job," he says, "is to see what the company *can be*—beyond what it is today" (emphasis added). The editors of *Fortune* magazine said, "The new paragon of an executive is a person who can *envision* a future for the organization and then *inspire* colleagues to join in building that future" (emphasis added). Vision, then, is not predicting the twenty-first century. It's much more pedantically seeing what the organization can be in 1996.

More important, vision paints a picture of what your organization must be if it is to survive. The essence of executive vision is saying, "Here's where we have to go, and here's a general road map for how we will get there."

John Akers, president and CEO of IBM, has a vision of what IBM must be in the future. It *must* be principally a software and services company, rather than the hardware-oriented company it is today. It *must* dominate the personal computer business as it dominates the mainframe business today. It *must* be fast in developing new products. It *must* "own" the applications that run on its hardware, as it owns the hardware operating systems today. John Akers sees what his organization *must be* if it is to retain its premier position.

This picture of what we must be tomorrow, rather than what we are today or were yesterday, forces us to think strategically. We must manage backward from the future, rather than forward from the present.

Customers Help You See the Vision

Vision flows from extensive contact with customers and suppliers. It does not flow from some mystical insight into the future gained by consulting one's gut (no matter how golden) or one's astrologer. There's no substitute for direct feedback from the people who make the marketplace.

One of my clients runs a regional payroll processing and bookkeeping business. He was struggling when he came to me, believing that "empowerment" was the answer to his business problems. He didn't have an answer to my first question, "In the best of all worlds, from the customer's perspective, what is great performance?" So I helped him find out from customers what they really wanted from him. He was surprised.

Rather than fancy programs and new products, his customers wanted personalized service. They were lost in the maze of his big competitors. They felt "unimportant." They were treated like "just one more account." Small businesses also felt intimidated by the large payroll processing firms.

Based upon this input from customers, he put together a new vision for his company. Rather than competing directly with the biggies in the business—Automatic Data Processing, the $1.2-billion leader in the field, or Paychex, the rapidly growing number two—he goes after the small business market with personalized service. Each of his neighborhood/storefront locations has its own computer, networked with the larger central computer. He emphasizes, "We're just around the corner—and just for you." He redesigned his organization, setting up integrated teams who sell and service each account. These teams are paid on the basis of profits and customer service ratings.

His vision, "We're here for you," comes directly from listening to what his customers want and need. He's grown at the compound rate of 50 percent per year for the past seven years and shows an average of 32 percent return on equity versus less than 20 percent for his larger competitors. He is successful because his vision is based on the needs of his customers.

Vision Inspires

Vision goes beyond carrots and sticks. Long-term successful companies stand for more than just profit and big salaries. They also stand for people: people who contribute net value to society. Henry Ford, in 1915, put it well: "Wealth, like happiness, is never attained when sought after directly. It always comes as a by-product of providing a useful service." Our experience tells us that Henry Ford was absolutely correct. Inspiring visions create value for others: employees, customers, and the community at large. Inspiring visions motivate people. People need to see use of the vision as a way to accomplish some greater good.

ServiceMaster's vision of "Honoring God in all we do" and "Grow people" is a classic example of a vision that inspires by adding value to others. The $1.6-billion cleaning giant lives that vision through opening and closing every meeting with a prayer and offering a wide range of educational programs. This vision inspires ServiceMaster's employees. ServiceMaster has the lowest absence rate in their industry and the highest return of any commercial company in the world.

The inspiration of a vision must exist at all levels of the organization. The clerical-pool supervisor needs a vision. The machine shop supervisor needs a vision. The engineering manager needs a vision. I worked with the department head of a clerical pool for a large insurance company. She saw the need to dramatically improve the department's performance. Her boss told her, "That place is a mess. Fix it or I'll disband the pool and assign the people directly to departments."

I helped her recognize the need to sharpen and clarify the department's vision. Historically, the pool emphasized efficiency as its primary focus. After much discussion she felt she could broaden the department's charter.

To clarify a new vision, she invited the departments who were users/customers to staff meetings to discuss how people in the pool could better serve their needs. After several of these meetings she announced a new vision for her department: "Helping people protect our customers." Her vision, she explained, included both helping users more effectively do their work and helping department members realize their individual career growth.

Almost immediately, productivity in the department rose, and her people started to go out of their way to help users. A clerk-typist in the department told me, "It [the vision] helped me to see how I was doing important work. Before, all I did was type forms. Now I see how I'm helping people get vital coverage they need to assure their peace of mind."

Vision Is Clarity

Clarity is power. Clarity motivates people to use the vision as a criterion to evaluate their actions. People ask, "Does my action support the vision?" The answer must be clear. Vision provides the tight focus on thinking strategically. It insists that everyone direct his or her energies toward creating the tomorrow we want.

Brevity helps. Use a short, simple, easy-to-understand statement of your vision to gain clarity and empower its use as a decisional criterion. Feel the clarity and inspiration in these examples:

The most successful IBM third-party distributor:

> To provide the highest quality specialty software products and services to the users of IBM midrange products.
> * Never lose a good customer.
> * Never lose a good employee.
> * Deliver what is promised.
> * Be #1 in all that we do.

The largest software and services company in the world:

> Climb the next tallest mountain, together, with customers, suppliers, and employees.

Vision Is a Worthy Commitment

People will go to extraordinary lengths for something they believe in and to which they commit. But a vision must be worthy of commitment. The following story illustrates this point.

An entrepreneur took her key executive to the top of a hill overlooking a city. She asked him, "Do you see that knoll down there just below the crest?"

He said, "Yes, I see it."

She then asked him, "Picture a house on that knoll overlooking the city. Can you see it?"

"Yes, I can see it," he replied.

"Now picture a swimming pool on the left and a tennis court on the right of the house. Can you see it?"

"Oh yes! I can see it," exclaimed the man.

She then said to him, "If you work hard for the next five years and the company does well, someday that will all be mine."

Does that sound like a vision worthy of a commitment? Obviously not. Yet that's precisely the kind of vision many organizations present to their people. "Work hard," the saying goes, "so the leader's program will succeed." It's so obvious that it hardly needs elaboration. People need to see the personal benefit from their vision of great performance.

Vision Generates Supportive Actions

Actions must reflect the vision. I learned that the leader must live the vision, or no one else will. People watch what we do as leaders and follow. They notice most what we *do,* not what we *say.* They follow most what we *do,* not what we *say.*

Another of my clients was in the nursery business. He specialized in roses. He learned about the need to live the vision. He specialized in roses because he knew how to grow them and felt that he could grow them better than anybody else. For some time his customers agreed, and his business boomed. He was so successful that he decided to expand into selling other flowers, which he bought on the wholesale market. Buying these other flowers, and expanding his selling territory, stretched him too thin, and he ran into trouble. When the cash flow crunch hit, he pulled back into his original rose market. In the process, he lost his dedication to growing the best roses. "I got sick and tired of roses," he said.

To rededicate himself, and his people, he wrote out his vision. He posted it in his greenhouse for his thirteen people to see. "I want us to grow the best roses in the world. Always do work of which we can be proud."

He funded his vision with action. He redrew the sales commission plan to pay commissions only when customers rated the roses as "best." Employee training in rose growing and monthly visits to customers became a required part of everyone's job. Within two months his business set sales and profit records as people really "lived" the vision.

Vision is the focus of action. It is a critical leadership task. It doesn't take a "special person." Vision is a statement of what your customers tell you your organization must be. It is a simple-to-understand, inspirational, focusing statement. It establishes the framework for all other leadership activities. Then lots of actions to live and support the vision must follow. Vision is much more "down and dirty doing" than fancy plans and words. Isn't that what leadership has always been about, anyway?

QUESTION:
What Must We Become To Prosper?

LEADERSHIP SOLUTION:
Develop A Vision or Your People Will Perish.

PART IV

DETERMINING FOCUS AND DIRECTION

DETERMINE *FOCUS* AND DIRECTION

- VISION
- CUSTOMERS
- GREAT PERFORMANCE
- VALUE-ADDED STRATEGIES

STIMULATE
SELF-DIRECTED
ACTIONS

DEVELOP OWNERSHIP

REMOVE OBSTACLES

- Systems
- Skills
- Structures
- Mentalities

Introduction

Leaders set direction. It's the first critical leadership activity in Leading the Journey. But "what direction?" is the critical leadership question. Is off the cliff the "right" direction? Not unless you're a leader of the lemmings. Leaders set the "right" direction, delivering great performance for customers.

Margaret Thatcher's words made a deep impression on me. "I can not manage the past. There are other people in my government who manage the present. It is my unique responsibility as the leader to shine a spotlight on the future, and marshall the support of my countrymen to create that future." That is the leader's job in this intellectual capitalism age, regardless of position. A salesperson needs to shine the spotlight on the future she wants to create, an effective partnership with her customer and all their business, and marshal the support of all the people she needs to make that happen. A janitor needs to shine the spotlight on the future he wants to create—a clean floor—and marshal the support of the people he needs to create that future. Leaders need to shine the spotlight on the future and then marshal the people to create that future. Inevitably, that future involves great performance for customers.

Leaders Focus on Great Performance for *Customers*

Great performance is critical for survival in any marketplace. Being the best at delivering products and services that are noticeably better than your competition isn't everything. It's the only thing! Red Sander's words, often attributed to coach Vince Lombardi, echo in many different arenas. This is the key to success and I can't stress it enough.

There may be twenty or more things that a customer would like to have. But there are never more than a few things that are critical to have. Focusing people on the few most important factors helps them separate the "must do" items from the mountains of minutiae they encounter every day. It also helps people feel effective, because the things they work on make a difference.

When people come to me to help them become better leaders, my first question is "To do what?" The "what" is critical. One of our definitions of leadership is to "get people to do the right things." The right things are everything that must be done to deliver great performance from the customer's point of view. My task as a leader and coach to others is to help design organizations so that every person is focused on delivering great performance to their customers.

QUESTION:
Is every person in your company focused on delivering great performance for his/her customers?

LEADERSHIP SOLUTION:
Focus provides motivation to delight customers.

CHAPTER 10

Focus Provides Motivation

Customers Are Where It All Begins

Nothing happens until somebody buys something. That's why customers are the central focus for the LTJ process.

Customers love firsts. They love new products. More, customers love feeling that they are first in your attention. Most of all, it's about being first in the hearts of your customers, so they don't even think of buying someone else's products. Coach Lombardi put it well: "There's only one place to finish, and that's first."

Maintaining long-term customers is about creating value—doing something customers want different or better than anybody else.

Customers are where it all begins. Delighting them. Talking to them in their language. Selling them what they want. Learning from them what they need.

Most of all, getting and keeping customers is about everyone in the organization owning the responsibility to get and keep customers. Every person, every day, views every activity, every procedure, every process, through the perspective of "What is great performance for my customer?" Each and every person owns the responsibility for delighting customers. That's the right and only focus.

Focus on What Should Be Done

At Johnsonville our customers want great taste and fun. Our people are focused on producing great taste every time. Our vision is to become the greatest sausage company in the world. Every sausage that is made has to pass a simple test: Will this sausage contribute to our being the greatest sausage company in the world?

Our people track and chart every day's production of every product. They compare it to the competition's. They compare it to our customer taste profiles. They study our customers for clues on how to make it even better. They are continuously working on new technologies that will revolutionize the industry. This is part of a never-ending drive to create the ultimate taste experience for our customers. Ask any person who works at Johnsonville, "What's the top priority?" and he/she will answer, "Making great-tasting sausage."

What constitutes great performance is different for every company. People probably won't stand in line for great-tasting airplanes. That means there are no recipes. Focus everyone in your company on owning the responsibility to find out what his or her customers want and then on consistently delivering that great performance.

Focus Tells You What You Shouldn't Have

I learned through bitter experience that most businesses suffer not from an absence of resources, but from an absence of focus. Several years ago we needed to expand one of our product lines. The product was made in Wisconsin, where we had strong market penetration. But it was tough breaking into other geographic areas. We concluded that buying smaller regional companies with similar products was the best way to expand geographically.

We bought a company in another part of the country. It had similar, though not identical, product lines. This new company was different enough that it took a lot of my time. Shortly after we bought this company, our R&D group developed several new production techniques that made it easier to penetrate new geographic regions. This presented us with an opportunity to create a national brand. But the resources consumed by our new company prevented us from capitalizing on the opportunity. This business was the tail wagging the dog. It took me four years to sell that business before we could afford to invest in the new technology.

I held on to that business three years too long, believing that the turnaround was always only a few months away. It took me eight years to do what I could have done in four. All because I was focused on the wrong things. I ran an incredible risk. If any of our larger competitors had discovered the new technology and used it in their product line, we could have been history. It was our competitors' passivity rather than my wisdom that saved us. I was lucky that time. I don't intend to press my luck again. I intend to keep focused on the right things.

People *Are* Motivated: They Need Focus

I work with many companies besides my own on this issue of focus. I talk about every person being responsible for satisfying his or her own customers. People invariably comment, "This sounds great, but how do I motivate them to do it?" Many people believe that the other people in their organization don't care enough to make great performance happen for customers. This has not been my experience. In fact, I find just the opposite to be true. The following incident is typical.

A group of technicians in a food processing plant operated a production machine with the guard off. The guard had malfunctioned and the machine would not work with it in place. Everyone knew it was against the rules to operate it without the guard and knew as well that they ran the risk of being disciplined if they got caught.

The plant safety team held a meeting with the production operators to ask why they had violated the safety rules. The safety team asked the operators if they would drive a car without any brakes. The operators' reply was classic. They said, "Of course we wouldn't use a car without brakes. But this is different. We can't short sales. They need the product. So we removed the guard so we could go faster." These people didn't need motivation. They needed focus.

What is the leader's job? Create the environment where people focus on customers. Build the systems and structures that focus people on customers. Develop the mentality that the customer is the boss. It's a tough job. But it's absolutely essential in this intellectual capitalism world.

QUESTION:
How can I focus every person on giving our customers what they really want?

LEADERSHIP SOLUTION:
Encourage your people to ask their customers. Set the example by asking yours.

CHAPTER 11

What Do Customers Really Buy?

What does Johnsonville sell? "Sausage," I used to say, or "Food." "Protein," a nutritionist might add. I was wrong. Johnsonville sells all of those—and none of them. My definition of what we sold was a big barrier to my progress. But the reason I got the wrong answer was that I asked the wrong question.

The question asks about the product from the supplier's point of view. What a waste! It doesn't matter what the supplier *thinks* he's selling. It only matters what the customer *believes* he's buying.

My leadership task in Leading the Journey is to provide the direction and focus for everyone in the organization. A central part of that direction and focus must be on customers and what they think they buy.

What Do Customers *Really* Buy?

What do customers really buy from Johnsonville? They buy great taste and fun. How do we know? We asked customers about our product, and we listened. We watched customers use our products, and we learned. We let customers teach us about our products. We didn't presume to know why customers buy—or how they used our products. We asked them directly. That's the only way to find out what customers are really buying from you.

Progress only happened when I recognized that my assumptions about why people bought sausage was the biggest obstacle to actually knowing why they bought it. When I stopped assuming I knew, started asking questions, and began encouraging others to ask questions, eyes began to open all over the company. We used to think about our products the way we made them: smoked, cooked, etc. When we started thinking about why people bought them and how they used them, sales took off.

IBM understands. What does IBM really sell? Hardware? Software? Solutions? They sell all of those—and none of them. An old IBM advertisement says it all. "At IBM, we sell a good night's sleep." IBM sells certainty. In a chaotic world, with too many technological choices, no one ever got fired for buying IBM. I have my favorite IBM story. Everyone has one, it seems. During the installation of our IBM mid-range computer, a glitch developed on Friday afternoon and the computer "crashed." Worldwide payroll was scheduled for Monday morning at seven. IBM people began to appear, seemingly dropping from the sky. A programmer showed up from Rochester. An analyst flew in from Singapore. All told, seven IBMers worked the weekend, and the payroll ran at 7 A.M. Monday. I bought certainty and a good night's sleep. I willingly paid a premium for it from IBM.

My specialty chemical company sold ink for ballpoint pens, a fiercely price-competitive business. We commanded a premium in that commodity market. How? We didn't sell ink. We sold a solution to the customer's problem. Ink is a small portion of the total cost of the pen. But nonavailability of the proper color can shut down an entire line at great cost to the pen manufacturer. We guaranteed delivery and posted a performance bond to back up our guarantee. The customer bought production continuity from us—and paid a premium for it.

A friend of mine runs a restaurant chain. When asked what he sold, he responded, "I sell a good time. We sell good food, but that's not the reason people come to our restaurants. People go out to eat as a treat—on an anniversary, birthday, or some other special event. Our job is to help them enjoy their special time." His chain is the envy of the restaurant business.

How Can You Find Out?

How can you find out what customers really buy from you? First, examine your own assumptions. Are they an obstacle to hearing what customers buy? Then ask customers. A few short questions, followed by lots of silence, listening, and note taking can be very informative.

Everyone has at least four customer sets, as shown in the following diagram.

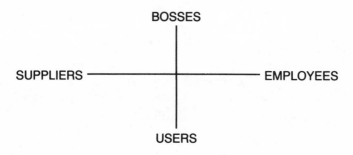

There are the people for whom you work—shareholders and bosses. There are the people who work for you—employees. There are the people whom you supply—with ideas, tangible products, services, information. There are those who supply you—with ideas, tangible products, services, information. Each set of customers has expectations and demands about your performance. Each of them wants and needs certain performances from you. Success is rooted in meeting those customer expectations and needs.

Leaders Focus on Customers— and So Does Everyone Else

The leader's job is to put his or her customers first. He or she does that by determining what each of them wants or demands in terms of great performance from the leader, and then by working assiduously to deliver that great performance. The leader encourages others by setting the example to follow and adopt the same methodology. The leader also needs to keep asking questions about end-user customers such as "What do your end-user customers really want? What is great performance for each of them? How do you know? How are you doing in meeting your end-user customers' needs?"

The leader sets the tone, provides the example, and stimulates through constant questioning. The leader leads by providing direction and focus on what customers really buy.

QUESTION:
How do I look to customers?

LEADERSHIP SOLUTION:
Find out what bugs your customers that you can fix profitably for them.

CHAPTER 12

The Market Is a
Great Place to Plant
Your Company

Focus on Finding *the* Location

"There are three keys to success in the retail business," my grandfather was fond of saying, "location, location, and location." He didn't invent that statement. Since the beginning of time, the business person went where the business was. Whether it was in the basement of the lord's castle, or a small shop off the square, or from the back of a horse-drawn cart, or from the piled-high shelves of a super store, the successful business person came to where the customers were located. It's amazing how this simple commonsense principle is so frequently violated.

My job as the leader in my organization is to help people focus on finding where customers are located, and then focusing the organization to satisfy those customers. Part of my focusing task is to locate the customer. In Leading the Journey we need a destination, and there's no better destination than the customer's location.

The Place Is Where *the* Customers Are

Johnsonville Foods began in Johnsonville, Wisconsin. We were a meat retailer. Unfortunately, the people in Johnsonville at the time did not need one more meat retailer. Our company would have collapsed quickly if it had stayed there. The market wasn't big enough to support them. My mom said, "Since they won't come to us, we'd better go to them." So my folks moved the business to a larger market and were immediately successful.

We've all seen two gas stations in the same neighborhood have widely different successes. One station, located on the median of a frequently traveled, divided highway, with easy access from both sides, is raking it in so fast they can hardly take it all to the bank quickly enough. Another station, located a few blocks off the freeway, is barely scraping by. The difference? Location, location, location.

Location Isn't Just a Physical Place— It's Also a State of Mind

Location is more than just a geographic spot. I learned the hard way that it is also a state of mind. My daughter was in the automotive parts aftermarket. She believed that she could create a competitive advantage in what is basically a commodity business by offering short-time product delivery. She would literally bring the location to the customer. The disinterest expressed by the customers, and the disbelief voiced by her suppliers, should have told her she was on the wrong track. But, no, she was certain that she had identified a way to gain a competitive edge, so she plowed ahead. She loaded up trucks with lots of inventory, set up an elaborate dispatching system, and hired enough drivers to blanket the area. Eight months of losses later she was forced to reconsider her position. Bringing the location to the customer was not what the customer wanted.

She began to notice what customers talked about when they called in to place their orders. She logged their questions and requests. She asked everyone who dealt with customers to find out "Where's the customer's head?" After only a few days an obvious pattern emerged.

Customers wanted advice and help. They were often mechanics who didn't know parts. They needed help in figuring out what parts could be substituted and what parts couldn't. It also turned out that most customers were more time-sensitive than price-sensitive. She was right in figuring that out, although they counted the time in hours, not minutes, as she had previously thought. Once she located customers' heads, she was in a much better position to figure out how to appeal to them. Her own predetermined solutions, and her unwillingness to think of location in other than physical terms, were obstacles to her success.

Seek and Thou Shalt Discover *the* Location

It's probably too simple but . . . it's almost always worked for me. The easiest and most direct way to find out where the customers' heads are is to find out from the customers themselves. In the automotive parts example, my daughter noticed what customers asked her. Then she went out and asked them if they really valued her consulting help and wanted more of it. They unanimously answered yes. She also offered to help them save time by stocking their most frequently used parts on a weekly basis, which she could identify for them from her computer files. They liked that idea, providing she was still available to them for consultation, and they could get special orders within an hour of ordering. The outcome was that each customer got his or her own consultant who took a weekly stock order, and who was available for assistance and special orders during the week. Business grew, costs dropped, and margins rose by seven percentage points. Seeking and finding your customer's mental location is profitable business indeed.

Location: The Certainty of a Marriage, Not the Thrill of a One-Night Stand

The auto parts example points to one inevitable truth: We are in the relationship business, not the product selling business. My daughter didn't sell auto parts. She sold advice, which helps the repair person do a better job. The parts are ancillary.

A typical conversation with her customer goes like this:

"I've got the following problem . . . What do you think?"

"Have you tried . . . ?"

"Yes, and here's what happens . . ."

"It sounds like your problem is . . ."

"Sounds right to me. What parts do I need?"

"It'll take a . . . Your cost is . . . We'll have it to you in an hour. Okay?"

"Sure, thanks."

Those parts cost 10 percent more than the same parts from another supplier. But the repair person was buying helpful advice, and was willing to pay extra for the certainty that the advice would be there when needed. That call with that customer is repeated dozens of times a week.

The same phenomenon exists in the software business. We sell a complete solution to a customer's problem. We do whatever it takes to give the customer absolute certainty about which toxic and hazardous materials are stored where. Customers pay only one price for "whatever it takes" to satisfy them—custom code, physical inventory, training, integration with other hardware—whatever it takes. We are there to help whenever they need us. They can count on us, and they do.

I've discovered that our software customers don't really care about bits and bytes. They have a problem. They want a solution to their problem. They want it now! And they want to know that we'll be there when they need us. It's like going to the dentist. We don't really care about the speed of the drill or the quality of the X rays. "Fix the tooth" is our main concern. "Make it right as fast and painlessly as possible" is what we want. "And be there at 2 A.M. if the fix fails."

My Blind Spots Prevent Me from Finding *the* Location

My daughter was the biggest obstacle to her success in the auto parts business. Her absolute insistence on a thirty-minute guarantee almost drove the company into bankruptcy. She was so busy listening to herself that she couldn't/didn't hear anybody else. She believed she knew better than the customers what they really wanted. She was so busy telling them what they *should* want that she couldn't hear what they needed. Such arrogance!

Many people suffer from this same arrogance. The leaders in Detroit continued to insist that customers wanted large cars well into the eighties, refusing to recognize the growing market share of the small Japanese imports as anything other than an "aberration." They lost a whole generation of car buyers and are struggling today to recapture them. They lost sight of where the customers were.

My Blind Spots Obstruct the Entire Organization

Worse, I infected the entire organization with my arrogance. In the specialty chemical business I believed that we had the best ink. At my insistence we told customers about our quality, over and over again. When customers didn't seem to respond, I insisted that we shout the message louder, and spent more on slicker direct mailers and trade shows. I insisted that everyone preach the quality message. I trained every direct customer contact person on how to "sell quality." I was an evangelist for our gospel of quality. For over a year I pushed it. Sales didn't budge. Competitors continued to eat into our market share. "What was wrong?" I wondered. "Maybe it will just take longer to get the message across," I thought.

Then it happened. A good customer told it to me like it really was for her. "I don't know what 'quality' means in your business," she said, "and I get annoyed with your self-serving, self-righteous statements about your 'quality.' My people get insulted when you tell them how to use your stuff. Sure I want quality, but I want a lot more also. I threw out your salesman last month because all he wanted to talk about was your product quality and not my real concerns. When are you going to listen to me!"

Whew! Talk about a cold shower of reality. I had trained, and thereby contaminated, our people so well that they stopped listening to customers. My entire organization was immobilized by my blind spot.

Leaders Design Systems and Structures That Help Keep the Focus on *the* Location

I relearned the lesson: My task as the leader in my organization is to keep everyone, including myself, focused on customers. We must find out where they are, physically and psychologically, and discover ever better ways to satisfy them. Systems and structures maintain the focus. My job is to design the systems and structures that provide and maintain that focus.

In the auto parts business my daughter's solution was to match consultants with customers. Consultants were then paid on the basis of continuing orders from the same customer. In the specialty chemical business, we established a system that encouraged our people to solve customer problems by meeting a set of specific customer expectations. In the software business, we set up multi-discipline teams to work with industry-based customer sets, and systems to reward those teams based on margins and long-term customer satisfaction. At Johnsonville, we converted the sales incentive system from one based on volume (as most sales incentive plans are) to one based on margin and customer satisfaction. That resulted in improved margins and a growing business as customers felt much better serviced.

QUESTION:
Am I with my customer?

LEADERSHIP SOLUTION:
If at first you don't succeed, you're not with your customers. Find them.

CHAPTER 13

The Customer Is the Boss: Productive Partnerships with the Boss

The selling game is old and well known. "Sell, sell, sell" is what I used to tell my people. When times got tough, I had a simple message, "Sell, sell, sell more!" I learned that I had the right target, but the wrong technique.

From Selling to Partnering

I always practiced the *sales approach*. In the ink business it was very clear. "Let me tell you why black is the best color," I trained my salespeople to say. "It looks great on the paper. It conveys an image of power and control. It's relatively inexpensive." I made my living selling features and benefits.

This approach worked through most of the 1970s and into the early 1980s, at which time customers became more sophisticated. There were more choices in the marketplace. Competitors got smarter. In an effort to stay ahead of the pack, I changed my tune. "What color would you like?" I trained my salespeople to ask their customers. We adopted a more *customer-oriented approach*. If a customer wanted pink perfumed ink, we'd mix them up a batch. If the customer wanted it next Tuesday, we'd get it to them next Tuesday. That worked for a while.

But, as usual, times changed. Customers got even more sophisticated. Competitors got even smarter. We had to change or run the risk of being buried. Now I train my salespeople to say, "Let's work *together* to discover how color can contribute to *your* goals." Notice the *partnership approach*. Notice the shift in emphasis from what I have in my bag (or can get from my factory) to what the customer needs. My job now is not to sell my products. It's to help the customer achieve his/her goals.

It's hard to get people trained in the selling approach to shift into a partnership mode. IBM has that problem. So do AT&T and most every other major organization. It's not easy—just necessary.

Be a Partner—or Be Gone

We've learned the hard way that the old sales approach doesn't work. Selling features and benefits almost always degenerates into a price competition in which there are no winners. In my software business, we sell $200 worth of disks and paper for $7.9 million. We must demonstrate our value added, or else we couldn't stay in business. I learned that lesson, again, through an experience early in the computer business.

We were competing for a major contract against several of the big firms in our business. We figured that the contract should go for approximately $17 million. Our costs were in the $13-million range. So we calculated that someone else could be hungry enough to bid in the $14–15-million range.

At the last minute we heard the customer worry about the accuracy of his inventory records. We also heard him worry about the huge job of entering fifty years of paper records into the new computer system. We decided to recalculate our bid. We got fixed price estimates from the best physical inventory firm and the best data entry firm in the area. We added their $4 million to our cost structure, and bid $32 million. In the bid we guaranteed to the customer's partner to "do whatever it took" to ensure the accuracy of the computer records, including doing the physical inventory and entering the data ourselves. We guaranteed the price.

Our bid was double everyone else's. Our bid was the only guaranteed price and the only one that addressed the inventory accuracy and data entry issues. We won the job. The purchasing agent told us later, "We really felt that you heard our concerns and were willing to work with us to handle them." Score one for the partnership approach.

Learning from this and other similar experiences, we've changed our entire selling approach. Every six months we sit down with every customer and review that customer's business. We've found that customers love to talk about their challenges and their successes. In fact, we've never had a customer refuse to meet with us.

Preparation, Preparation, Preparation

What happens *before* a customer call will often determine what happens *during* the call and *after* that call. We've learned to prepare the ground before we attempt to plant the seed. We take three significant preparation steps before every partnership interview.

First, we search the data bank of the information service to which we subscribe for significant trends, developments, and issues in the industry and the company. We identify a few significant issues to serve as a launching pad for discussion and the tangible demonstration of our interest in and knowledge about their business. We know we've succeeded when we hear such statements as "We didn't know that." Or "How did you find that out?" We intend to bring substantive and, we hope, new information to the interview.

Second, we plumb our own internal data base to identify the personal interests and issues of the people with whom we'll be talking. We gather and track personal information about all customers. Our data base contains such important data as birthdays, anniversaries, names of family members, favorite sports, colors, vacation spots, and other personal information. We shape what we present and how we present it to meet the personal preferences of the listener.

Third, we call in advance to review the purpose and agenda for the meeting. We ask customers what they want to accomplish in the meeting and how they will know when they've achieved it. We inquire about their preparation and what preparation they expect from us. We clarify expectations and get on the same wavelength. No surprises or blindsides.

Begin with the Customer's Business

We begin by working to understand the customer's business. We pose a version of the following general directive:

- Tell me about your activity.

We follow up with these more specific questions:

- What are the few keys to success in your unit?
- What is your unit's advantage in the marketplace (why do customers buy from you?), and how do you contribute to that advantage?
- What is great ICBIH (I can't believe it's happening) performance for your unit, and for yourself, for the coming year?

One supermarket chain customer of Johnsonville surprised us with a unique set of answers to these questions. The meat manager for this several-hundred-store chain was an old antagonist. We believed that he favored our largest competitor. He always gave us the difficult orders, those with short time deliveries and big discounts. We suspected that he kept us around just to keep his preferred supplier honest.

He surprised us by granting an interview. I expected to have the door slammed in our faces. During the interview he stressed his need to be the industry innovator in his categories, something we never heard before. His chain was the higher cost supplier, so he felt that they needed to differentiate themselves by being innovative. He wanted to know the impact of his strategies on the marketplace, but his internal systems weren't fast or accurate enough to give him the data he needed. Compounding his information problem was his head office location, which was many miles removed from his stores, so he couldn't personally visit the stores to see for himself.

This was a golden opportunity. We made three proposals: (1) link our two companies electronically, so he would get shipment and sales information per category, per day; (2) keep him posted monthly on developments we saw out in the marketplace upon which he might capitalize; 3) develop together a year advertising and promotion program. In return we wanted a year's minimum order. He accepted the offer, doubling last year's order. Had we not asked this series of questions, we would never have gotten his attention. We'd still be competing on price against a preferred competitor.

Peering into the Cloudy Crystal Ball Can Stir Partnering Desires

Next we focus on the future. Often the uncertainty of what can happen tomorrow encourages customers to look to suppliers to help them deal with those risks. So we ask a general question:

- What current/future developments will change the way you and your unit do business?

We follow with a subset of more specific questions, such as:

- What developments are impacting both your department's activities and the company's?
- What do you see coming in the future that will change the way you and your company do business?
- What do you and your unit plan to do to prepare for these coming events so you are ready *before* they occur?

This line of questioning is where our preparation pays off the most. We are almost always able to put some new information about the customer's business on the table—information of which the customer was not aware. Most often this leads to very stimulating discussions. In our software business we discovered that talking about the future is a potent line of questioning when dealing with hazardous waste. The rules change so rapidly while the consequences for noncompliance escalate. Customers are always interested in the rules we think will emerge in the future.

We cemented our first large contract in the chemical process industry when we brought to the plant manager's attention a recent process development which would both improve his productivity and decrease the amount of toxic material in his plant. We'd already been approved by the purchasing department, but after our interview the plant manager became our champion and sponsor. We helped him look good and he never forgot it.

Problems Spur Partnerships

When things are going well, we are loath to change what we do or whom we buy from. We work to help people get in touch with the things that cause them discomfort, so we can help them eliminate the causes of discomfort. We ask the general question:

- What are the biggest problems you face?

We follow with a specific question:

- What prevents you from being a great performer?

One of our customers in the specialty chemical company was a large automobile manufacturer. We supplied an ingredient for their bright metallic paints. During an interview they shared with us their internal quality data, which showed reject rates in excess of 35 percent on the metallic paints. They exhaustively tested the chemical components and felt the problem was in the application. They blamed poor factory supervision.

We weren't certain, so we conducted a few tests of our own. We discovered that the chemical interaction between the paint and the metal in the spray nozzle was causing a slight congealing. When baked at certain temperatures, the paint beaded and cracked. We reviewed our data with the factory and R&D people and urged them to run a few of their own experiments. They replaced the metal spray nozzle with a plastic nozzle and developed a new baking process which ameliorated any beading and cracking. Yields went up to 98-plus percent. We made lifetime friends, and customers. I believe that we are the only supplier to have a key to the factory and access through their electronic-mail system to all company information. We are an integral part of their new product planning and development team.

We're Here to Help *You*

All of the preceding discussion is "make ready." It's table setting. It's designed to establish the climate and identify the issues on which the partnership is going to work. Now we go to work. We move to defining our contribution to the customer's great performance by asking the following general question:

- How can we help you?

We follow up with the more specific questions:

- How can we help you be a great performer today?
- How can we help you remove the obstacles that prevent you from being a great performer today?
- How can we help you prepare to be a great performer in the future?

A learning-center private education business faced a tough market situation. Whenever they entered a new geographic area, they encountered suspicion and opposition from public school officials. After all, their business opportunity was created by the failure of the public· education system. They wrestled for a long time with methods to overcome this significant obstacle. They tried advisory boards, donations, and massive advertising, all to little avail. Growth was inevitably slow, with heavy losses in the first several years, and the perpetual threat that the wrong word from the local superintendent would put them out of business. Then we worked together.

"What do the superintendent and the school staff really want?" I asked.

"Don't know," they replied. "Keep their jobs maybe?"

"Maybe, but there's got to be other professional and personal issues." So we put together a partnership strategy, much like the one I'm writing about in this chapter. We went out and spoke to the superintendents, principals, teachers, and parents. The answers surprised us. These education professionals were frustrated with the bureaucratic rules that prevented them from fulfilling their education mission. Parents were frustrated by their sense of isolation from the education process. Everyone was feeling like a victim. It presented us with a great opportunity.

We crafted a program to end these feelings of victimitis. We made our education technology available to any teacher or principal who would recommend our after-school tutoring program. We offered training sessions for teachers who wanted to learn how to use our educational approach and technology in their own classrooms. We set up joint education goals and individualized learning programs with teachers and parents for children in both our after-hours tutoring and our regular school. We planned a seamless joint education effort, so that the child received similar instruction in both our center and his/her regular classroom. For every ten students recommended from a school, we offered one scholarship to be awarded by the school. That enabled local school professionals to make our special assistance available to all of their students, even the less fortunate.

In most areas, opposition from professional educators melted like snow in July. The company grew into a nationwide system, with high margins and excellent education results. They forged a partnership with public education officials which helped both achieve their goals, and improve the education of children.

Extend *Your* Hand

Up until now the discussion has been in the generic "we." But "we" don't deliver great performance. "We" don't help customers achieve their great performance. All work is done by an "I." Move to the more micro level of "I" by asking the following general question:

- Based on the above, how would you define great performance for me in the coming year that will best contribute to your great performance?

An incident that occurred to one of the product/market groups in the specialty chemical business reminded us all of the power of personalizing the partnership effort. This six-person team worked with a large chemical company under an annual contract to supply a chemical binder component. The contract was profitable and stable, or so we thought.

One of the team members worked most closely with the plant superintendent who ran the facility we supplied. In the course of the multiyear relationship the team member had helped the superintendent with such personal and professional issues as getting additional education for one of his children and installing a new process at the plant.

In the course of our semiannual partnership meeting we uncovered a potentially big opportunity for the plant and a big threat to our contract. The chemical company was "thinking about" changing their overall marketplace strategy. The change would significantly reduce, if not eliminate altogether, our current product line. This particular facility would double in capacity, so the plant superintendent would gain importance in the organization and likely a big salary increase.

As partners we went to work on converting this potential win/lose situation into a win/win. Our team member suggested that great performance for her was to help the superintendent's staff make the plans necessary to have a seamless start-up when and if the company decided to enter the new market. Great performance for her was to have the fastest and most trouble-free product start-up ever recorded in the chemical industry. Her offer was not purely altruistic. She knew that if she was involved in the detailed planning, she'd have the best opportunity to find the future niche that she and her teammates could best serve.

The plant superintendent accepted her offer and matched it by agreeing to search for ways that we could continue to be their supplier. The story has a happy ending. She became critical to the superintendent's team in planning and executing the product switchover. The start-up was flawless. Their trade magazine called it "the future model for what all new start-ups should be." Oh yes, she also found several new products we could supply, which tripled our volume.

Get on with It *Now*

Talk is cheap. Action pays. So we close every partnership session with the following question:

- What would I have to do this week to earn a rating from you of 10 out of 10 for perfect contribution to your great performance?

We review partnership actions with customers every week. In that way both partners stay focused on the mutual great performances we need to create.

My first leadership task in Leading the Journey is to focus everyone on identifying and delivering great performance for customers. Building partnerships with the *boss* is one way to Lead the Journey.

QUESTION:
Are you a supplier or a partner?

LEADERSHIP SOLUTION:
Sit with the customer, or don't get in the door.

CHAPTER 14

Reading the Tea Leaves

The future is a puzzlement. Economists disagree about the next three months. Yet we need to plan for the next three years. I believed my responsibility was to climb up into the corporate crow's nest, peer into the swirling mists of uncertainty, and pronounce the future corporate direction.

Dealing with the uncertainty of the future is difficult. It's too easy to wallow in the mire of *what could be* and never get on with *what must be*. I spent a lot of time wallowing and worrying until I realized that I should be sharing the wallowing and worrying. When we all learned to share the responsibility, things got much better, for me and my company. As I gradually moved into the intellectual capitalism age I discovered better ways to lead.

My leadership task: Focus individuals on identifying and delighting tomorrow's customers.

What's Coming? Who Knows?

I struggled to read the future. Even though it was difficult, I knew it was essential if I was going to lead my company to prepare for that future. The time to build a seawall is *before* the high tide comes crashing in.

I tried several crystal ball techniques. I hired futurists, like Alvin Toffler, to talk with us about what he saw. He was fascinating, but my people just couldn't make the connection between his "global village" and our business. We talked to industry "experts." Every industry has a "guru," and ours was no exception. I was faced with the problem of deciding which "guru" to believe, if any, because the different "gurus" gave different predictions. For all I knew, maybe they all were wrong. I inevitably fell back on my own "golden gut," believing that my intuition was the most reliable future predictor I had. I guess that's why I "owned" the responsibility for forecasting the future and planning for it. Ah, the leader's burden is indeed a heavy one!

When the Going Gets Tough, It's Usually Too Late to Get Going—Anticipate Problems Rather than Solve Them

I persisted in trying to predict the future. I knew that if I didn't prepare for it, the future had a strange way of creeping up on me and becoming the present. I knew that great leadership is not solving problems after the fact, but foreseeing potential problems and eliminating them before they occur. It is easier, and cheaper, to pay the $10 to change the oil in your engine and prevent engine seizures than to pay the $1,000 to repair the engine after the seizure locks it up.

The lesson was brought home to me by an experience in one plant. We were producing specialty chemicals for the textile manufacturing industry. We felt that we "had the niche sewed up" because we had a cozy relationship with the leading textile manufacturer. Then "It" happened. A competitor came out with a very inexpensive substitute. Their product didn't do everything ours did, but it did everything the manufacturer needed to get done. Within months we had lost the account. No matter how hard we tried, we couldn't get back in. "You've got a good product and I like working with you," the manufacturer said, "but business is business, and your price is much higher than his price."

"How could this happen to us?" I asked over and over again. In retrospect the signs were all there. There were articles in the journals about this new competitor coming on stream. He'd been building the plant for two years. Some of his early product had been tested by the labs and reported in the technical literature. I knew he'd be substantially subsidized by his government, so that his prices would be low. Yet I ignored all the signals. When the times got tough, it was too late for our company to get going. My traditional leadership had failed to anticipate the problem. I was forced into the crisis micromanagement role.

Business Is a Cycle: What Goes up Comes down, and Vice Versa

I realized then, and repeatedly in many other situations, that I don't choose the cards in this poker game of life. My only leadership job is to learn how best to play the cards I am dealt. There is no point cursing the darkness. All the curses in the world won't shed one point of light. I know it is better to spend my energies finding matches and candles to create my own light.

After I got over the shock of losing the textile account, I rolled up my sleeves and went to work. I realized that even in the best of times, I must prepare for adversity. That's my leadership job. Adversity is always just around the corner. The converse of that is also true. While I'm experiencing difficulty, I must get ready for prosperity. It always follows right behind adversity. What goes up comes down. My leadership challenge was to get people focused on what to do about the cards they had been dealt, rather than to curse the picture cards they weren't holding.

I began by asking the people two thinking-strategically questions:

1. What will it take to have a profitable textile business?
2. What will it take to never be surprised again?

This was my effort to work the new leadership paradigm.

Given the existence of this low-cost subsidized supplier, the people answered the first question by abandoning the low-end commodity textile coloring business and focusing attention on the specialty color market. They went back to the textile manufacturer and worked with him on his particularly difficult coloring problems—such as the bright-bright and the metallic colors. He was pleased to have us solve those problems for him, and was more than willing to pay us a premium price for those products. We wound up making more profit from his account with this new approach. It took us two years to recover, however. Given the investment required and discounted cash flows, our inattention cost us five years of profit. That's a steep price to pay for arrogance—and an inappropriate leadership approach.

We then answered the second strategic-thinking question: "What will it take to never be surprised again?"

Create Your Own CIA to Avoid Surprises

I began with the following observations: First, there's a long period from invention to commercial application. Powered flight took thirty years to commercialize successfully, for instance. Most often, the process of commercialization occurs by putting together already extant technology into a new format. Douglas produced the first commercially successful aircraft, the DC-3, by combining five existing technologies. Several years earlier, Boeing's entry into the commercial market had failed because it only combined four technologies.

Second, most new developments occur from *outside* an industry. Most often individuals within an industry develop a trained incapacity to see developments that threaten their current activities. As an example, the silicon wafer (and the computer miniaturization process) were driven from outside the traditional computer industry. I need to help people look for developments outside our current fields, in parallel fields that pose both threats and opportunities to the areas in which we currently function.

Third, I need to sensitize everyone to future developments to which we must react. Responsibility to discover the "right" future actions needs to rest with those who can take current actions to deal with them. That's the new leadership paradigm at work.

I established a system called scan, clip, and review. We borrowed it from John Naisbitt and from the CIA. In academic circles it's called content analysis. It's simple and works like this:

Everyone in the company *scans* ten periodicals he or she does not normally read each month. These range from highly technical journals to such popular periodicals as *Prevention, Rolling Stone,* and *Mother Jones Good Earth Journal.*

Each person *clips* all articles he or she thinks are interesting regarding future trends and puts them in a file folder. People clip advertisements, articles, opinion letters, anything they think will have any potential impact on the business in the future, no matter how farfetched it may seem at the time. The entire company is divided into seven-person interdisciplinary, interdepartmental "review cells." Monthly, people circulate their file folders of clipped articles to the other members of their review cell, so that everyone *reviews* the clippings in all seven file folders.

Quarterly, the seven members of the review cell meet and discuss the important trends they noticed in the clipped material they reviewed. The discussion is built around three questions:

1. What is the future event that will have the greatest impact on our business?
2. What will happen when that event happens?
3. What can we do now to prepare for that event?

We use a process called a future wheel, which is shared throughout the company. Every six months, the trends are reviewed and appropriate changes in strategy are made.

An example of a future wheel is shown in the illustration on pages 132–133. First, we identified the most likely future events that would have the greatest impact on our business. There were three of them:

1. Our insecticide delivery system is approved for use in the United States and throughout the world. This system marries our chemical formula with a dry, flowable insecticide produced from either bio-engineered products or current chemicals.
2. The reformulated, restructured food business grows and our formulas receive FDA sanction.
3. New materials, which include our formulas as a binder (such as ceramics, gallium), find wide commercial application.

Because we believed that the insecticide delivery system held out the greatest opportunity for us, we did a future wheel on a current chemical insecticide (called product 1) and the delivery system we proposed to a large integrated chemical company (called Company C).

Then we identified what would happen when our insecticide delivery system is approved for use in the United States and throughout the world. We identified first-, second-, and third-order consequences by answering the question "What will happen when . . . ?"

First-order consequences:

1. EPA mandates it.
2. There's a wider application of product 1. The market grows.
3. Other countries adopt the "new" safer system, growing the market still more.
4. Company C (the integrated chemical company) and Company I (the largest manufacturer of product 1, also an integrated chemical company) reject our system in favor of another.
5. We become the exclusive supplier to Company C of the delivery system.
6. We go into the business of supplying the dry flowable product to Company C.

We decided to explore the second-order consequences of two of these first-order consequences in greater detail. First, alternative 5 above. If we become the exclusive supplier to Company C of the delivery system, we see the following second-order consequences:

1. Company C's competitors will want the technology. Our credibility in the business will rise dramatically. The following are third-order consequences of this alternative:
   a. We will need to develop more capacity and this will require more capital.
   b. We will be encouraged to enter the joint venture with Korea/Taiwan to develop more capacity.
   c. More opportunities with others, including nonagricultural activities, and more joint ventures. We identified the following fourth-order consequences of this alternative:
      i. More market-directed product development with more technological sharing and joint ventures.
      ii. Company C reacts negatively to our success and attempts to cut us off from other business.
2. Company I (the manufacturer of product 1) sees us as a threat and takes action against us. The following are third-order consequences of this alternative:
   a. Company I will try to intimidate Company C into refusing our product.
   b. Company I will file a legal attack on our patent in an effort to slow us down.
   c. Company I will try to pressure us to drop the system.
   d. Company I will develop/market an alternative system.
   e. Company I will discontinue distributing our product.
   f. Company I will make a deal with us either to use our system elsewhere or to try to cut out Company C. The following are fourth-order consequences of this alternative:
      i. We generate megadollars and it improves our position vis-à-vis others in the field.
      ii. We have a worldwide system—increased sales and profits.
      iii. We more aggressively seek the joint venture with China to acquire additional capacity.
      iv. We develop other opportunities with Company I.
3. We become intellectually committed to the agriculture business, devote more resources to it, and explore additional agriculture activities. The following are third-order consequences of this alternative:
   a. We will find more agriculture activities.
   b. We will set up a separate division/entity to handle the ag business.

ANTICIPATING FUTURE CONSEQUENCES
OF FUTURE EVENTS

COMPANY C COMPETITORS WILL WANT TECHNOLOGY, OUR CREDIBILITY IN THE BUSINESS WILL RISE DRAMATICALLY

COMPANY I SEES US AS A THREAT AND TAKES ACTION AGAINST US

WE BECOME COMMITTED TO THE BUSINESS, DEVOTE MORE RESOURCES TO IT, AND EXPLORE ADDITIONAL ACTIVITIES

WE BECOME THE EXCLUSIVE SUPPLIER TO COMPANY C OF THE DELIVERY SYSTEM

OUR UNIT COSTS GO DOWN AND PROFITS IMPROVE

COMPANIES C/I REJECT OUR SYSTEM IN FAVOR OF ANOTHER

SEEK LARGE NEW CHEMICAL COMPANIES

JOINT VENTURE OR USE CURRENT KOREAN/ TAIWANESE PRODUCERS AND GO INTO THE PRIVATE-LABEL BUSINESS

DO THE WHOLE JOB OURSELVES

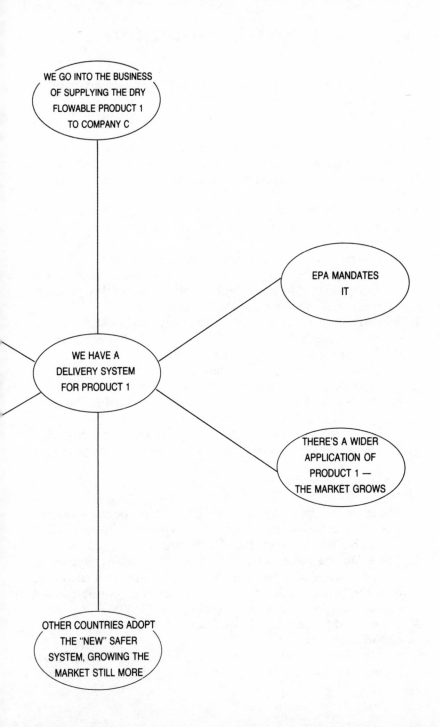

    c. We will devote more resources to ag ventures.

    d. Our business mentality will change to being more open to other ventures.

4. Our unit costs go down and profits improve.

We explored another first-order consequence—alternative 4 above, in which Company C and Company I reject us for another system. The following are the second-order consequences of this alternative:

1. We find another large agricultural chemical company with which to market. The following are the third-order consequences of this alternative:

    a. Several ag chemical companies decide to join us.

    b. A European-based ag chemical firm who wants to trade on the strong dollar and enter the U.S. market with other products and can use product 1 as the leader joins us.

2. Joint venture with current Asian producers and make product 1 ourselves through the private-label business. The following are the third-order consequences of this alternative:

    a. These secondary producers enter the U.S. market through the private-label route and grow in size and importance.

    b. Big guys in Europe, particularly those in central Europe, become interested in doing business with us.

    c. We secure approval from the regulatory agencies in Europe.

3. Do the whole job ourselves (become a producer of product 1).

We concluded from this exercise:

1. The exclusive supplier to Company C is the most desirable alternative. We can handle any threats from Company I (particularly if we can become the world supplier through Company I).

2. Going into the business ourselves with the secondary suppliers is mostly valuable as a leverage threat. We don't want to do so, however, because of the capital requirements and because it would take us away from our primary business.

3. We decided to take the following actions now to prepare for the opportunity:

    a. Organize seminars to pique the interest of the new biotech firms in our formulas. We will look for opportunities for joint projects.

b. Identify relevant equipment makers and give them technical presentations to see what they can do with our formulas.

Everyone's a Futurist

In my company everyone in the company scans, clips, and reviews. Everyone climbs up into the crow's nest, peers off into the swirling mists, and attempts to discern the best future direction for the company. Everyone is responsible for choosing the right future direction for "their" company. That's leadership with a capital "L."

We get lots of ideas. Imagine having seven hundred people all scanning, clipping, and reviewing! We don't get blindsided anymore. We hear the footsteps. Our customers come to us to find out what's coming. We get lots of discussion about appropriate actions. And we get lots of commitment to a future course of action once the discussions are done.

Although the future is difficult to discern, you need not keep all the worry for yourself. Share the burden, and gain access to considerable brainpower. That's what intellectual capitalism is all about. Your leadership task? Focus people on identifying the future needs/demands of their customers so they can be ready when the future becomes the present.

QUESTION:
**Do you know what's coming? Do your people
know what's coming? Are you and they ready
for what's coming?**

LEADERSHIP SOLUTION:
**Everyone should be responsible for managing the future
if he/she doesn't want to become a thing of the past.**

CHAPTER 15

Focus on
Great Performance for
Your Customers

In *Leading the Journey*, focus yourself and others on "great performance." Not "good" performance. Not "average" performance. Not "acceptable" performance. But "great" performance from the perspective of your customers. The leader's task is to focus the entire organization on the "right" direction of providing great performance for customers.

Is This the Best You/We Can Do?

I asked the question listed above of one of the CEOs I currently coach. We'd been reviewing the performance of one of his division presidents. The division president was an excellent salesperson. He sold his division into a delivery and cash flow crisis.

"He always does this," the CEO said. "He creates a crisis. Then drives his people to solve it, and they usually do."

"What about margins?" I asked.

"They're low to nonexistent, and have been for years," the CEO replied.

"So," I summarized, "he drives his people from crisis to crisis, and doesn't make any money doing it. He's really the world's greatest salesman, because he keeps selling his problems to you and his customers.

"Is that what you really want? Is that what your customers really want? Is that great performance? How would you like to see the division run? In a constant crisis mode, or as a finely tuned Swiss watch? What would the customers prefer? No-hassle delivery of perfect products, or sweating the delivery of the usual first-run product glitches?"

Leadership, Not Status-Quo-ship

Leaders move and direct organizations. Leaders marshal resources—people, facilities, equipment, money, ideas—and get them into motion. Otherwise we'd call it status-quo-ship rather than leadership. In what direction? That is the question. Movement to where? That's the key leadership issue.

I learned that successful leaders ask the following thinking-strategically questions:

- What do we *really* want to create for our customers?
- What will it take to create what we want?

It wasn't always that way. I was accustomed to thinking incrementally, not strategically. My businesses, and I personally, suffered as a result. I kept urging my buffalo to "run a little faster." It wasn't until I helped them to see themselves flying that they even arranged themselves in that "V" and began to think about what it took to get off the ground.

Thinking Incrementally Manages Forward from Today

Thinking incrementally is an American disease. We learned it early in life. Our parents were always admonishing us, "Try a *little* harder.

You're *almost* there. Just a *little* bit more." The mentality was reinforced in the classroom: "Eighty-eight percent is *almost* an A. Study *just a little bit more* and I'm certain that you can get it." Our bosses taught us: "Next year we need to reduce another 5 percent in costs." "Our goal is to gain 2 percent in market share this year." "If we could only knock off 20 percent in this product development cycle, we could beat the competition." "We'd be in great shape if we could improve quality just 1 percent; that would get us past the competition."

It's not that thinking incrementally is bad. It's just that in that thought process you begin from where you are now and add a little more to it. The view from your current position includes the limitations of all of your current assumptions, your current paradigms, your current prejudices. All of that baggage clouds your vision of what's possible in the future. After all, if Christopher Columbus had looked out at the horizon and accepted the then-current paradigms and assumptions that the world really ended where the sky met the ocean, who knows where we'd be today?

As the leader of my organization, my responsibility is to set the right tone, to determine the right direction. For too long I set the "a little bit better is okay" tone—the "5 percent more" direction. That tone, that direction, limited my progress and success.

Thinking Strategically Manages Backward from the Future

Leaders who engage in thinking strategically begin with where they want to go. Then they look backward from the future and ask, "What will it take to create that new tomorrow?" It's the looking back from tomorrow that gives thinking strategically its power, because that perspective helps you escape the limitations of today's situation.

Remember, success is the leader's enemy. Yesterday's paradigms created yesterday's success. Since today is different from yesterday, and tomorrow will be different from today, the paradigm that created success yesterday will not create success tomorrow. That's why we need to escape the limitations imposed by beginning with today's situation. That's what thinking strategically enables us to do. Unfortunately, too few of us who sit in the corner office use this escape mechanism.

How Many Bugs Is One Bug Too Many?

You can't see "what can be" through the blinders of "what is." In the software business we struggle with errors/bugs/glitches. All too often we've asked the question "How can we minimize the number of bugs?" That's the wrong question. In the software business one bug is one bug too many. So I learned to ask the strategic-thinking leadership question "How can we be absolutely certain we never have *one* bug/ error/glitch?" We haven't had a bug problem since I asked the right, strategic-thinking question.

Some time back, I had a bad case of incrementalism and it was killing me. At one specialty chemical facility, our quality was good— but not good enough. We were among the leaders in our segment. Yet we still dumped 5 percent of our product due to poor quality. At least a dozen times a month we had to take product back from customers because it didn't meet specs. Try as we may, and we tried mightily, we stayed just about where we were. "We're doing okay," the people told me. "We've improved from more than 15 percent spillage when we started a year ago and have one of the best records in the business. We'll keep tweaking the process and improving over time. Just you watch. Don't worry so much."

But I was worried. Very worried. How many times will a customer reorder after sending back a bad batch? How many precious dollars were we spilling down the drain every day? How long before someone started to lean on us about where we put our toxic waste? How long before some competitor figured out how to lose only 1 percent and price us out of the market? I spent lots of sleepless nights worrying.

Finally, one day it hit me. We'd never get to 4 percent without first getting to zero percent. My insight happened at a circus. I was watching the trapeze artists fly through the air when I remembered the story of the Flying Wallendas, the famous trapeze family. For years they never used a net and never had an accident. Then, after a fall, they began to use a net, and had so many accidents that they abandoned the act altogether. That's when I realized that only when the Wallendas *pictured* a perfect performance, and *focused* on what it would take to get that perfect performance, did they *achieve* performance. Once they lost that picture of the future, they lost their performance.

Excited, I came to the plant next day and asked, "What will it take to make perfect product? What will it take never to get a shipment back? What will it take to dump not a drop of bad product down the drain?" After a chorus of "It can't be done," people's eyes began to light up. "Well," one technician said, "we could do this, and that, and . . ." Four weeks later, after rearranging the line and changing several procedures, we had our first perfect day. It took a lot of other changes in paradigms and assumptions to maintain that high-quality performance, particularly in developing the sense of ownership for the "perfect product" activity. But it never would have happened if I had not escaped the bonds of yesterday by asking the strategic-thinking question "What will it take . . . ?"

Begin with the End in Mind—the Federal Express Example

Federal Express knows the importance of thinking strategically. They begin from the end state they want to create: "Absolutely, positively, it has to be there on time." With that end state firmly in mind they ask the strategic-thinking question "What will it take to get it absolutely, positively there on time?" Answering that question strategically has helped them build one of the most successful businesses in America.

It's Easy to Fall Back into the Incremental Trap

Thinking strategically begins with me, not them. This is a difficult transition. I fall back easily. Recently, an issue came up in a software group. The group representative wrote on the E-mail, "There's a tough competitor here who's promising an incredible delivery time. We don't think he can deliver but . . . it's got the client's attention. We'd win this bid on a three-year project if only we could improve delivery by two months."

My first reaction was to ask, "Where can we cut two months out of the delivery cycle?" I was ready to sit down and problem-solve about how to cut a day here and a day there. I caught myself. Thank goodness for the delay in typing an answer rather than speaking it! I was about to fall into the incremental trap. Instead, I typed the strategic-thinking question: "What do we really want to create? Do we really want to just nose out the competition, or do you want to win by a mile? What will it take to deliver the job in two years—not two years ten months?" As usual, my first reaction is still wrong, even after all these years.

QUESTION:
What will it take to create what I really want?

LEADERSHIP SOLUTION:
Ask for enough or you will get less than you need.

CHAPTER 16

How High
Is Up?

I am frequently asked, "How high is up?"—and not just rhetorically, particularly when I've been pushing individuals to raise their sights. I have found that too many people "settle" instead of reach. I've learned how expensive that can be. I also learned that my task in Leading the Journey is to help people focus high enough. I need to encourage individuals to "reach" for great performance for their customers, rather than "settle" for acceptable performance. Part of providing focus and direction to my organizations is to keep all the noses pointed straight up.

Best Today . . . Gone Tomorrow

This company was the founder of its industry. It created the category thirty-seven years ago and dominated it for some time. The owners lived well, reaping the harvests of their creation. They disdained defending their territory against encroachers, saying that there was more than enough for everyone. The result was that several major firms copied their activities and became competitors, consuming large chunks of the market. The owners were still satisfied: They had the reputation for making the best products, sales continued to grow, and the company did well.

To continue to maximize earnings, the owners cut back on research. "We have more than enough patents ready to market for some time to come. The pipeline is overflowing," they said.

Competitors continued to gain share. Eventually, after eight years of no R&D, the company fell into the red and stayed there for several years. When I was called in to help, the patient was terminal. The owners were forced to sell on the steps of the bankruptcy court for pennies on the dollar. They escaped with their personal assets intact, but got virtually nothing for the business, which had been their principal financial asset for their entire lives. They were the victims of their own inability to set their sights high enough.

This story is repeated all over the corporate landscape today. Too many business leaders fail to see how good they *must* be in order to survive. Being the best in an industry today is no guarantee that you will be the best tomorrow. In fact, you can probably count on the fact that the chances are exceptionally good that you will not be the best tomorrow—unless you are doing something to assure your continued success. Look at General Motors, IBM, Alcoa, U.S. Steel, Goodyear, and Kodak. The list of yesterday's stars that are today's "also-rans" reads like the Fortune 500. Success really is the enemy.

Winning Isn't Final. There's Always a Game Tomorrow

A long time ago, I was in the construction business. One of our suppliers had a difficult time buying tile. One of my partners invented a process for applying a substance that dried into a tile-like finish. It was a new product, and we attempted to sell it to other contractors through hardware distributors. The product caught on. We were doing very well.

We didn't have the distribution, however, to capitalize on our product advantage. We were delighted when a major distributor came along and offered to buy the product outright. He offered some up-front cash and a royalty percentage on each future shipment. The future potential numbers he talked about made our eyes grow wide. We were already spending the downstream royalty checks when we signed the agreement. Who cared if we didn't recoup all of our investment in the up-front cash payment? Who cared if all of this was speculative? Who cared that it took us a long time to put the business in shape to sell? With the need for documenting processes and formalizing procedures, we didn't have time to do any sales or talk to customers for better than six months. Who cared? We didn't.

We waited and waited for our checks to come. Very few did. We discovered that within days after signing the agreement, the major competitor in the industry came out with its own similar product with superior distribution and swept the marketplace. We were so busy basking in the glory of our newfound "wealth" that we took our eye off the ball (the market, the customers, the competitors) and were hit in the head with it. As leaders we had failed ourselves. We learned a very expensive lesson: Leaders must keep helping people prepare for the *next* match, rather than savoring the win from the *last* match.

Up Is Never Where You Are Now

No matter how well you are doing now, you can always do better. Leaders must keep challenging people to continue raising the bar for themselves. Like most lessons, I learned this one the hard way. I had a very successful company, or so I thought. In a business dominated by 11 percent returns, it averaged 27 percent net profit before tax. It grew sixteen times in a seven-year period. Imagine my delight when another company came along and offered me a rich cash flow multiple for the business. I couldn't wait to sign.

After the new owners took over the business they revealed why they had paid so much. They saw a new market for our product lines, which, according to their projections, would result in a much larger company at even higher margins.

When I realized I had left considerable money on the table in the deal, I felt completely deflated. My blindness to this potential market caused me to miss seeing how high up the business could go. Not only did I miss the chance to harvest some of the low-hanging fruit in my orchard, but I would miss future harvests by not asking enough money for the sale of the business.

If I Set the Sights Too High, I'm Afraid I'll Fail

"Why don't people stretch themselves more?" I keep asking myself. As usual I had to look no further than the mirror to find the answer.

One of my managers was struggling. I knew it. He knew it. He spent his days in my office trying to figure out what I wanted, rather than out and about, doing his job. He probably spent his nights worrying about whether he'd gotten it right or not. I know I spent my nights also worrying about whether he'd gotten it or not.

The travesty went on for months. It got better for a while. Then it got worse. Then promised to get better again. It never improved enough, however, that either of us had a solid night's sleep.

Finally, I saw the dawn. I was the problem, not the manager. My problem? I was afraid my expectations were too high. Maybe I couldn't find a better manager.

My fear of setting my sights too high drove me to accept less than great performance. My fear blinded me enough to ask the question "How high is up?" I was afraid to look. When I, as the leader, am afraid to look up, imagine how low others will set the bar.

Customers Help Us See How High Up Is Up

Customers are not blinded by our current lofty position. They are remarkably immune to the dazzle of our success. Dealing with customers provides a bear hug on reality. One recent experience reminded me of the necessity of that sometimes unpleasant activity.

Our software company is the best in its marketplace. We have the biggest market share and the best functionality. It's easy to rest on our laurels from that lofty position.

One of our teams had just come back from visiting a large customer. We have a multiyear, multimillion-dollar contract with them to install our system throughout their worldwide operations. It's the biggest contract in our company. The customer was very pleased. At least until now.

The team reported that one of the customer's other consultants had developed software that automatically converted their present program to run on any hardware platform. Before conversion the program ran on only one hardware platform. One of our principal selling points was our software's compatibility across hardware platforms. The company had a wide diversity of platforms throughout their various sites, so our compatibility feature was particularly attractive to them.

That programmer's software could offer a much cheaper solution to the customer. Even though our software was richer in functionality, the customer could save money by converting their current configuration at several of their smaller sites. We'd lose some business on this particular contract. But we could potentially lose many others if that feature became available in the marketplace. Here was a first-class threat to our business.

The team informed everyone through the E-mail system. The team, supported by ideas from the entire company, went to work on enhancing our software. The goal: make our product so valuable that our customer would reject any solution other than ours, even the inexpensive conversion of their current software. We worked for several weeks with that customer and developed many new enhancements. Our customer is still "our" customer.

I breathed a big sigh of relief—for a moment or two. I know absolutely that there are very bright programmers out there, right now, working on ways to put us out of business. I know, without doubt, that they will be talking to our customers, both current and potential, whispering in their ears about the superiority of their program to ours. Our customers will listen, and we need to be ever alert to keep working with our customers to continually improve what we have. We must stay one step ahead of everyone else.

This is an excellent example of leadership at work in the intellectual capitalism age. I had set up the systems so that the people talked frequently with their customers. The people knew they were responsible for raising the standards for their own work. The people owned the responsibility for meeting their customer's expectations. They had the capital. They had the power. They had the responsibility. They delivered.

There comes a time in every business when getting better at doing the things you have been doing is not the answer. Challenge your assumptions. As the leader ask yourself and your people the thinking-strategically question "What is great performance for you and your customers?" Then get everyone involved in determining what it will take to deliver it. Getting better at delivering great performance for your customers is the only answer to the "How high is up?" question.

QUESTION:
How much higher is up than I think it is?

LEADERSHIP SOLUTION:
Don't look back. They may be gaining on you!

CHAPTER 17

It's Their Checkbook

Most businesses are charities. Mine were. I suspect that we lost money on every sale, because we didn't have good product costs, and only stayed afloat through sales growth. I was leading my people off the financial cliff. I definitely had them focused in the wrong direction. I turned it around and headed in the right direction when I got good product/program/function costs so that everyone knew which products really contributed. Every person spent company money then as if it were his/her own. That's a major focus and direction in LTJ.

Just as there is great performance for customers, there is also great performance for the financial owners of the business. Stockholders are entitled to great performance in the financial arena, just as customers are entitled to great performance in the quality/service/product arena. Leaders help people focus on great performance in all relevant areas. Lead the Journey in the direction of both great service and great profits.

Dollars Determine Your Destiny

Your current financial position inevitably determines what you can and can't do. Unfortunately, most business leaders don't know their current financial situation.

One distributor told me he was doing "very well." Upon closer questioning he discovered that he was losing money on every sale and staying in business only because of the cash brought in by the increasing sales volume. When sales increases slowed down due to seasonal factors for a few months, he almost went bankrupt.

Another small manufacturer, typical in rapidly growing markets, grew himself into bankruptcy. His cash couldn't support his increasing sales volume. Just at the height of his manufacturing phase he ran out of money, and lost everything through a buyout to avoid bankruptcy.

That almost happened in my learning-center business. We were growing rapidly, more than trebling every year. Money seemed to be no problem, until D day—"D" for disaster, that is. We were opening two new centers that week. Everything was in order: the property, the director, the staff, the advertising. Everything except the equipment that goes in two days before opening. The equipment package costs $125,000 and I didn't want it sitting around idle; so we waited until the last moment to order and ship it. The panic call came from my office manager. The bank refused the financing and the manufacturer wouldn't ship. The bank had looked at our credit line and saw that we were overdrawn. For the bank it was a simple decision. Overdrawn means no advances. For the manufacturer it was a simple decision. No money means no shipment. Since we couldn't open without the equipment, it was also a simple decision for us. The ultimate result was panic and trauma.

What went wrong? The simple answer was we were out of cash. Our growth had sucked up cash like a black hole consumes light. Worse, I didn't know what was going on. Of course, only I was responsible for knowing it. Since I was so busy opening centers, I didn't have time to worry about money. What I didn't worry about, nobody else did either. I almost went under. Chalk that close call up to my old leadership philosophy of making myself the center of all decisions. So much for the joys of being the head buffalo!

I learned a fundamental lesson. The first day you can't meet your payments is your last day in business. I also learned another important lesson. I learned that all businesses are cash businesses. Hard as it is, I learned to ignore the profit-and-loss statements and ask, "Did we make money on sales, in cash terms? How can we manage the receivables, payables, margins, to generate more cash for investment?" I learned to track cash and to be certain I have enough. Too many of my business associates learned this important lesson sitting in the bankruptcy court.

The Scoreboard

I learned to avoid disasters by tracking both the overall financial health of the organization and the financial contribution of each product, service, and function. Here are a few measures I've discovered are essential to any business. Without drowning in accounting details, get the following figures. Monitor them as vital signs of your organization's financial health:

1. Track on a frequent (weekly and monthly) basis:
    *   *Cash on Hand* and *Projected Cash Flow*. There are three essentials in any business: cash, cash, cash. All businesses are cash businesses. There are two ways to track cash. The first is using a funds flow analysis. There are many good ones available.

        The second way is a little more complicated. In the final analysis, cash requirements are a function of four factors: daily expense rate, manufacturing cycle, down payment, and collection time. Here's the formula:

$$\text{Daily Expense Rate} \times \left[\text{Installation Cycle} - \text{Advance Payment Days} + \text{Collection Days} \right] = \text{Cash Required}$$

    *   *Expenses ÷ Orders*. Increasing expenses often go hand in hand with increasing orders. But often, expenses continue to increase after sales level out. Monitoring this ratio of current expenses to

current orders (which will be future sales) will ring an early-warning bell and help you prevent expense inflation and profit deterioration. The ratio also tells you when you can expect future cash problems.

The ratio should be your projected margin. If you want 15 percent margin, then your current expenses should be 85 percent of current orders. When it creeps up past that point, know that you are not earning the margins you want. When your expenses exceed your orders, your ratio is greater than 100 percent, so anticipate a cash crunch in the coming months.

- *Receivables.* Nothing is more insidious than not collecting the cash that customers owe you. You're usually so busy with other "important" things, like sales and deliveries, that you don't notice when your customers reach into your pocket and rob you of your cash. Look up the standards for collection periods in your industry (in most industries it averages forty-two days), and figure out how you can beat it. Arrange your business so you minimize receivables. Collect money in advance. Collect deposits with orders. If you have a lengthy installation cycle, collect progress payments. Be certain that you are not investing your money in your customer's business.
- *Sales ÷ Working Capital.* This critical ratio shows the stretch in your working capital. (Working capital is current assets—cash and accounts receivable—minus current liabilities.) Working capital supports sales. With too little working capital, you grow yourself to bankruptcy. Typically, each dollar in working capital supports eight dollars in sales. When your ratio is below 5:1, you are likely not using your cash well and are not earning good enough margins. When your ratio exceeds 15:1, you may be technically bankrupt.

2. Track on a less frequent (semiannual/annual) basis (primarily for the banker):
- *Current Ratio* (Current assets ÷ current liabilities). This short-term solvency ratio tells you (and your banker) whether you have the short-term funds to pay your short-term liabilities. Ratios of 2:1 are considered good. That means there are two dollars in current assets for every one dollar of current liabilities. When the ratio falls below 1.5:1, the bankers get nervous. When it falls below 1:1, they start looking at pulling the line.

Make Every Product/Customer/Function
Pay Its Own Way

Almost all accounting systems are designed for accountants, bankers, and stockbrokers. They are not usually designed for leaders and operators of businesses. That's because most accounting systems came into existence during the 1920s when valuing inventory was the biggest challenge and short-stroke manufacturing was the dominant business activity. Times have changed. Unfortunately, most accounting systems have not.

You need to really know your costs. How? Use a real-time direct costing system. Assign every penny you spend to a product, a customer, a function.

Without drowning you in details, here's how we do it. We work on a cash basis—no depreciation or overhead allocations. Everyone directly bills every hour to a product/customer/function. Each person's hourly wage cost includes his/her direct hourly wage plus his/her "burden rate," which represents his/her portion of the occupancy costs (heat, rent, light), benefits, and management costs (the costs of local site management allocated as a proportion of the total time spent during that day on various products/customers/functions). All other expenses, including supplies, materials, and travel, are billed to a customer/product/function. Every day the computer automatically totals all of the allocations and reports a thirty-day rolling average cost per product/customer/function. All income is similarly distributed. Since everyone is paid a bonus based on net margins before tax, this data is an important decision-making and control tool. It is studied assiduously and used extensively.

Fire Some Customers—You Can't Afford Them

One of the biggest fallacies going around is that customer service doesn't cost, it pays. The cost of serving some customers can pay you right to the bankruptcy court.

One of my clients learned this lesson the hard way. He was in the metal fabrication business. He did well during the good times, but when the cycle turned down (as it always does), he was hurting. "Sell your way out of the downturn" was the advice from one consultant. So he went out and sold-sold-sold and almost landed in Chapter 11.

One of his unique selling points was an extended warranty. He felt that his warranty gave him a leg up on the competition. When he sold to customers in his geographic area, he was fine. Trips across town don't cost much. As part of his sell-sell-sell program, however, he took any customer, including many in foreign countries. The sales looked great. The top of the statement looked great. Short-term profits looked great.

When the after-sales support costs started to roll in, he began to choke on warranty costs. Trips across the ocean cost a lot. That's when he called me.

I helped him think strategically by using a version of the four empowering questions: "What do you really want to create in your business? What obstacles prevent you from creating that dream? Who owns those obstacles? What actions will the owners take to remove the obstacles?" He decided that he actually did not want to expand overseas or into other geographic territories. He had more than enough work where he was. He wanted to get out of the warranty obligations, preserving goodwill in case he chose to reenter those markets at a later time. He visited all of his out-of-area customers offering to "buy out" their warranty. Most customers requested modest prices, to which he readily agreed. When the price was too high, he offered to refund the original price in full. When he finished, he thought that he had minimized his losses and made a little money on the overall venture.

I could have quit there. But I was not quite done. I helped him analyze his actual costs. He was shocked to discover that because of his downstream warranty work he was actually losing money on virtually all of his products. The absence of full cost accounting and rising sales deluded him into thinking that he was making money.

To remedy the situation he installed a real-time, real-cost accounting system and repriced all of his products. He also changed his leadership. Recognizing the imperatives of the intellectual capitalism era, he shared the new data with everyone. He got them involved in reducing the customer problems that caused warranty work. The net result was that he not only quadrupled his margin but also successfully reentered those foreign markets and grew the business tenfold. Because his people shared in the profits, they did well also. Only this time, he carefully chose customers who were bunched together geographically, so he could minimize his warranty work if it ever arose.

"It's tough to turn down an order," he told me. "Particularly when you want to make that sales quota this month. But it's easier to say no before they're a customer than to fire them afterward. I learned that the hard way through having to do it. Believe me, I don't ever want to do that again."

Busy Assets Are Happy Assets

I learned the importance of managing assets. One product line enjoyed many years of sales growth. That was the problem, however. As sales went up, the need for cash went up faster. The product line sucked up cash faster than Donald Trump's yacht. The product never generated enough cash to fund the necessary capital expenditures. Borrowing became a way of life.

We've Always Done It This Way, It Must Be the Only Way

I believed that new asset investment was essential to business growth. My bankers had a different perspective. I got a rude shock one day when they shut down my credit line and insisted upon higher margins before they'd lend me another dime.

As I struggled with the credit-shutoff dilemma, another shock occurred. One of our best products was growing rapidly. The line that produced it was at capacity. The plant manager requested a duplicate line to double capacity. I routinely approved such requests in the past. Without the credit line, I didn't have any choice. I turned him down.

The plant manager was shocked. I had never said no before. I explained the credit situation to him. Once he understood, he went to work on the problem. I was surprised when he came back with a recommendation that redesigned the product flow, doubling capacity at a cost of less than $50,000.

I was delighted in his ingenuity. But it caused me to wonder. How many other similar opportunities are there out there that we are missing? Was this an isolated example, or was this the tip of the iceberg?

I saw my problem in the mirror one day. I was proud of the size of my factories. I enjoyed buying equipment. I liked to brag that there was always construction going on at my company. It was fun being the head of an expanding herd of buffalo. I encouraged people to spend, spend, spend.

I immediately launched a cost-control program. I questioned every expenditure. Then I asked myself, "Why am I the only one pushing on this? Why aren't others concerned? Why am I owning the problem?"

The answer was simple. Only a few people received the cash flow statement. No one had return-on-capital criteria for expenditures. Everyone else's job was to recommend expenditures. My job was to approve their recommendations. Head buffalo at work.

This clearly had to change. The people had to be responsible. I gave them the information. I explained the cash situation. I established a bonus program with an ROA hurdle.

The Only Good Idea Is One That Works: Get the People to Take Ownership

Remember the Palmer Sausage situation from Chapter 2? The amount of product they wanted would have put us way over capacity. The people wanted the business because they knew it would improve their ROA substantially—and give them bigger bonuses.

Their plan was predicated on working a seven-day-a-week schedule. They bet that they could develop ways to get more out in less time. They were right. In eight weeks they were back to a five-day-week schedule. I still don't know the capacity of that plant. What amazes many people is that the people who made the decision to take the business, and then developed the capacity to produce it, were not engineers or managers. They were the plant production staff. It didn't amaze me. After all, they *are* the experts.

That part of the business is still growing rapidly. But it is now generating a cash surplus. I'm not quite sure what great performance in that plant is, but I am having a lot of fun trying to find out.

It's Their Checkbook

The key to financial health is getting everyone to make financial decisions as if they were spending their own money out of their own checkbook. Too many people spend a "budget" of someone else's money. Witness the spending sprees at the end of each year. I am frequently contacted by people who want me to come, on short notice, and give a presentation. They say, "We've got the money in the budget this year and we must spend it or else we won't get it next year."

I learned that my leadership role is to set up systems that focus people on being responsible for their own spending. When it's a "budget" with no financial consequence, there is no control. The software company is furnished in "modern Salvation Army." The financial reporting system shows the people every day the consequences of their own financial decisions. They recognize that they spend fifty cents out of their own pocket for every dollar of "company" money they spend. So they buy used furniture, travel coach, and rent small cars. They see themselves as the instruments of their own destiny. That's leadership in the new intellectual capitalism age.

QUESTION:
Are you sitting on your assets?

LEADERSHIP SOLUTION:
It's their checkbook or it's the creditor's assets.

CHAPTER 18

Your Competitor Is Your Best Friend

Competitors Are Friends in Disguise

Love your enemy as your best friend. Enemies are very valuable. They help you organize and focus on what must be done. Part of the leader's job is to use competitors' actions as a way to focus individuals on great performance for their customers.

I learned this lesson by chance. My specialty chemical company was doing very well. After struggling for several years we had identified and dominated a number of highly profitable niches. We were on easy street, and that was the trouble. We became careless. Quality slipped. Deliveries were "just a little late." We were a little slow returning phone calls. We had eased off. My exhortations to "shape up" fell on deaf ears.

Then "It" happened, as it always does. A competitor came from out of nowhere and began to take market share, initially not so much as to worry anyone. Then the message came home when one of our oldest customers "fired" us in favor of the new kid on the block. When I called the customer to ask why, the answer was direct and simple. "You stopped taking care of me and my problems," she said. "They're going to do what you used to do for me, only at a lower price." The message was a two-by-four across the forehead.

I put the customer's comments on the E-mail. The usual fire storm of doubts and accusations followed. "She's wrong! We took care of her. We're probably better off without her. Just wait, she'll be back because the new kid on the block doesn't have the resources or staying power we do."

I let the storm run its course, then pointed out the significant immediate financial loss to each and every one of their pocketbooks. I asked them to consider what would happen if other customers took the same action. "Can you really afford this?" I asked patiently and persistently. "Do you really want this situation? What is the best of all worlds? How can we create that best of all worlds for ourselves and our customer?"

The people saw the need to prevent this situation from happening again. They galvanized into action. They went out and visited every customer. They resolved that they'd never let this happen again and that they would do whatever it took to win that customer back. We changed our systems to get regular customer feedback. We modified the reward system to encourage continuing customer feedback. This situation never happened again. The story has a happy ending: Two years later we won that customer back. We had a champagne celebration, and I relearned the value of continuing customer feedback.

I was so caught up in the excitement of the "new" program, I didn't take time to reflect on what it all meant. Some time afterward, over dinner in an airport waiting for a plane, I was ruminating about the incident with several employee-partners. I felt the lightning bolt of insight hit me. That competitor did us a great favor. He was able to convince us to keep our guard up. He moved mountains in the organization with the simple act of winning one customer. He was probably puzzled by the flowers I sent the next day.

Competitors easily become the greater enemy against which we can all rally. Why fight with the person in the next office when there's someone outside the gates looking to destroy us all? In most organizations, the people may not agree on much among themselves except that they all dislike the competitor. I learned to use my competitors as a weapon to keep everyone in my organization, including myself, from getting complacent.

I learned to use the competitor as a rallying point to focus everyone on great performance, and continuously raise the standards. One of the leader's best friends, therefore, is the competitor who's planning to steal your lunch.

Identify That Villain—and Get out the Black Paint

Lead people to learn about their competitors: who they are and what they plan to do. Enter the intelligence business—legally. I'm not recommending that you dig through someone's trash or tap their telephones. Such activity is unethical and illegal. More important, it creates an atmosphere in your organization that "anything goes" and "the end justifies the means." That poison results in lying and cheating internally as well as externally. You don't need that headache.

You can find out about your competitors without resorting to unethical or illegal means. Competitors will tell you if you just ask. Competitors' salespeople love to brag about "conquests." Let them, and pay attention when they do. Clipping services can collect trade and other news. Often research and technical journals tip off a competitor's plans long before any specific product announcement. Many companies "test" customer response to proposed products. Often your current customers, who are their potential customers, are included. Stay in touch with them to find out what competitors are planning.

Then get out the black paint. Communicate with everyone about the "enemy." Keep everyone posted on what the "villain" is attempting to do. In my own company, I generate competitor information and share it with everyone. I talk frequently about what "they" are trying to do and what "we" will do to counter. One of my favorite question routines goes like this: "Have you heard about XYZ's latest ploy? What are we going to do to beat them to the punch?" As the leader I work to keep the competitor clearly in the forefront of everyone's thinking.

Watch Your Neighbors. Customers and Suppliers Can Become Competitors. Beware of Left Field

Villains are hiding everywhere. Sometimes competitors are disguised as customers, sometimes as suppliers. Sometimes competitors come from entirely different industries, as the Swiss watchmakers can attest. The Japanese electronic parts manufacturers virtually wiped out their fine watch business.

One of my sons provides supplies to automotive repair shops and garages. He carries small-item supplies such as paint buckets, light bulbs, and sandpaper. One of his biggest suppliers decided that they'd integrate forward into direct product distribution, becoming his direct competitor. To enter the market, they hired and trained a direct sales force and established a large warehouse in the area. They were a significant threat to his business.

This is another good news story, however. Customers actually wanted the diversity of products my son carried, as opposed to the single product line of the manufacturer. In addition, years of personalized customer service paid off as customers remained loyal. After a year, the manufacturer withdrew and again signed an exclusive distribution contract with my son.

The Tale of the Tape

Analyze your position vis-à-vis your competitors. Every marketplace player—you and your competitors—has strengths and weaknesses. Identify your strengths and weaknesses compared with your competitors. Understand your current market situation, and you improve the chances of your success.

Examine your principal competitors and their current strategies. Identify your standing vis-à-vis those competitors *from your customers' perspective* in terms of:

1. Cost structure: Do you have higher or lower costs than your competitors? Check out such things as comparable salaries, locations, cars, number of employees, competing bids.
2. Differentiated value of the product/service you provide: How do your customers see the value of the product/service you provide in comparison with your competitors? How would your competitors' customers answer this question?
3. Price: How do you compare with your competition on price? Are

you lower priced, about the same, or higher priced than your competition?

4. Delivery: Do you deliver on time more or less frequently than your competitors do? What would your customers answer? What would your competitors' customers answer?

5. Quality: How does your quality compare with your competitors'? How would your customers answer this question? How would your competitors' customers answer this question?

6. After-sales support: How good are you at being there to solve customer problems after you've made the sale? How would your customers answer this question? How would your competitors' customers answer this question about them?

Include specific factual data. Understand your competitive advantages and disadvantages. Know what you must do in the market in order to survive and prosper. Most important, include everyone in the game of sensing competitors. Lead everyone to see that it is in his/her best interest to pay attention to competitors. After all, it's his/her job that's on the line.

See It from the Customer's Point of View

Most firms practice the cruelest form of deception—self-delusion. They continue to tell themselves that everything is all right, right up the steps of the bankruptcy court. The inward focus is responsible for more business failures than anything else. Above all, this is a leadership failure.

One of my clients was a very successful computer firm. They swept the market with a hot new box. Then one of their designers came up with an even hotter box. They worked for two years developing it and released it to the market. The market yawned. Sales never took off. Stunned, they came to me to figure out what had happened. "I can't tell you," I said. "But I can help you figure out how to avoid this debacle again."

I helped them go back to their customers and ask why. Their customers gave them a long list of reasons, many of which my client had never anticipated. They set up a system of conversations between customers and computer designers which enabled the company to identify customer needs and develop specific products to address those needs. Their record of new product acceptance is unequaled in the industry.

At another client, the sales manager was convinced that they had the best service in the market. In the face of persistently falling sales he continued to maintain, "We are the best in the industry. We need to do more of what we're doing to overcome the economic slump." The customer survey data showed a very different picture. Customers rated the company "below average" in most categories. It took several months of talking about the survey data to break through the old complacent attitudes. This is not a good news story. By the time the sales manager changed his tune it was too late. The customers were lost. He's history, and the company is a shadow of its former self.

See it from the customer's point of view. Great products are great only when customers buy them.

Everyone's a Tracker—Everyone's an Executor

Inspire everyone involved to find out what customers want and how we measure up against the competition. Winning in business is not a spectator sport. It requires everyone's contribution.

I helped one of my clients learn that lesson. They were an international insurance firm based in Europe. As the European market shifted, they were very adept at buying local firms at good prices in expanding areas. That strategy worked well in western Europe, particularly when local management remained. The strategy didn't work at all when they attempted to apply it in the new free-market economies of central and eastern Europe.

Initially, they set up insurance companies in several eastern European countries headed by western European managers from headquarters. When sales faltered, they called me. I suggested that they use the local staff as a sounding board and resource for figuring out how to beat the competition. They discovered a complete absence of any information about or appreciation of the need for insurance. People in these countries had never thought about insurance before. Until very recently the state had provided everything and made all of their financial decisions. The competitor wasn't another insurance company. It was ignorance.

They began by educating the employees so they could participate in fighting the ignorance. The employees became so enthusiastic about the concept of insurance that they asked for, and got, permission to run information seminars in their own neighborhoods for their friends and relatives. News spread rapidly about these insurance seminars, and soon people were calling in to attend. It became the "in" thing to attend one of these seminars and buy insurance. It was "the way" to demonstrate belief and participation in the new market economy.

Everyone in the company took part: clerks, secretaries, actuaries, as well as managers and salespersons. They mobilized all employees to fight the competitor, ignorance. In doing so, they created one of the most profitable units of the insurance company. The parent company, recognizing a good thing, is now busy applying the same principle throughout their worldwide operations. While the strategy and tactics vary from country to country, the principle remains the same. Everyone is an evaluator of competition, because everyone is involved in beating that competitor.

I learned that lesson myself when I took over a struggling specialty chemical company. It was doing $4 million and losing $400,000. I cut and focused the units to bring it to break-even or a little profit. It was slow going, like walking waist-deep through molasses. One day as I was dragging myself home at 2 A.M. from a trade show, I realized I was owning all of the responsibility for beating the competition. Although I loved being the center of that particular decision set, it was killing me. I did not execute any of the actions necessary to implement my great strategies; so I got less than great execution. Being head buffalo is tough work.

I went in the next day and announced that next month I'd pay for each person to visit one customer, within a 400-mile radius of the location, provided that the person come back with a brief report. The report would be shared with everyone, answering four questions:

1. What are we doing right that we should continue?
2. What are we doing wrong that we should either stop or improve?
3. Who is our chief competitor for that customer's business?

4. What do we have to do to win the customer's business?

The first month approximately one quarter of the people visited customers. They came back with valuable golden nuggets of information about competitors and what we needed to do to win the business. We talked about what we had all learned from the visits, and the people decided what needed to be done by whom. The second month even more people made visits. By the fifth month virtually everyone was visiting and reporting. Moreover, they were taking actions to win customers. In the year we launched the visitation effort, our volume doubled and our margins tripled. I believe these results were a direct consequence of getting everyone involved in identifying competitors and doing whatever it took to beat them and win customers.

QUESTION:
**How can I hone in on and get everyone involved in
beating that competitor?**

LEADERSHIP SOLUTION:
My competitor is my friend.

CHAPTER 19

Create Value-Added Strategies

Leaders provide focus and direction to their organization. The art of effective leadership is to focus people in the "right" directions. I've argued that the "right" direction is to deliver great performance for customers and shareholders. Leaders set up systems and structures that provide that focus. Leaders influence mind-sets. Leaders create value-added strategies that enable everyone in the organization to deliver great performance. Leaders Lead the Journey.

Much of the talk about "empowerment" misses the mark. Empowerment is required in this intellectual capitalism era. But empowerment to do what? Empowering people to leap off the cliff is not particularly productive. Leaders must focus empowered people on the "right" targets. I believe that those "right" targets are executing the value-added strategies that help you win in the marketplace.

Stay Close to Customers

"Get close to customers," I repeatedly admonish people with whom I consult and the people in my own company. "All right already," they tell me. "We hear you." To which my response is, "All right already, I believe you. And how can we do it better?" You can't get too close to customers.

I learned that building close relationships with customers is a tonic for arrogance. Even though our specialty chemical business was very successful, there were always new challenges. New compounds. New applications. New competitors. When one of our low-cost competitors decided that they could enter our higher end market niche, they put on a full-court press with several key accounts, offering lower prices, better delivery, and even brighter colors. They had some "gee whiz" samples to show, which looked very appealing. It wasn't ten seconds after their salesman left our customer's office that she was on the phone to tell us about this new incursion. She even sent us the sample to analyze. We were shocked. We didn't believe that this competitor was capable of delivering such high quality; but there it was, in very bright living color.

We went back to the customer and asked her what she wanted to do. "Can you match this color?" she asked.

"Of course" was our easy reply. "But do you really want that color? It's awfully bright. Will your customers buy it? Let us show you some surveys we've just completed of your customers and their color preferences. Maybe that will help you make up your mind. If you decide you want it, we'll give you what you want. And what's more, we'll absolutely guarantee you'll get it when you need it, exactly how much you need, and with the quality and color that meet your complete satisfaction. We guarantee it and back up our guarantee with the one-million-dollar performance bond. Will *they* do all that?"

The customer grew uncharacteristically quiet. After a thoughtful long pause, she agreed to look over the survey material and get back to us. "Your guarantee is very persuasive," she said at the door. "I look forward to continuing our relationship."

What won the day for us? Was it our superior product? Maybe. Was it our sparkling personalities and great salesmanship? Maybe. Was it our going the extra mile for her in doing the customer surveys? Maybe. We're not certain. All of those contributed. But I believe that her last comment tells it all. At the end of the day she was swayed by the guarantee. That guarantee was one of our key value-added strategies.

We sold a commodity. Our products could be made by virtually anyone with a Bunsen burner and a kettle. Our colors were bright, but anyone could easily copy the formula through reverse engineering.

We won in the marketplace because we were willing to go the extra mile for our customers (witness the survey), and we had the guarantee. Our products were a small part of the overall costs for our customers. But not having the right colors at the right time could cost many dollars in lost production time. So our guarantee bought our customers a good night's sleep. They could count on our products being there. If the products weren't, the customer would be made financially whole.

The Tough Strategic Question: "What Do I Do?"

"What do I do?" the president of a very successful small business asked me recently.

His company was a Cinderella story. Starting with nothing but an idea, he built a rapidly growing business. Customers seemed to come from everywhere, and anywhere. His products were the talk of the industry—the state of the art. He had all the business that he could handle. Yet his face was creased with worry.

"There are too many opportunities," he said. "Which one, or ones, do I take? And how about those product problems we've had? We don't seem to be able to deliver the same quality anymore. Why are we behind so much in the schedule? And why am I always so short of money? The harder I work, the further behind I seem to get. To tell you the truth, I wake up a lot at night worrying about what will happen if someone else comes along with a better product. What do I do?" he asked.

I understand that young president's question. My own business experience tells me, and my years of consulting confirm, that every day we confront this tough strategic question: "How can I maximize both value for my customers and profit for myself?"

The answer? Create value. Customers don't buy price; they buy value. What is value? Like beauty, it is in the eye of the beholder. So I learned to ask my customers to tell me what value was for them. And guess what? They told me with clarity.

It wasn't always that way. For too long I worked hard trying to figure out what customers really wanted. I tried everything under the sun. In the specialty chemical business, for instance, I had a dye-tracing product which I thought would be great for the booming do-it-yourself market. I tried off-price promotions to induce retailers to carry the product. I tried coupons to get consumers to try the product. I even direct-mailed samples to stimulate customer interest. I knew I had a great product. It could do so many things in the home; I just knew customers would go wild over it, that it would walk off the shelves once they tried it.

I spent millions of dollars in marketing and promotion. Many people in the organization spent hours worrying about, and working on, the problem. I woke up competitors to the potential. Ultimately, I sold so few packages that I didn't even cover the packaging costs.

"What went wrong?" I asked myself after I sold the operation to a larger, better financed competitor. When I talked to a hardware store manager a few weeks after the sale, it became painfully obvious. I packaged the product as a liquid because that maximized its flexibility. Consumers were concerned that the liquid would spill or dry out. "Either the liquid container had to be different, a package like WD-40, or it had to be put into a dry pellet form," he told me.

"Why didn't you tell me before?" I asked. "We could have easily changed the package or the form. In fact, pellets were the original form of this product."

"*You never asked,*" he said. "Your people were so busy selling me that they had no time left over to listen."

So much for being smarter than the customer. Without knowing what value is for customers, it's impossible to deliver it consistently.

Value Is Solving the Customer's Problems

Customers usually don't care about features. Bells and whistles attract lookers. It's the answer to the "What will it do for me?" question that converts lookers into buyers. And the best "What will it do for me?" answer is inevitably related to solving some immediately pressing problem.

A friend in the travel agency business struggled to survive. She worked long hours and provided good service to her clients. But she never seemed to have enough money left at the end of her month. She organized a focus-group meeting involving several of her best clients. At that meeting she asked her clients to describe the problems they encountered in traveling and how the "perfect" agent could help them.

She made detailed lists of customers' problems and how they wanted travel agents, in the best of all worlds, to handle them. She didn't defend or attempt to explain what she did now or why she did it. At the end of two hours she had a complete picture of what her customers really wanted from her agency.

The next day she began to change her agency to help her customers solve their travel problems. The changes she made included: joining a twenty-four-hour reservation service to accommodate clients who said they needed to change reservations at other than regular business hours; setting up a travel club, complete with frequent newsletters to keep people posted about alternative travel destinations; arranging for subscriptions to travel magazines to help people plan vacation locations; establishing fax contacts with frequent travelers to pass on short-term bargains; and negotiating regular discounts for her volume business travelers. Her business tripled and she opened two new offices within a year. Solving customer problems pays big dividends.

Value Is Doing It Better than Anybody Else

Providing a product or service that solves important problems for customers is necessary, but it is not sufficient to succeed. You must provide that solution in a different way or better than anyone else. In business there's no place to finish except first.

A trucking-firm client of mine focused on providing distribution for less than full truckloads for small to midsize packaging firms. They had the market mostly to themselves for some time, so they got a little sloppy in their service and quality—not much, just a little here and there. As inevitably happens, a competitor moved into their territory. They were concerned, as they should have been. By talking to their customers, they immediately saw their problem clearly: The new kid on the block had heard the customers' need for greater predictability in delivery times. The competitor promised deliveries within a half-hour window and met that more rigid schedule through use of two-way radios. Our client had heard that request before from customers, but hadn't gotten around to doing anything about it.

The president called her people together and asked them, "What can we do to provide the best-in-the-marketplace service to our customers?" The people made a list of over thirty items that they had heard from customers. She told them, "Do whatever it takes to be the best in the business for your customers." The drivers put on a full campaign with their customers and dedicated themselves to do whatever it took to get them back. Drivers went out and stacked orders. Drivers called ahead to notify customers when they would deliver. Drivers even arranged their hours to pick up and deliver items early in the morning and late at night. Customers were impressed with their dedication and service. Their business doubled.

Value-Added Strategies Solve the Problem that Drives Purchasing Decisions

Customers have lots of problems. You have limited resources. Choose the right customer problem on which to focus. What is the right problem? The right one is the one that drives the customer's buying decision. Inevitably, there's one overriding problem, the solution to which will encourage your customer to buy from you and not your competitor.

I know that Johnsonville's products are not necessities. People don't "have to" buy Johnsonville sausage in order to survive. People must "want to" buy the product. How can you get people to "want to" buy this nonnecessity? Provide such great-tasting sausage that when people see it in the meat case they remember the great taste. Their mouths water and they feel compelled to pick up the product and put it in their shopping cart. Johnsonville sells great taste. Every action in the company is designed to build a great-tasting product. Their value-added strategy is to produce a product with a noticeably better taste than their competitors.

In the late 1970s and throughout the 1980s the Japanese car companies were able to outproduce the American car companies in delivering what drove customers' buying decisions. Toyota, Nissan, Mazda, and others understood what drove customers' buying decisions about new cars: gas efficiency, lower prices derived from manufacturing efficiency, and quality. They outdelivered American car companies on those dimensions, and their market share quadrupled in that period.

The examples are legion. Every successful company can point to a value-added strategy that solved the customers' problems and drove their buying decision.

Learn How to Focus Yourself and Get Others to Focus on Solving the Customer's Problem

I know that the leader's job is simple to say but not so simple to do: to identify and solve the customers' problem that drives their purchasing decision. I learned the hard way to identify those few problems that drove my customers' purchasing decisions, and then focus all of my energy on them. It's tough to ignore the rest. I am subject to drowning myself in details, or becoming preoccupied with all those "other problems," particularly those I know how to solve already. These inevitably tempt me off course. I know I must fix firmly on identifying what drives the customers' buying decision; then decide what it takes to solve that problem, creating value for the customer better than anybody else in the market. That's the simple-to-say—and not-so-simple-to-do—way to succeed.

QUESTION:
Do our products and services stand out head and shoulders above our competition?

LEADERSHIP SOLUTION:
Stay tuned in to customers and do whatever it takes to create value for them.

CHAPTER 20

Nichemanship/Domination: Own It or Forget It

Question: Who makes the most money? Answer: The person who leads the pack. Lead and get the cream. Follow and get the crumbs. Which would you rather have?

Until recently I chose the crumbs, believing that that was all I could get. Once again, with my old leadership mentality, I was the biggest obstacle. Only when I learned to believe that I could dominate the market did we begin to make progress.

As the leader Leading the Journey I learned to establish value-added strategies that focus everyone on providing great performance for their customers. One of the most powerful value-added strategies I've discovered is to identify the most profitable niche we can successfully serve, and then dominate that niche. Once I learned how to lead my organization on *that* journey, we became much more successful.

"Hit 'em where they ain't": That was Wee Willie Keeler's motto. He did that through a very successful baseball career. The motto of a successful niche player might be "Hit 'em where the big boys aren't, and the big money is."

Find Niche Applications for Commodity Products

Find the crack—the crevice—that piece of unfulfilled demand. That's what successful niche players do. That's the lesson I learned when I took over a specialty chemical business on the steps of the bankruptcy court.

I set out immediately to find profitable niches. I shifted the emphasis from low-margin, high-volume products to higher margin specialty products using the same basic chemical formula. In the ink business, for instance, we continued to supply large-volume purchasers, like Papermate. Simultaneously, we sold a variant of our inks to a growing number of specialized users, like Cross and Waterman, who were willing to pay higher prices for higher quality and better service. We were successful in taking basic commodity products and finding upscale, higher margin applications. Volume grew twelve times in six years, and margins increased twenty-seven times. I learned that's one value-added strategy in the niche game.

Know Your Customer—and Use That Knowledge

You can't find a more basic commodity product than food supermarketing. Yet I took my niche-oriented value-added strategy and helped one local supermarket chain move from number seven to number three in their region. They found and serviced specific niches. They had a store in a poor, Portuguese-speaking neighborhood. It was an old store and looked it. To appeal to a different customer set, I worked with them to completely restock the store. Out went all the "yuppie" items, which sold well in other locations, such as pasta and whole-wheat bread. In came many new items specifically aimed at the Portuguese taste, including antipasto salads and dough cookies. Sales rose significantly and profits doubled.

Learning from this experience, they surveyed their neighborhoods and in-store customers on an ongoing basis in an effort to understand and focus on their customers. The employees, hired locally, played an active role in these surveys. Using this customer information, this supermarket chain sells 50 percent more per square foot per year than the industry average. Using locals, who understand and can relate to the customers, is one way to ensure the customer focus to identify value-added strategies.

Minimize Your Dependence on Any One Customer or Product

One of my clients learned how to be a successful niche player by spreading their risks. They produce a wide range of computer couplings. In the three years during which we worked together, they came to realize the value in small accounts. They sell today to over one thousand companies, none of whom represents more than 2 percent of their sales volume. That means that they are largely immune from strong price pressure. They stay away from large customers and long production runs. They specialize in supplying customized components. Competitors seek out the large jobs and shun the custom work. This leaves the custom market virtually competition-free. As a result, they earn 10 percent to 12 percent return, rather than the 3 percent most component firms eke out. I learned, and helped them learn, that minimizing your dependence upon any one customer or product can help you be a successful niche player.

Stay Away from the Big Boys

I learned that niche players usually survive by following the "avoid the big guys" strategy. My textile coloring business is a good example. It was an absolute disaster. We had a foreign competitor who was paying five cents an hour in wages, and was being subsidized by his government. To say that we faced tough price competition is to understate the obvious. Yet we continue to survive and prosper in that business. How do we do that in the face of such awesome foreign competition? It's obvious! Pick a niche in which low-cost labor doesn't count and where we can move faster than our competition. We focus our efforts on solving textile manufacturers/dyers' tough, "it can't be done" coloring problems. No one else is willing to commit the resources we have to this particular activity. As a niche player in a tough industry, we survive by avoiding competition. That's good advice in any industry.

Stay Nimble or Else. "If All Your Eggs Are in One Basket, Watch That Basket"—J. C. Penney

You must stay nimble! Taking your eye off the ball can lead to disastrous results. I did some work for a regional department store chain. They had eleven stores in a large metropolitan area. They had a good niche strategy, convenient locations, and low prices on particularly high turnover items like budget clothing. The low margins on these products were offset by higher margins on off-size clothing. In this region they owned the local discount retailing business and showed net margins double the industry average. Then they got sloppy. They became preoccupied with opening two new stores. No one was minding the eleven stores they already had. My job was to help the management wake up. We got the employees involved in defining and living the "discount retailing" vision. They actively participated in drawing customers back into the stores. Unfortunately, customers once lost are hard to get back. While the business turned around within six months, it was too late. The owners had to sell at fire-sale prices. One mistake in this niche business could be your last.

There you have it. The basic niche player's strategies:

- Avoid the big boys.
- Be flexible.
- Find upscale applications for commodity products.
- Stay close to your customer.
- Avoid dependence upon a few products and/or customers.

Focus your people on these value-added strategies. That's the way you Lead the Journey using the intellectual capitalism paradigm.

QUESTION:
What do my customers want that they are not now getting?

LEADERSHIP SOLUTION:
Niches are gold mines. Find them and start digging.

CHAPTER 21

A Rose by
Any Other Name
Probably Wouldn't
Sell

Pictures Create Focus

Many executives complain about increasing competition. Translation: Their customers don't see enough reasons to buy their products rather than their competitors'. Price competition almost always means that customers don't see enough differentiation among products, so price is the only way to distinguish.

The customers' perspective is often different from what we initially think. I've discovered that people talk rationally and buy emotionally. People buy a car not because of the great gas mileage or the price. They buy it because it makes them feel good. That "feel good" dimension is critical to every purchasing decision. People "feel" on the basis of the words used and the pictures painted by those words. Literally, a rose by any other name probably wouldn't sell.

As a leader I learned to use words, and the pictures they paint, to help keep people focused on creating and executing value-added strategies—strategies that deliver great performance for their customers. My job as a leader is to provide that focus and direction by using the right words that paint the right pictures. In that way I Lead the Journey in the right direction.

Pictures Create Feelings—and That's What Customers Really Buy

Customers buy the feelings that pictures evoke. Can you imagine selling a cactus as an "I love you" message? The picture painted by a cactus is incongruous with that of the feeling of the words "I love you."

The feelings, which the picture creates, stimulate the customer to buy your product. Picture the Coors advertisement with the running mountain stream. Feel the coolness of that stream as the mercury heads toward three digits. With the sweat running down your neck, feel the saliva start to flow as you feel the impulse to reach for a Coors—to cool you down. Why Coors sells so well is the picture that triggers the feelings. Feelings, triggered by the appropriate picture, move the hand to reach for the silver can.

Where the Hell Is Johnsonville?

In 1968 Johnsonville began marketing outside its traditional Sheboygan County, Wisconsin, home. It began selling in Racine, eighty miles south. Since few people had heard of us there, we ran in-store samplings to introduce our products. Our sampling people wrote down the comments they heard.

Our customers' response shocked me. One question was asked far more times than any other comment. They wanted to know, "Where the hell is Johnsonville?" I talked with some of them. They thought the product was the best they had ever tasted, but they were reluctant to switch brands. They didn't know enough about the company. They didn't want to know *where* Johnsonville was. They wanted to know *what* Johnsonville was and *that* Johnsonville was okay to buy.

The Picture Must Inspire Customer Confidence

Sausage has not benefited from a sterling reputation. People are a bit skeptical about what is in it. They want to know that the people who make their sausage have values and can be trusted. They want the people they buy from to care about them. They felt that small-town companies would be more interested in making great products than a fast buck.

None of our marketing conveyed this image. Our labels are a good example. They simply had the company and product name, the ingredients, and our address on them. I was proud of them. My name was big. I liked the colors. My conceit convinced me that our sausage was so good we didn't have to have "fancy" labels. I loved them. Our customers didn't. Guess who was winning!

I decided that our labels had to convey exactly who we are. Our company is located in a small farming town. We pride ourselves on using the finest ingredients in the world to make the best sausage in the world. We *will* go the extra step to make sure our customers are totally satisfied. I changed our name to Johnsonville Foods. I put a picture of a small country town on the label along with cooking suggestions. I told people we were committed to making the best sausage in the world. I asked them to let us know how we were doing. Sales started to climb but still weren't what I thought they should be.

The Product Name Must Paint the Picture

The answer was in the information customers gave us. Our product names were Bologna, Bratwurst, Wieners, Summer Sausage, etc. Product names paint pictures in customers' heads. I asked myself, "What picture does our product name create?" In the sausage industry, products are almost always named for the process by which they are produced—cooked, fried, stuffed, or fresh. The kind of picture that creates in the minds of my customer was not the kind I knew would stimulate sales.

That's why Johnsonville sells products, not with the usual name of the process by which it is produced, but by the name of the taste it creates or by how the customer uses it—Italian, snacking, barbecuing. The picture that "Italian" sausage paints in one's mind evokes many more memories of enjoyable sensations than "smoked" sausage. We changed the names of most of our products, adding sensation-loaded names to our standard products to make them more exciting to our customers. We now have Beer City Grillers, Italianti, Now That's Italian, Irish O'Garlic, Snacking Sausage, and many more. Sales have taken off.

Every Activity and Every Person
Must Create the Picture

Next we changed the advertising to reflect the image. We repainted the trucks. Our people answer the phone, "The best to you from Johnsonville." Our invoices, statements, and letters all convey the image. Most of all, our people convey the image in everything they do. Our customers know that we are committed to be the best for them.

Everything must contribute to creating the picture. Everything. The operant question must be "How does this activity or action contribute to the picture we want customers to have of our organization?" Each person needs to think strategically and then own the responsibility to do whatever it takes to please customers.

Every person is in marketing. Every person must do whatever it takes to create the right picture in the customer's mind. The telephone operator who's the first point of contact has to convey that picture both with the opening greeting and with the handling of the customer. The accounts payable clerk has to create that picture with how he handles suppliers. The engineer has to create that picture with how she designs the product. Every activity and every person must contribute to painting that picture.

My Actions and Words Cast a Long Shadow

As the leader my words and actions shape my people's words and actions in creating the "right" picture for customers. As the baseball umpire said, "It isn't a ball or a strike until I call it." People watched my every action and interpreted it as either supporting or detracting from my stated customer orientation. People wanted to see if I really did "walk my customer-oriented talk." I looked at my every action for its possible picture-painting impact. Early on, I did some simple things to demonstrate my sincerity. When people came to me with a possible action, the first question I'd ask was "How does this contribute to the picture we want to create for customers? How will this impact your customers? What do your customers really want?" Invariably, people didn't know, so I sent them to find out and discussed possible answers with them. Very few problems returned to my desk, as customers and employee-members worked out solutions. My actions in pushing for customer reactions contributed to the "We're in the customer-satisfaction business" picture I wanted in every person's head.

Every action and word on the part of the leader paints a picture for internal (and often external) individuals. Anticipate their potential picture-painting impact and use them to create the mentality that "I'm responsible for ensuring that the customer has the right picture of us."

QUESTION:
How do customers see us now?

LEADERSHIP SOLUTION:
Paint a Rembrandt or forget it.

CHAPTER 22

If You Don't Lose 20 Percent of Your Business on Price, Your Prices Aren't High Enough

Pricing Provides Focus on Great Performance for Customers

Pricing is a critical strategic decision. It dictates who your customers will be, how much money you make, and your position in the market.

Pricing is also a key leadership tool in providing focus and direction on great performance for customers. As such, it is a value-added strategy which helps you, as the leader, to Lead the Journey.

I learned to use pricing to help everyone think strategically about the business, and focus on customers. In that way I became the lead goose, using the intellectual capitalism paradigm.

In Reality, Do Customers Buy Price? Or Is It Something Else?

I recently worked with George, a contractor. When I first started working with him, his company was in serious financial difficulty. He served the public utility market. All work was done on a bid basis. Competition was intense. He was focused on cutting costs because he felt pricing was set by the bidding process. He wasn't optimistic about his chances for survival. He was competing against larger, well-financed competitors. His banks were very nervous. He didn't have much time. He was in a downward spiral from which bankruptcy was the only exit. George was homesteading his house and thinking about "other options" when we first talked.

We reexamined his fundamental strategy through the prism of his pricing policies. I asked him, "What prices would you have to charge to make a great return on your investment? What are your customers really buying? What would they have to believe about your company to pay the prices you needed?"

The questions helped George rethink his situation. He realized that his customers were focused on buying pipe laid in the ground as cheaply as possible, because that was all anyone offered them. He realized that what they really wanted was no-problem service for their customers.

Armed with this new insight into his business, George developed several value-added strategies. His principal value-added strategy was to promise no-hassle service. His second strategy was to build the systems and infrastructure to deliver that perfect service. Both of these strategies enabled George to raise his prices considerably.

Several months later George called me. He was very pleased with the changes in his business. He told me about a recent rush job for a major client and how his new strategy worked to get him more profitable business. The utility didn't have time to go through the normal bidding process, so they solicited informal bids from several contractors. George offered them his no-hassle service guarantee and increased his prices 30 percent. The utility accepted. The work went smoothly. His crew went back several times to fix unexpected difficulties. Overall, George felt that the job went well and the utility was pleased.

Several weeks later the utility called George back and asked him to do twelve years of work. They wanted the work on the same guarantee basis. They even agreed to a substantial price increase. George was delighted. Within the same week George won another bid on which he was the high bidder. That bid also included guaranteed service. George's comment was very interesting. He said, "They aren't buying pipe. They're buying a good night's sleep." Shades of IBM.

What Customers Do You Want to Have?

Newport Beach, California, is a very affluent community. It is home to many expensive houses and yachts. Some of the largest and most expensive are on Balboa Island, in the Newport Beach harbor. I learned a valuable lesson when I visited the island.

The largest house on the best lot on the island also had the largest yacht moored to its dock. The name of the yacht: *High Bidder*. At first I thought that the owner had outbid everyone else for the yacht. Later that evening the owner explained to me how the yacht got its name. He owned a contract services company. He told me, "I learned years ago that the secret to success in my business was not winning most of the bids, but losing the 'right' ones. I only want to win the ones that I know I will do well on. I'm willing to walk away from business that is marginally profitable. I don't need marginal business. I need the profit. I've learned that being the high bidder is the way to succeed."

What a great insight. There are some customers you don't want. Who needs the unprofitable customer? Why not leave those to your competitor? I've used this insight many times in my own business. I've learned that being high bidder is one sure way to be the high earner.

Create Value for Customers in Every Market

I worked with a consumer products company. They had a large market share but poor profit margins. They made the best products but sold them at the same price as their competitors. Previous price-increase efforts resulted in lost market share.

They missed a very important point. If their products were so good, why didn't customers recognize their value and pay more for them?

Successful companies differentiate themselves by adding *real* value for their customers. Helping customers see the real value you bring marks the difference between high and low profits. The question is "What is *real* value from the customer's perspective?"

The consumer products company decided to examine their present business to learn why their customers were not seeing them as providing real value. There was obviously a gap between their perception and their customers' perception of their products.

They discovered their real advantage. They sold their product by the pound. Their customers took the product, performed another operation on it, and then sold the combined new product by volume. A pound of their product produced 30 percent more volume of the new combined product than their competitors'. That's a significant advantage. They had tried to sell this benefit in the past, but it was obvious that the message wasn't getting through.

The company sold to distributors, who in turn sold to thousands of small customers. They decided to change their marketing. They put together demonstrator kits so distributors could show the difference in volume between their product and the competition's. They built projected income statements for the final end-user customer that showed their product's significant income advantage compared to the competition's. And they added a minimum income guarantee.

These value-added strategies demonstrated *real* value, for which their customers were willing to pay. They were also able to use this value-added strategy as a way to focus their people on providing great performance for their customers. They charge a 20 percent premium and take the money to the bank. They are now very profitable.

The Biggest Battle over Price Is Not with Customers. It's with Myself and My Sales Force

Our company used a similar value-added strategy. We'd been upgrading one product line for some time. We were clearly the industry leader in everything except price. Our goal was to be the best and to be perceived as the best by everyone in this industry. Our measurement of great performance was to have the highest selling price and the highest market share.

We were slow to increase prices in our local markets. We were afraid of losing market share. Our sales force told me that the market would reject higher prices. Our initial attempts at increasing prices met with resistance from our long-term customers. At the same time, however, we were expanding into new markets and charging more for our products in those markets. Our new customers were quite satisfied with our prices and our products. What was different?

After thinking about it I realized the problem. Over the years, we'd trained our sales force, our customers, and especially myself that our product wasn't worth more than the competition's. Once I saw the light, the hardest battle I had to fight was not with our customers. It was with my own sales force, who had difficulty believing that they could sell the new value in the product. As a way to help them learn, I sent some of them out to sell in new markets where we were achieving higher margins. I brought people from the new markets back to our home market to work with people who wanted to learn how to sell at higher prices. The result? Customers accepted the new price-value relationship. We achieved our goal of highest market share and price.

Pricing Creates Value

In one of my first marketing classes I remember the professor using the case of a hardware company that experienced difficulty when introducing a new item for $1.95. They had a good product, got it in the "right" locations, and advertised it strongly. But it still didn't sell. After many frustrating months the company withdrew the product. A new management came in several years later and decided to reintroduce the product at $4.95. The product was a big hit.

The professor used the case to illustrate his point that price was an important determiner of value. Selling a Cadillac at Chevrolet prices would probably sell fewer Cadillacs, he said. Interestingly enough, Cadillac proved his point many years later when their small Cadillac not only failed to sell but also detracted value from the entire line.

Leadership in the intellectual capitalism age demands that we think about our leadership tasks in a totally different way. Pricing is one prism through which we can see the differences: between being the head buffalo and the lead goose, between commanding and controlling or leading and enabling. Pricing is one way to help everyone, including ourselves, focus in the right directions.

QUESTION:
Do your prices reflect your great performance?

LEADERSHIP SOLUTION:
What your customers are willing to pay tells you what they—and you—think about your products.

CHAPTER 23

Sharing the Sandbox

Focus on Finding Partners

Dizzying change has forced us to rethink our relationships with suppliers and distributors. Our previous strategies of integrating through purchase and direct ownership are out. The new way to add value is through business partnerships.

Because I always felt that I had to do everything myself, that new way was an amazing revelation to me. The old leadership paradigm stressed independence and control—with suppliers and distributors as well as employees. Then I learned that I need not do it alone.

Just as I learned to develop more productive relationships with my people, I found business partners who could supplement my strengths. They could help me break into new markets, leapfrog technology, develop new technology, and apply current technology to new areas.

Building these business partners became one value-added strategy. It enabled me to stay focused on the delivery of great performance for our customers—another way in which I Lead the Journey. I also helped the people in my organization learn to work with others from different backgrounds and organizations and with different functions to solve together what each of them could not solve alone.

The Old Way: Big Dictates

For decades the large vertically integrated organization used its size to force concessions from smaller suppliers. Sears, for instance, often used the lure of its huge potential market to squeeze suppliers' prices down. Landing a big contract with Sears was often the first step on the road to financial ruin for a small supplier.

Owning small companies, I knew firsthand about the big bully who was our customer. In the specialty chemical industry, "net 90" were payment terms practiced by the big customers. When they needed to generate a little more cash, it was easy to "stretch out" the payment to 120 days. And we got stretched. We were unwillingly financing our customers.

On the downstream side of the distribution channel, large manufacturers often bullied distributors to carry more inventory than necessary, usually of slower selling models. Arm's-length adversarial relationships dominated the scene.

Again, I've been on the downstream distribution side as well. I am a distributor for several computer manufacturers. The manufacturer decides, "We're going to push this product line this year." So they put in place a whole set of incentives to sell that line. It usually takes the manufacturer several months to get their act together and several more months for us to get up and running on the new thrust. It's usually the dog days of summer before we are really ready to roll. By then the manufacturer has shifted emphasis and is off pushing another product line in order to meet revised corporate earning and revenue targets. Meanwhile, of course, the rest of my business suffers from a lack of attention. The scene got repeated several times before I decided, "Never again."

The New World Order: Partnership, Not Domination

The giants have learned that it takes both size and flexibility to meet rapidly changing customer demands. Healthy smaller firms, surrounding the giant, provide the flexibility to focus and capitalize on the giant's size. Take the computer industry.

Haughty giants have long dominated that industry. IBM and DEC were very good at telling customers what they needed—usually their own internally developed proprietary systems. The "we know best" attitude carried over into distributor relationships.

Today, relationships with downstream distributors is the biggest challenge confronting computer manufacturers. IBM's strength, for instance, lies in its direct marketing efforts to large mainframe customers. IBM is the premier large-account marketing company. However, the mini- and midrange markets, the most rapidly growing segments of the industry, are much too fragmented to capitalize on IBM's strength.

Critical success factors in these markets include specialized industry knowledge, application-specific software solutions, and custom-tailored implementation. In these markets customers buy solutions, not hardware. One survey showed that fewer than 10 percent of the customers in these markets relied upon the hardware manufacturer's name in choosing a system. Instead, the quality of the solution drove more than 50 percent of the purchase decisions. Those solutions are offered by the small, independent software distributor. Partnerships with these large manufacturers is maturing for downstream distributors.

Initially, the manufacturers sabotaged partnership efforts. They set up competition between distributors and their own internal salespeople. Local branch offices owned customer leads and turned over only the ones they couldn't handle. Needless to say, internal salespeople cherry-picked the plums and left the dregs for distributors.

They also set up competing partner channels. Dealers, agents, and remarketers all competed with each other to sell the same systems at differing discounts. It was very difficult to compete in a market where the distributor earned an 11 percent discount on the hardware (the largest dollar portion of the sale), when others received a 45 percent discount.

New product information was also closely guarded. Downstream partners often read about new systems in the newspaper.

Why were these disruptive actions practiced when it's clearly in the manufacturer's interest to help the distributor partner be successful? At its base lies a substantial mentality gulf between the giant hardware manufacturer and the smaller software partner. The large manufacturer, with elaborate staff and financial resources, couldn't understand the small company's reluctance to hire more marketing staff. Highly leveraged and always cash poor, the distributor couldn't understand why the large company couldn't pay its commissions faster than ninety days. The staffs of the large firms often resented the partner's economic success. Many of the small-company employees, often escapees from the big corporate world, resented the risk-aversive, big-company "let's study it to death" mentality of the manufacturer's people with whom they dealt.

Experience is a great teacher. Both have been avid learners. Manufacturers now involve partners early in the hardware development cycle, so that software can be developed and available when the new system is announced. Manufacturers also endeavor to provide a wide range of support services. Consulting services, strategic planning assistance, and a wide range of free education activities all help smaller companies operate a more successful business. They also received direct financial grants for hiring marketing people and/or migrating application software.

The partnership is now in the adolescent stage of development. Arm's-length relationships still prevail in many instances. There's still a lack of understanding of the different basis for each one's success. There needs to be more willingness to work for the partner's success with the same intensity as you work for your own success. There's been growth. More needs to happen. Adulthood is still waiting in the wings.

Technology Helps Build Partnerships

Our relationships in the specialty chemical business offer another model of successful business partnerships. We successfully built partnerships with several larger customers. That partnership helped them combat the pain of restructuring caused by competition in their primary markets. The problem confronting most of our customers was simple to understand: Lower the break-even point so that you can make money when production levels fall. We helped them find a simple answer also: Use strong technology-sharing relationships with suppliers. Together we jointly used just-in-time inventory, joint product development, and flexible manufacturing technologies. These helped several of our customers reduce inventory levels by one third, break-even levels by as much as 50 percent, and product development cycles by more than 72 percent.

We did it with one large pen manufacturer. We make nine just-in-time deliveries a day to this manufacturer. They provide us the technology to use their just-in-time inventory planning system so we know precisely the minute when they are going to produce what product. They also helped us automate our production line. In turn, we work with one of our second-tier suppliers, a large commodity chemical company, to use the manufacturer's JIT technology to tie them in with us so we do not have to carry additional inventory.

The giant firm with the resources developed the technology. It then shared that technology with us, their first-tier supplier. They then helped us apply the same technology to help the second- and third-tier partners. The result was by tying in first-, second-, and third-tier business partner suppliers through technology exchange, this manufacturer produces nineteen hundred different-colored products on the same production line, with a lead time of less than two days. Business partnerships have overcome the potential cost disadvantage of specialized markets. Better yet, everyone wins.

Win/Win or Lose/Lose

The message is clear: Supplier and distributor business partners can capitalize on the advantages of both size *and* flexibility. I learned that unless both parties work as hard for the partner as they work for themselves, they are both doomed to fail.

I learned this lesson through experiences in two offices. Both offices are business partners for the same computer manufacturer. Both compete in the same market in different geographic areas. In office A there's a close relationship between that office and the manufacturer. The manufacturer's local branch manager sits on the local board of directors. She's always ready with advice, counsel, and assistance in piloting the office through the shoals of the inner workings of the manufacturer and in making joint presentations to customers. Her marketing staff "works" for that office, and the office staff has input into the manufacturer's personnel performance evaluations and business discussions.

Office B is in a different world. There's an arm's-length relationship between the office and the local branch manager. He sees the partner as a threat to his local bonus goals. They compete with the local marketing staff for leads and customers. They never make joint presentations. The partner never informs the local branch manager of their activities, as they're afraid he'll sabotage them.

Office A is highly profitable. Office B is a disaster. As the leader in the intellectual capitalism era, I posed several questions: "How can we change Office B to be more like Office A? What is the leader doing or not doing that causes this breach of confidence and poor working relationship?" I asked the entire staff at Office B.

The first response was a lot of finger-pointing. "They won't cooperate. They'll steal our ideas. I don't like that branch manager, and he doesn't like me. Our personalities clash." I listened . . . and listened . . . and listened.

Finally, I asked, "How would they answer the same question?"

The room was silent for a long time, followed by lots of stammering and halting guesses. "We don't know," everyone finally admitted.

"How about finding out?" I suggested. I urged them to meet with the branch manager and think strategically together. Surely, they both shared a deep desire to succeed in the market. That they needed each other to succeed was clear, if they could only focus on their common purposes, rather than their differences in personalities and backgrounds.

They met several times and put together a business plan for working together. Progress was difficult. They slipped back several times. I kept urging them to keep focusing on their common interests. The office showed a remarkable recovery. Thinking strategically helps focus on the common purposes and keeps partnerships on the win/win track.

Expand the Sandbox. Full-Stream Manufacturing Builds Win/Win Partnerships Within the Organization

The win/win game not only involves finding partners "out there." It also involves building win/win partnerships within the organization. For example, for many manufacturing people their plant becomes their prison. They can't see beyond their four walls. In today's rapidly changing market that perspective is a sure recipe for disaster. As leaders we need to help the factory people reach out beyond their walls and form alliances with *all* the partners necessary for their success.

I work with the manufacturing leadership of a large high-technology company. Their story is familiar: dramatic downsizing of domestic operations, transferring operations to low-wage areas, and outsourcing of production to generate lower cost products that can be OEMed by the sales force. The leaders see clearly the need to change. They see the requirement to influence the *full stream* of activities necessary to satisfy their customers.

The leaders changed the information system to present all employees with the realities of their new world. Internal customers came and explained how manufacturing added to their costs of design, distribution, installation, or service. External customers came and explained that competitive products were cheaper and better. The employees, and the union, saw the need to work together with their internal partners to save their jobs.

Everyone in manufacturing got focused on adding value throughout the *full stream* of building, selling, and servicing the company's products. Now teams of people, including production workers, regularly visit their internal and external customers. They ask the partnership questions listed in Chapter 13, such as:

- What must you create in the marketplace in order for you to succeed, and how can we help you achieve your goals?
- What are your biggest frustrations, and how can we help you eliminate them?
- How can we reduce the total cost of getting the product to market and servicing it once it's there?

Teams go out with installers to learn how to redesign products to cut installation costs. Teams work with service technicians to produce products that are easier and less costly to service. Teams meet with designers and marketers to shorten the product realization process.

The manufacturing staff's full-stream approach extends their influence beyond the walls of their factories. Their vision, of adding value throughout the *entire* chain, is the future of manufacturing in our country. It also saved a lot of jobs as the holders of the intellectual capital extended their leadership across formerly inviolate organizational boundaries.

QUESTION:
How can we both be on the same side of the table?

LEADERSHIP SOLUTION:
Hang together or we will surely hang separately.

PART V

REMOVE THE OBSTACLES
THAT PREVENT
GREAT PERFORMANCE

DETERMINE FOCUS AND DIRECTION

- VISION
- CUSTOMERS
- GREAT PERFORMANCE
- VALUE-ADDED STRATEGIES

STIMULATE
SELF-DIRECTED
ACTIONS

DEVELOP OWNERSHIP

REMOVE *OBSTACLES*

- Systems
- Skills
- Structures
- Mentalities

Introduction

Focus and direction allow your people to deliver great performance for your customers. Knowing the "right" direction is the first step. The second step is to identify and remove the obstacles that prevent you from achieving great performance. My job as the leader is to remove the obstacles that stand in the way of my people being great performers.

Focus on Those Obstacles You Control or Directly Influence

We have little or no control or influence over many things in our lives: inflation, interest rates, the future of Russia. These issues make great conversations over dinner or around a fireplace, but have little relevance in a business setting. We control our own behavior, and directly influence certain other issues that impact people's behavior. More than a thousand people work in my company, none of whom I control, but all of whom I can directly influence on some issues.

Obstacles Come in Two Arenas:
Systems and Mind-sets

While most of us are drawn to the mind-set obstacles of motivation, communication, and teamwork issues, the biggest obstacles are organizational obstacles, like the systems and structures. I've found that the systems and structures dramatically affect the mind-sets of everyone else.

Your leadership task in this age of intellectual capitalism is to remove the obstacles that impede people from delivering great performance for their customers. In that way you increase the probability of successfully Leading the Journey.

QUESTION:
**How can I identify and remove those obstacles that
prevent great performance?**

LEADERSHIP SOLUTION:
**Ask your people what prevents their great performance.
Get to work on those obstacles.**

CHAPTER 24

Systems and Structures Call the Tune

Align Systems and Structures

Systems are the most powerful drivers of performance. Before I learned that lesson I tried many other "do it yourself" classics. Early on, I identified communications as an obstacle to great performance. I put everyone through an intensive communications course. Surprisingly, communication actually got worse. I worried about the lack of team-work. So I took everyone on a white-water rafting experience. We had great fun out there, and we even all survived. Afterward very little improved back at the plant.

I assumed the people's attitudes needed to change first. If I could only change their attitudes, I believed that would improve bottom-line performance. The more I worked on changing mind-sets, the worse the situation seemed to grow. For instance, I was an early believer in employee involvement. I assumed that involvement would trigger attitude change and that attitude change would improve the organization's bottom-line performance.

A number of failed efforts convinced me that my assumption was flawed. I was attempting to change performance by changing attitudes directly. Of course, it never worked. Once I stopped pushing whatever I was pushing—quality or cost reduction or service improvement—the people stopped working on it. After many frustrating failures, I realized that what I was doing wasn't working. Attitudes are shaped by the environment within which people function. The environment is made up of the systems and structures in the organization. Although I could not change attitudes directly, I could change them by changing the environment. I learned that incorrect attitudes are a symptom of incorrect systems, structures, and practices.

Systems Send Powerful Messages

Unfortunately, systems usually reinforce the "don't change" mentality. The leader's job is to encourage people to question and challenge those systems that prevent them from delivering great performance for their customers.

For example, one high-tech manufacturing company I've worked with had a problem: bulging order books and serious delivery delays. Although the factory was months behind, because they couldn't get the engineering drawings in time, the engineering section was receiving bonuses for on-schedule performance. The bonus system was the villain. Engineering met its deadline, and earned its bonus, by issuing "white drawings"—blank sheets with the correct drawing numbers on them. The bonus system was the obstacle to achieving great performance.

At Johnsonville the marketing department received all customer complaint letters. The marketing people sent out good answers. That wasn't the problem. In that system we could not achieve great performance because the people who made the sausage were insulated from knowing what customers thought of the products they made. Simply by changing the system, sending the letters directly to the people producing the sausage, they saw, for the first time, what turned customers on and off. Now Johnsonville people could work to change customer problems. The people on the line responded to complaint letters and did whatever was necessary, including sending coupons for free product. To prevent complaint letters, the line workers asked for, and received, responsibility for measuring product quality. They used those measurements to improve production processes. The simple systems change, connecting people with direct feedback, developed the ownership of responsibility.

Three systems hold the key to focus people in the "right" directions and allow them to own responsibility for their behaviors. Compare your current systems with these "model" systems. If your current systems do not have the same characteristics as these model systems, you have an obstacle to overcome. The sooner you begin the work of removing it, the sooner you can enjoy the success of the new leadership paradigm.

Performance Management System

How are the standards of performance determined in your organization? How does your current system compare to the following model?

1. *Manager determines the overall parameters/objectives.* Define the playing field. Are you playing American football? Canadian football? World football? Or is it arena football? All four are called football, but the rules in each game are significantly different.

For example, one fine-dining dinner house company defined their great performance objectives as: (1) be the dinner house of choice for customers; (2) be the investment of choice for investors; and (3) be the employer of choice for people in the local labor market. These three great performance objectives became the parameters for all managers and employees in the organization. Everyone set objectives that contributed to one or more of these three.

You as the leader establish the parameters, the overall objective, the vision. You need to articulate great performance standards for the overall organization. You need to be certain that everyone's nose is pointed in the same direction.

2. *Set standards between performers and customers.* We need to ensure that standards are set between performers and their customers. Each performer must meet frequently (weekly) with his or her customers to agree on standards of great performance. Then the performer must meet with other performers to coordinate activities with them. The leadership job is to make certain that this standard setting and coordination take place on a regular basis.

3. *Reduce the expectation to a specific, measurable number.* What gets measured gets produced. For a long while I measured sales and wondered why there was so little profit. Everyone's attention was focused on getting that order. Delivering it profitably, or selling it at a price that would make money, was always an afterthought.

People love to be measured. But measure the "right" stuff. The right stuff is that which creates great performance for customers. The right stuff is what helps you keep learning. The right stuff is what helps you continuously improve.

Do you have a performance management system where performers define, with *customers,* specific numeric standards of performance? Every machine operator, every janitor, every secretary, must know exactly what great performance is for their jobs. If your current system does not do that, you have a serious obstacle.

Information System

Does every person in your unit know how he or she is performing? At the end of every day? Every week? If people don't know how well they are doing relative to some target, you can't ever expect them to do it well. To back up your performance management system, you need an information system that tells every performer frequently how well he or she is doing in creating great performance for his/her customers. How does your information system compare to the following model?

1. *Makes performance visible to every employee.* Every designer, every secretary, every maintenance person, needs to see how he or she is doing in terms of the standards of performance agreed upon in the performance management system. That information should come directly to the performer—not through some third party like a supervisor.

2. *Real data in real time.* The data must be real data. Not sanitized accounting/financial data. And it needs to be in real time. Real time means "Now!" We need an information system similar to that in the

game of golf. How long would a golfer wait to find out where his or her shot went? Seconds, probably. He or she certainly wouldn't wait six weeks, or six days, or six hours. Yet that's the usual lag time between performance and reporting in most information systems. People need to know as close to the actual performance as possible how well they hit the ball.

3. *Based on continuing conversations between performers and customers.* Customers are the best source of feedback on performance. The best information system structures-in continuing conversations between performers and customers. These two systems form a loop—the performance management system and the information system. Both rely upon a stream of performance-based conversations between customers and performers about the standards of great performance and feedback on actual performance.

Do you have an information system that structures-in continuing conversations about great performance between those who receive the work and those who deliver it? Do you have an information system where everyone in your unit knows his/her standards of great performance and exactly how well he/she is doing in meeting them? If you don't, you have another serious obstacle.

Reward System

Unfortunately, I succumbed to the folly of rewarding "A" while hoping for "B." In the past, my reward system focused on attendance. I paid people to show up and then worried why they didn't perform. I learned that if I wanted quality, I had to reward quality. If I wanted service, I had to reward service.

The performer is the best person to determine what needs to be rewarded, and what is an effective reward. Begin with the performer-customer established standards of great performance, the performer-customer established feedback mechanisms, and the performer involvement in the definition of the appropriate reward. The reward system closes the performance standard/feedback/reward loop.

1. *Assure the consequences of behavior.* Performance must have consequences. Performance must matter. It must be clear that "them that

does it, get it, and them that don't do it, don't get it" or get a significantly different and much less desirable outcome.

F for effort. A for accomplishment. Pay for results, not efforts. I learned the hard way that throwing water uphill for sixteen hours a day will only result in standing knee-deep in mud. Get clear on what great performance you want to accomplish. Then be certain that the performer has measures so that he/she knows when he/she does it. Only then can you reward those who achieve great performance. Too many people are rewarded for working hard, rather then getting the "right" things done.

2. *Blend monetary rewards* (such as gain sharing, profit sharing, onetime bonuses, merit increases) *and nonmonetary rewards* (such as recognition, promotion, job assignments, autonomy). We can find as many ways to reward people as there are people. We don't suffer from a lack of ways to reward. We suffer from a lack of imagination in identifying what turns people on, and in ways to distribute rewards fairly and equitably. Many leaders wrestle with "equity" issues: "Is this reward system fair?" They also struggle with "motivation" concerns: "Will these rewards motivate the behavior we need?" Both of these concerns can be dealt with by involving performers in designing the reward systems. As long as leaders own the responsibility for designing reward systems, they will also own the responsibility for making them "fair" and "motivational." My experience tells me that owning that responsibility is an impossible task, doomed to frustration and failure. When performers design and administer the reward system, it is both equitable and motivational.

Here's an example of the reward system we have at Johnsonville, designed by the members.

JOHNSONVILLE COMPENSATION POLICY

1. All members are paid the average/median salary for their classification in the local area.
   a. There are nineteen classifications for hourly member. This includes the office and plants. They are as follows:

Job Group 1
Production Loader
Rework
Sanitation I
Hanger/Sticker
Trayer
Truck Washer
Twist Hanger/Tier

Job Group 2
Casing Soaker
Batcher
Boxmaker
Stacker I

Job Group 3
Boning I
Grinder/Blender
Kill Floor I
LBB Utility
Packer I
Machine Operator I
Rework Coordinator
Sanitation II
Scaler

Job Group 4
Shipping I
Polyclip
Frank-A-Matic Operator
Pre-Price
Stacker II
Weigher
Yards/Grounds
Stuffer I
Information Support

Job Group 5
Grinder/Blender II
Boning II
N/C Hanger/Tier
Processing I

Job Group 6
Lab Technician
Stuffer II
TQC Coordinator
LBB Lab/Fat Analysis
Machine Operator III
Boxer/Scaler
Palletizer/Scaler
Boning III
Grinder/Blender III
Production Support

Job Group 7
Shipping II
Sanitation IV
Local Drivers
Kill Floor II
Hiring and Stats
Wastewater Operator

Job Group 8
Team Leader I
Boning IV
Scheduler
Smoke House Operator
Inventory Control

Job Group 9
Kill Floor III
Processing II

Job Group 10
Team Leader II

Job Group 11
Coach

Job Group 13
Maintenance I
Maintenance II
Maintenance III
Maintenance IV

Sanitation III
Packer II
Machine Operator II

Office/Technical

Group 1
Office Support

Group 2
Records Retention
Switchboard/Receptionist
Mail Coordinator
Member Store

Group 3
Administrative Assistant Buyer
Computer Operator
Billing I
Production Assistant

Group 4
Order Entry
Accounts Payable
Payroll
Indirect Compensation
Production Coordinator (WT)
Assistant Traffic Control
Accounts Receivable/Billing
   (NE)
Consumer Labeling Response
Graphic Services Specialist
General Accounting
Accounts Receivable

Group 5
Engineering Coordinator
Accounting Coordinator

Group 6
Administrative Ass't
   Coach
Pricing Coordinator
Customer Service/Food
   Service Lab Tech
Credit Coordinator

Group 7
MRO Buyer

b. Each classification has three to six Result Blocks which identify the most important things a member must learn and accomplish in his position. The following is an example.

RESULT BLOCK 1
(New in the position)
Stuffer I

ITEMS SKILLS/TASKS	YES	NO	EVALUATION OTHERS
Identify different linkers—AC, Kielbasa, Big Link, OM			Verbal quiz
Able to read production and people schedules			Verbal quiz
Knowledge of GMPs and safety procedures			Written quiz
Able to stuff 1,000 pounds per hour			Time the member
Rework percent 11% on Big Link all day			Monitored by reworkers
Properly dispose of inedible			Demonstration
AC rework 6% all day			Monitored by reworkers
Check plastic/paper on meat wagons 100% of time			Check work records
Able to identify and read different product labels on wagons			Verbal quiz
Able to identify foreign objects, hair, straw, plastic, glass, metal			Quiz
Identify rework pans from inedible pans			Quiz
Identify inedible pans from waste containers			Quiz

RESULT BLOCK 2
(Learning, developing, contributing)
Stuffer I

ITEMS SKILLS/TASKS	YES	NO	EVALUATION OTHERS
Able to stuff 1,200 lbs. per hour			Time the member
Rework percent 9% on Big Link all day			Monitored by reworkers
AC rework 5% all day			Monitored by reworkers
Linkers full on AC			Observe
Able to adjust linker tension			Demonstration
Know stuffing speeds for different products			Verbal quiz
Know different horn sizes			Verbal quiz
Identify causes of inedible			Written quiz
No accidents attributable to member negligence			Check safety record

RESULT BLOCK 3
(Strong performer, hitting expected results)
Stuffer I

ITEMS RESULTS/TASK	YES	NO	EVALUATION OTHERS
Able to set up and tear down stuffer			Demonstration
No accidents due to member negligence			Check safety records
Stuff 1,200 lbs. per hour on Big Link			Time the member

Big Link rework no more than 8%; AC rework 4% all day	Monitored by reworkers
Produce accurate paperwork (casings, inedible, rework)	Check records/ Customer feedback

    c. Members receive an increase in compensation as they complete their Result Block. A member completes a Result Block Evaluation Request Form and presents it to their Coach. The Coach then sets up a Team Review. The Review Team will be composed of the Coach, Team Leader, and two to four members who are able to distinguish between the achievement and nonachievement of a Result Block Evaluation. At that time they will determine if the member has accomplished what is needed to justify the pay increase for the Result Blocks they have requested.

2. Great Performance Share (GPS). Johnsonville Foods is now organized by three distinct team categories, and every member is on at least one of these teams:

    a. Product Performance Teams (PPT)
        Fresh Grilling Sausage
        Country Sausage
        Heat 'n' Eat and Smoked Cooked Sausage
        Snack Sausage
        Food Service Sausage
        Perri Brand Sausage
        Pathmark Brand

    b. Customer Focus Teams (CFT)
        Retail Sales
        Food Service Sales
        Processor Sales
        New Ventures Sales
        Mail-order Sales
        Pathmark Sales

    c. Performance Service Teams (PST)
        Member Development
        Purchasing
        Procurement

Financial Services
Logistics
MIS
(All other teams)

3. Establish a pool of dollars for the GPS fund. The source of GPS dollars is pretax net income (PTNI) set aside by the owners.

4. How many pools for the GPS fund? Participating in this pool will be seven Product Performance Teams, six Customer Focus Teams, and eight Performance Service Teams.

5. Who should be eligible?
   a. Both Full Members and Associate Members are eligible to participate.
   b. *All* new hires must serve a thirty-day probationary period prior to being considered for eligibility. After that, it is strictly a team decision as to when they become eligible.

6. How do members qualify for their Great Performance Share?
   a. Qualifications:
      Completion of 100 percent of agreed-upon weekly goals
      Average scores of 8.5 on the monthly customer feedback survey
      Error-free work
      Teams and individual must write Weekly Action Plans on electronic mail.
   b. Each team must achieve its Great Performance "gates" to receive its share of Great Performance fund. Other teams (customers) will review and approve the gates of your team. If your team does not pass its gates, no individual team member will receive his/her share for the period of measurement.
   c. When a "miss" occurs: *Team:* The GPS dollars are dumped back into the central pool for distribution to other qualifying teams. *Individual team member:* Team gets the GPS dollars for distribution as they choose.

7. What happens when you serve on multiple teams? Salaried members negotiate with the team they will be working with prior to start of service to the team. Hourly members will be allocated based on estimated labor hours.

8. How will GPS dollars be distributed to the teams? An example is given for clarification of how the pool is distributed. Country Sausage Product Performance Team Payroll represents 10 percent of total Company payroll. If the Country Sausage PPT achieves

Great Performance for the month, that team receives $10,000 ($100,000 Company GPS Pool × 10% Team Payroll %).
9. How often are bonuses paid?
   a. Once a month money will be paid out to all that have achieved their Great Performance weekly goals.
   b. Money will be paid out in one of the following three ways as chosen by the member:
      Regular payroll/check/direct-deposit system
      Deposit into your profit-sharing account (as legal)
      Deposit in your 401(k) account (as legal)

Does your reward system distinguish between great performers and the not-so-great performers? Is great performance really rewarded in your unit? Do performers have a significant input in the reward system design and administration? If your answers to any of these questions is anything less than an unqualified yes, you have an important obstacle.

If you don't expect, measure, and reward great performance, you'll never get great performance. In short:

- Does every person know at the start of every day what great performance is for him/her?
- Does every person know at the end of every day if he/she has been a great performer?
- During the day is everyone motivated to do whatever it takes to be a great performer because he/she knows that he/she will be rewarded on the basis of performance?

Structures Sound Clarion Calls

Systems are powerful message carriers that too often prevent the achievement you want. Structures do also. Many organizations need to get products faster to market. Demanding speed, though, doesn't work. Often the functional organizational structure is a governor, preventing speed.

One organization with which I've worked needed to reduce its time to market from six years to three, the best of their competitors'. They struggled for more than a year using training programs and internal communications to urge faster development time. They set up task forces and committees to work the issues. When asked, "What prevents you from speeding up developments?" almost everyone answered, "We can't get the information we need from other departments."

Development time fell dramatically when they broke down the organizational barriers created by the functional structure and adopted a project structure and co-located people.

Does your organization structure meet the following model? If not, you have structural obstacles that prevent your achieving great performance.

1. *Decentralize decision making to the point of customer contact*. Those closest to the customer should make the decisions about servicing that customer. When that isn't the case, you get organizational "handoffs," a major obstacle. In the software industry one person sells the system, another designs it, another installs it, and yet another person supports it. There's always a finger of accusation being pointed. "He promised you what?" the designer asks. "How can I install that mess?" the installer asks. "I've never seen such a screwed-up installation," the help-desk person says. All the while the customer stews—and great performance gets frustrated.

2. *Multidiscipline teams where everyone is present*. Parkinson's law was written based upon the absence of teams. When the secretary of the navy wished to write a memo, he asked his assistant to draft it for him. His assistant asked an assistant who asked another assistant who asked another assistant until six other assistants had been asked to participate in the drafting. After seven weeks of passing drafts back and forth among the seven assistants they finally gave it to the secretary. The secretary read it, didn't like it, tore it up, and in twenty minutes wrote what he wanted. This is a classic example of what happens in the absence of teams.

3. *Simplification of processes and procedures*. The only things that grow automatically seem to be weeds—and administrative procedures. Stem administrative procedure growth by emphasizing continual simplification of processes and procedures. One organization eliminates every policy and procedure every year. Anyone wishing to continue a policy or procedure must reapply for it *de nouveau*. They call it zero-based administration.

4. *Focus on one customer, one product, one product/market combination.*
Structure focuses people on serving a homogeneous collection of customers. This focus develops expertise in what customers want/need and facilitates a customer focus throughout the organization.

Does your structure encourage the decentralization of decision making to the level of direct customer contact? Does it facilitate the use of multidiscipline teams to solve customer problems? Does it force continual simplification and focus? If your answer to any of these questions is no, you have another serious obstacle to overcome.

Systems and structures obstacles prevent great performance for customers. The leader's task is to remove those impediments as quickly as possible. Systems and structures provide focus and direction. Do yours provide the "right" focus?

QUESTION:
What message do my systems and structures send?

LEADERSHIP SOLUTION:
Systems and structures call the tune to which we all dance.

CHAPTER 25

Measuring Performance for Fun and Profit

Bad Measurements Are Big Obstacles

If you want it, measure it. If you can't measure it, forget it. Peter Drucker wrote and spoke those strong words many years ago. I believe they are just as true today as they were when I heard Professor Drucker say them. My perspective on the meaning of those words is different now, however.

Back in my old buffalo days, I believed that it was the leader's job to measure a subordinate's performance. Now I believe that the leader has to help people (not "subordinates") set their own measurements with their customers. This belief came when I learned to change the systems to what enables me to be more effective at Leading the Journey. It is the basis of my new lead-goose behavior.

The old theory implies that people at every level aren't motivated enough to manage their own affairs. They need someone to control them. In the head-buffalo days, a leader added value by motivating and controlling. Now I know that people can and will produce great things if they know what those things are and can track their results.

Measurement becomes one more way in which leaders focus the

organization in the "right" direction, consistently providing great performance for customers. Measurement is a powerful leadership tool when the performers and customers establish the measures.

People Who Know How Well They Are Doing Will Do Well

People need measurements to excel. Bowlers are good examples. How many would keep bowling if you hung a sheet over the pins so they couldn't see how they did on every roll? This situation is similar to how most companies work. The people have no means of knowing how the things they do affect the company. Any information they receive is unrelated to what they did, or it is so old that it is no longer relevant.

A few years ago, I bought a company that was performing poorly. The plant's tradition of mediocrity continued under my ownership. I spent a year working to turn it around. I tried management changes, extra pay, and other things to motivate them. Nothing worked. People didn't seem to care how they did. The packaging department especially reflected this indifference.

When I asked that department how they were doing, they answered, "Pretty well." When I asked them what they meant, they responded, "We've been working hard and we got all the product packed." When I asked them how they were doing compared to last week, they just shrugged their shoulders. They didn't know. They developed a crude system that measured how much product they packed. That was it. I learned something from those people I've seen reaffirmed in companies all over the world: People want so much to measure their performance that if they aren't given a way to do that, they will develop their own. The people needed better measures, and it was my leadership job to help them develop effective, relevant measurements.

We worked to create measurements tied to the company's goals. Most of these were short-stroke—hourly and daily recaps. They began charting their progress. Their performance improved continuously from that day. Moreover, their attitudes changed. People who hadn't seemed to care much began to be involved. They said that their work was much more fun.

Right or Wrong, People Will Produce What Is Measured

One unit was a consistent underperformer. I thought the goals for this company were clear to everyone: growth and profit. We got good growth—25 percent per year—but profits lagged.

Every year we budgeted a sales and profit increase. Every year we hit the sales number and missed the profit number. By this time, I knew it was time to take stock of my leadership behavior. Everyone knew the sales numbers and tracked them daily. Profit numbers, on the other hand, were confidential. Most people couldn't correlate their performance with profits.

I compounded the problem by always asking about sales, not profits. I didn't expect them to know about profits. In fact, I didn't want them to know.

We changed the systems so people could measure how they contributed to profitability. We stopped setting goals *for* them. Instead, we worked *with* them to set goals for themselves to stretch sales *and* profit. They've been attaining their goals since that time. We stopped measuring the wrong things. Now we measure, and get, what we want.

Those Who Have to Produce It Have to Measure It

I recently worked with the president of a major food company. Although his company was successful for years, it was under attack by an aggressive competitor. Hal's company was known for quality. The competitor's products, however, were as good as, or better than, several of Hal's biggest sellers. Hal and his managers spent an unsuccessful year in an intense effort to upgrade the quality of their products. He was very frustrated when we first talked.

"We can make products that meet every one of our specifications, and still they aren't as good as our competitor's! Why can't our QC people write better specs?"

"Are they the best people to write them?" I asked. "Are they the experts?"

"Of course they are," he said strongly. "And they're the best in the business."

"Are you sure? Please don't misunderstand me. I'm sure they are very good technically, but they work here in headquarters. Do they know how the machines are running today? Do they know how the raw materials are reacting to the process? Are they aware of the hundreds of variables that are happening right now while we are talking? You have forty plants. You can't control them from here. Your operators must be the experts on your process, because they are the only ones who can control it. Do they know what quality profile you are trying to achieve? Have they had any input into what should be measured?"

When Hal realized that "no" was the answer to all of these questions, he grasped the situation immediately. The only people who could ever produce great products were those who actually made them. He reorganized to put the operators in control of the process. QC's new job was to support the operators with the information and technical know-how they needed to measure and improve their performance.

Within weeks the operators had the data they needed, and the products started improving. The company is now back where it was— leading the market.

Notice Hal's use of the intellectual capitalism leadership paradigm. As the leader Hal decided the direction. He revised the systems so the people who did the work, the owners of the intellectual capital, could focus on delivering great performance for their customers.

If It Were Easy, Everybody Would Be Doing It

Truly outstanding results are not achieved by being slightly better than the competition. Greatness is different. It stands onstage as the star of the show. In my own business, I use many of the "standard" measures—ROA, margins, sales/employee—as well as other, nonstandard measures.

For instance, my business is in a fast-moving market. We must adapt continuously. Rates of learning and adaptation are critical to our survival. We must measure these two factors if we have any hope of managing them. It sounds impossible to quantify something like this, but it is possible if the right people are measuring it. I've worked with the people to develop the best measures of these "impossible to measure" activities. Here is the plan they developed: The people write down every customer-driven change they make. They count the aggregate number and then categorize them to spot trends. When they see trends, they review the internal systems and structure to see if they are aligned with where the market is going. They discuss among themselves what it will take to do better. They measure how long it takes to make the improvements and spot the trends. They track it against past performance.

Their plan works. We seem to be one or two jumps ahead of our competitors. Sure it's difficult. But isn't it worth it? What's the alternative?

Notice that the intellectual capital owners own the responsibility for both measuring and responding to the measures. My leadership task is to provide the focus and direction, and work with the capital owners. They establish the measures that will tell them how they are implementing that direction and focus. By changing the systems, I Lead the Journey.

What's Good for the Goose Is Good for the CEO

For many years, I envied people whose jobs provided more feedback than mine. A salesperson knows when she gets an order. A machine operator knows how many pieces he made. I didn't have the luxury of knowing how well or poorly I was doing. I believed that the things I worked on were so long-term that I couldn't expect good feedback on my performance.

In retrospect, I am certain that the absence of real-time performance measurement encouraged me to act like the head buffalo. Being the head buffalo gave me the opportunity to get feedback on my performance. I ran the meetings, had the ideas, and made the decisions. This was my way of measuring my performance. I knew immediately when I solved a problem or had an idea. As I proceeded on my leadership journey, it became roaringly obvious that I needed to change how I measured my own performance. I understood the principle that what gets measured gets produced. If I wanted to change from being head buffalo to lead goose, I had to alter what I measured about my own performance.

I used my own model. I met with my employee/"customers." Using the company's "great performance" definition as the guideline, we established my great-performance contribution, which would help my "customers" achieve their great performance. Together we developed measures for each element. My "customers" measure each of these elements monthly. Here's what a recent version looks like.

GREAT PERFORMANCE FOR THE PRESIDENT

1. Coach of strategic thinking
   Measure: Number of helpful contributions I make to the strategic thinking of others. Indicated by member/customer evaluations of the president in the monthly surveys. A rating of 10 is expected.

2. Learning and growth
   Measure: Attainment of 100 percent of the president's educational goals.

3. 100 percent of the people believe they own the right problem and are capable of handling it.
   Measure: As indicated by ownership comments on the weekly reports.

4. Coach of personal development. Facilitator of learning for everyone in the company.
   Measure: 100 percent of direct reports attain 100 percent of their educational goals and report complete satisfaction with their development. 100 percent of all employee-partners attain 100 percent of their educational goals and report complete satisfaction with their development.

5. Ensure that all transactions are characterized by caring and integrity.
   Measure: Measured by employee responses of being important, respected, valued, and cared about personally on the quarterly all-

employee survey. Other indicators are number of personal messages exchanged, number of personal celebrations acknowledged.

Feeling Good Versus Being Good

There's been lots of words written in the past few years about making work more fun and rewarding. Many pundits believe that if we can make people happy they will perform better. I started down that path years ago and concluded that just the reverse is true. I discovered that when people perform better, they are happier. My experience is that everyone wants to excel. Everyone enjoys winning. Everyone loves being part of a winning team. Winning reinforces itself. Everyone takes pride in his/her accomplishments. That is why most everyone loves sports. Sports give instant feedback on performance. We all share a deep desire for feedback on our performance.

Harness this deep well of energy and commitment in your organization by helping people build systems that measure their performance against those things critical to success. These efforts will remove one of the biggest obstacles to Leading the Journey successfully. You and your people will be astounded by the results.

QUESTION:
Do all the people in your company know how well they've done before they go home every night?

LEADERSHIP SOLUTION:
People perform what they measure—help the performers to measure the "right" stuff.

CHAPTER 26

Making the Customer the Boss

The injunction "Measure it or forget it" applies in most settings. I discovered that it particularly applies when it comes to keeping the focus on customers.

An executive friend of mine discovered the truth in this injunction, much to his chagrin. His company was faltering. The sales and marketing group, formerly the strength of his organization, was in particular trouble. He learned that his salespeople spent only 18.7 percent of their time in front of customers. What did they do with the rest of their time? They spent it making budgets, preparing plans, briefing the boss, explaining why they didn't get the order or why this category of expenses was over budget while that category was under budget. In other words, the principal strength of his company spent over 80 percent of their time saluting the internal organization, virtually ignoring the main reason for the company's existence—serving customers.

He saw clearly what he had to do. He declared "The Year of the Customer" and transferred thousands of people to the sales force. At the end of the year he discovered that the average time in front of customers had *fallen* to 16.2 percent. The attraction of the internal organization is so powerful that it drowns out the words of even the chairman.

"Why is this?" he asked me.

"Do you expect, measure, and pay for customer contacts and service?" I asked.

"We talk about customer service all the time. We expect it from our people. But, in truth, no one has ever been fired for not delivering it. We haven't been able to come up with good measures of customer satisfaction, with the result that we haven't been able to build it into our compensation plan."

"I'd bet, in fact," I responded, "that having perfect paperwork is more likely to get a person promoted than having perfect customer service."

The conversation triggered thought on my part, which led to several significant changes in my organization. If I wanted my people to delight their customers, I had to help them design systems and structures that focused them on delivering great performance for customers and not fulfilling internal organizational requirements. That was my lead-goose role in this intellectual capitalism era.

Get the Experts to Measure Customer Satisfaction

Using the LTJ process, I engaged the intellectual capital holders, the people who delivered great performance to customers, in determining the right measures of that service. Each product/market team met with their customers to design the "best" way to measure customer satisfaction. Using the E-mail system, the entire employee-partner population participated in the design of a generic form. Here's the form they designed:

Dear Customer:

Please complete the following BRIEF survey to help me improve my service to you and your organization.

On a scale of 1 (very poor) to 10 (excellent), please evaluate my performance during the past month:

1. The quality of the service you received from me.

Very Poor   Excellent

      1   2   3   4   5   6   7   8   9   10

COMMENTS _____

_____

_____

2. My contribution to your great performance.

Very Poor   Excellent

      1   2   3   4   5   6   7   8   9   10

COMMENTS _____

_____

_____

3. How well I've done being your partner.

Very Poor   Excellent

      1   2   3   4   5   6   7   8   9   10

COMMENTS _____

_____

_____

4. Your overall satisfaction level this month.

Very Poor   Excellent

      1   2   3   4   5   6   7   8   9   10

COMMENTS _____

_____

_____

Thank you for your cooperation.

[Name of employee-partner]

Every month we mail a computer-generated customized survey signed by the employee-partner to each customer with whom that person worked during the month. The survey form itself is designed every six months by the employee-partner and his/her particular customer set. The responses are tabulated by the branch office. Approximately 60 percent of the customers return their survey forms. The customer survey data is posted in the E-mail system, which is open to everyone.

This system provides frequent feedback to employee-partners about their customer service performance. The data is studied assiduously and taken very seriously, because it represents real data about one of the most important reasons for great performance: delighting customers. This system helps keep the focus on the customer and removes one of the biggest barriers to great performance. And it pays off in the pocketbook for everyone.

If You Want Service, Pay for Service

We recognized that customer service was essential to our long-term survival. So all employee-partners decided to tie their bonus payments to meeting agreed-upon levels of customer satisfaction. Currently, employees must average 10 from their customers each month in order to qualify for the monthly profit-sharing payment. The qualifying number began at 8.5 and rose each period to its current level of 10. In 1991, in only three instances did people not qualify for the bonus because they received less than a 10 average rating.

Customers' eyes light up when we tell them that our pay is dependent upon their ratings. "Really?" they usually say in disbelief, followed by a smile. "I guess I'll get very good service, won't I?" We work very hard to deliver even better service than they expect, because that's what earns 10s.

Eliminate the Organizational Barriers to Focusing on the Customer

Functional organizational structures drive the internal focus. Engineers are focused on doing great engineering work, rather than satisfying the end-user customer, because their salary increases and promotions are controlled through the engineering department. Satisfying the engineering boss is more important than satisfying the customer end-user boss.

Use Systems to Build Partnerships for the Future

In addition to ensuring great customer service today, I've learned that in these rapidly changing times you need to build productive customer partnerships for the future. In a previous chapter I outlined the way we go about building those partnerships. However, we know that if we don't expect it, measure it, and reward it, we will likely not get it. So each month we review one sixth of our current customer accounts. We discuss the answers to the six partnership questions:

1. Tell me about your activity.
   - What are the few keys to success in your unit?
   - What is your unit's advantage in the marketplace (why do customers buy from you?), and how do you contribute to that advantage?
   - What is great ICBIH (I can't believe it's happening) performance for your unit, and for yourself, for the coming year?
2. Tell me about current/future developments that will change the way you and your unit do business.
   - What developments are impacting both your department's activities and the company's?
   - What do you see coming in the future that will change the way you and your company do business?
   - What do you and your unit plan to do to prepare for these coming events so you are ready *before* they occur?

3. Tell me about the biggest problems you face.
   • What prevents you from being a great performer?
4. How can we help you?
   • How can we help you be a great performer today?
   • How can we help you remove the obstacles that prevent you from being a great performer today?
   • How can we help you prepare to be a great performer in the future?
5. Based on the above, how would you define great performance for me in the coming year that will best contribute to your great performance?
6. What would I have to do this week to earn a rating from you of 10 out of 10 for perfect contribution to your great performance?

A spirited conversation usually follows each presentation. This presentation to peers is both an information system and a reward system. Everyone sees what's going on with each account, so the process exposes both progress and problems. Since partnering with the customer is one of our principal values, this presentation provides the opportunity to be praised or reprimanded by your peers for your performance.

The leader's task in this intellectual capitalism age is to fix the focus on great performance for customers and then help remove the obstacles that prevent that great performance from happening. As the lead goose my task is to create the environment in which the individuals establish measurements and rewards with their customers. When that happens, the buffalo fly.

QUESTION:
Who's the boss: the customer or the person in the corner office?

LEADERSHIP SOLUTION:
Build systems and structures that focus people on the end-user customer, not on the corner office.

CHAPTER 27

The People Who Do It Must Know About It

It sounds so simple. Get the information to the people who use it. It's common sense. Unfortunately, it's not common practice. I know for a long time it wasn't common practice in my organization. I used to horde information like some people horde gold coins. Information is power, I believed, and I was determined to maximize my power by maximizing my stash of information. Worse, I kept as much information as I could to myself. Then I realized that not getting information to the people who used it was a big obstacle to great performance in my organization.

Getting the Right Information to the Wrong People Is a Big Obstacle

Great performance depends on having the information you need to do your job. Measurement is vital. You can't correct your course until you know the course you're on. Useful measurement requires useful information. That fact seems obvious. Yet for years information in my company went to the wrong people, thus making it useless. When I shifted my leadership mentality, I learned to redirect the information to the people who used it. That's the only place information is useful.

One of my biggest leadership tasks is to remove the obstacles to great performance. One of the biggest obstacles I encountered was this misdirection of information. The company dramatically improved when I clarified who needed what information.

I spent years trying to improve my company's results. As the head buffalo I asked for more and more information. My accounting staff grew larger and larger. My reports proliferated. I worked Herculean hours and the results got worse. What could be wrong?

I kept asking, "Why aren't the people taking responsibility?" My traditional command-and-control leadership paradigm was failing. I saw that I couldn't control the business by trying to control people. I needed people who could and would control themselves, people who knew what great performance was and were committed to achieving it. Gradually, I began to see that in the intellectual capitalism era, the capital holders have to manage their own performance. They, and no one else, are in a position to know how they are doing in real time, quickly enough to control their performance.

At first I resisted the implications of that insight. It was so alien to everything I'd learned. It seemed so complicated. It would be so much work. I didn't have the time. I didn't know how to do it. I didn't know how it would turn out. In short, I *couldn't control it*. Finally, I had to let go. The head buffalo simply couldn't control the herd.

Managing the Present

My traditional leadership mentality showed in my diligent effort to manage the present. I spent hours poring over cost data. I knew where every dollar went last month and last year. I assiduously studied sales account performance. I knew how much of each product each customer bought last month and last year, and why they did or didn't buy what we planned. One day I realized that I was actually attempting to manage the past. The past can't be managed. It is already gone.

I saw that I needed to help people manage the work they did today, not yesterday. Something was missing. I had already made it in their best interest to improve, so why didn't they do it? They were buffalo standing around waiting to be told what to do. As long as I kept being the head buffalo and telling them what to do, and rewarding them for doing it, they would be buffalo and stand around and wait to be told. I had to change from head buffalo to lead goose before they'd change from being dependent buffalo into independent geese. So, rather than *telling* my people, like head buffalo to his herd, I *asked* my people, as a lead goose of his gaggle. Their response was instantaneous.

"If we are to control the work we do today, we need better information. The data we get is worthless. It comes too long after the fact. It measures the wrong things. It does not tell us what we need to know to do our work today."

I was shocked to discover that their assessment was accurate. Very little of the information they received could help them control their work today. The data was prepared by accountants for accountants. Most of it was designed to produce accounting numbers at the end of the month. Just think of all the wasted time spent on reading and trying to see the relevance of useless information, not to mention all the lost opportunity for increased performance we could have realized if the "right" people had the "right" information. The thought made me sick.

People told me they needed better control information. Control information is short-stroke in nature and tells people how they are doing in a given task. It is tied to the process cycle. The people who do the work need this information in order to do their job. Almost every person, senior management to the janitor, needs control information. The performer is in the best position to determine what control information he or she needs.

Control information provides timely information that helps people manage and improve their results. I saw a good example at Johnsonville.

We sell breakfast sausage products in a guaranteed-twelve-ounce tray. Since every tray must have at least twelve ounces on it, anything over twelve ounces per tray is given away to the customer. We put exactly fourteen links on every tray. This means the links must be as uniform as possible.

Our sausage stuffers had a hard time controlling the amount of product stuffed into each link. A small variation in the temperature of the meat, for instance, would cause variations in the size and weight of each sausage. Or the diameter of the casings varied, which changed the weight of the sausage. Our giveaway was costing us bundles. I talked a lot about the "giveaway" problem and made certain that everyone knew how much it cost us everyday. The stuffers complained that they never knew how much each tray weighed. Without that information, they couldn't control their process and be great performers. Not knowing was a big obstacle to their, and my, success.

I worked with the sausage stuffers to remove this obstacle. They redesigned the product line. Previously, the trays dropped onto a conveyor and went into another room to be weighed and wrapped. They reassigned one person to stand at the end of each stuffer line to weigh the unwrapped trayed product on a scale set for twelve ounces. The sausage stuffer watched the scale and recycled for repacking any product that was over or under the twelve-ounce standard. The performers designed and implemented a measurement system which gave them continuous information that allowed them to control their process. Our giveaway on that product dropped to 25 percent of the original amount in three days.

The people now strive to get all control information (costs, margins, inventories, etc.) in real time to the people doing the work. When the holders of the intellectual capital get the power to make a difference, they become great performers. My leadership role is to help them remove lack-of-information obstacles that prevent their great performance.

Improving the Present

In addition to information that measures present activities, the people also told me that they need trend data. Trend information is historical in nature. It provides comparisons over time (year-to-year, month-to-month, or day-to-day) of the critical elements of great performance. It deals with such things as return on assets, return on sales, sales ratios, cost comparisons, sales per account. I always kept these company secrets closely guarded, because I was afraid it would fall into the hands of our customers or competitors. My paranoia reduced the value of this data to zero. If I wanted to change the trend, I needed to get the data in the hands of those who could make a difference.

At first the accounting staff objected. They said, "What if competitors get it?"

I said, "I'd mail it to the competitors myself if that's what it takes to overcome this obstacle."

We now share trend data with all members to help them plan long-term improvements. Once we started to share this data, I noticed two behavior changes. First, many more people talked about how their activities impacted these trends. Sausage stuffers talked about how their activities impacted return on sales and return on assets. These conversations never took place until I shared this data. Second, the trends improved. Return on assets went up, as did return on sales, while inventories actually declined. People were not only talking about the data, they were using it to take actions that improved the trends.

Other companies also share control and trend data with their people and get similar positive results. Susan is the president of a service company with twenty facilities around the country. The market was expanding, but the business did not generate enough cash to support the growth.

Susan kept all the control and trend information at national headquarters. For instance, only the headquarters staff knew the return on assets for the entire company. No one knew the return on assets for any plant. She didn't calculate return on assets for each facility because the nature of each facility's assets varied so widely. She knew that the people in each plant needed more information to improve their operations. But she couldn't figure out how to get them the information they needed. I knew how she felt. I spent a lot of time in the same place, feeling the same frustration. I shared with her my insight that the leader's job isn't to develop the information. Rather, the leader's task is to focus the people who use the information, and help them develop the system to get them the information they need.

She met with her division managers and explained the situation. She challenged them to decide the information they needed and designed a system to get it. It wasn't easy. They argued and debated. Within six months they implemented their information system. Using the new system, each plant set financial targets. Susan reinforced this new information system by establishing bonus payments based upon meeting the agreed-upon targets. Financial results improved dramatically. Cash is no longer a problem.

Managing the Future

We made a lot of progress when I finally stopped trying to manage the past and started helping others manage and improve the present. But something was still missing.

I still held on to certain key information about the future. I believed that I was responsible for planning our future. I didn't think the employee members could or would do that task. As usual, I was wrong. My old buffalo mentality dies hard.

In Chapter 14 I described the scan, clip, and review process. That process helps every person in the company manage the future. I've discovered that not only do the people want to also manage the future, they are very capable of doing so.

In one situation the scan, clip, and review process revealed a new application developed by a university laboratory for one of our specialty chemical compounds. We licensed the technology and were first in the marketplace with it. Before our competitors knew what was going on, we locked up the niche. "How did you know about it?" the national sales manager of our largest competitor asked me at a trade show. I smiled and said to her, "Just lucky, I guess," while to myself I said, "Thank you, Shauna." (Shauna is a technician at the Delhi, India, facility who first found the article about the new technology and included it in her scan, clip, and review package.) I've learned that you can see the future before it happens when you have enough of the right eyes searching for it.

Leading the Journey requires that I remove the obstacle of the misdirection of information. Inevitably, that means that the performers get more of the information they need to control and direct the organization in both the present and the future.

QUESTION:
Are you managing the past, the present, or the future?

LEADERSHIP SOLUTION:
Help the right people get the right information and they will do the right things.

CHAPTER 28

Beware
the Siren Call

People Are an Obstacle to Great Performance
for Customers

From the point of view of the staff, most hospitals would be better places if it weren't for the patients. From the faculty's point of view, most universities would be great places if the students didn't get in the way. And most executives would agree that their businesses would run better if only they could be rid of the pain-in-the-neck employees or customers. Even in tourist-based vacation spots, hotel personnel are often "inconvenienced" by guests. Though it sounds a bit facetious, the sentiment is familiar. People obstacles dominate the list of obstacles that prevent great performance.

Employees' mentalities pose big obstacles. One executive said, "It's so clear what we have to do. We are losing market share. We are losing margins. We are falling further and further behind in product development. Yet all my people do is stand around the water cooler and complain. The bulletin boards are full of anonymous letters saying, 'Why don't you do something, Mr. President.' Why is it my responsibility? They've got to get with it, or else we're all history. What do I have to do to get them to shape up?"

Listen to the traditional leadership paradigm at work. "I know what needs to be done." "They have to shape up." As long as we try to fix them it will never work. They must see the need to fix themselves. Creating that need to own the change—that's our leadership role in the decade of intellectual capitalism.

It is easy to generate a list of people obstacles. Ask any executive, "What prevents you from realizing your goals?" and the answer will almost always include, "Teamwork—nobody works together. Motivation—no one seems to care. Communications—people just don't talk to each other."

People obstacles prevent great performance. Like Mount Everests, they stand in our path.

Symptoms Are Sirens—They Attract the Sailor to the Rocks

Be careful, however. People obstacles are most often symptoms, not causes. Like Odysseus, we are pulled right to the rocks as we struggle to answer the siren song of people issues. Early in my career I identified many people obstacles. Like Odysseus, I sailed my ship on a course to change people's mind-sets. It cost me tons of money, lots of lost opportunities, and pieces of my stomach to realize that while mind-sets were important obstacles, they were symptoms of a deeper cause, the system and structure factors. Once I went to work removing the system obstacles, the people obstacles disappeared.

The Best Way to Get Teamwork Is to Give the Team Work

"Siloism is killing us," the frustrated president of a large company told me recently. He's not alone. Many executives complain about the lack of cooperation among departments. Siloism (keeping others out and information in) is an epidemic.

Teamwork is the answer to this serious problem. Many companies are on a crusade to develop cross-departmental teamwork. Yet, when I ask executives how it is working, they are less than glowingly enthusiastic.

Usually, the talk goes something like this: "It's going a little slower than we expected, but we are plugging away at it. We've got to get better at it. We have no choice."

They are right. Teamwork is absolutely essential. Executives who do not learn how to work together will not survive. But the current solutions aren't working.

So much of the failure of the teamwork crusade lies in the traditional leadership paradigm. Teamwork efforts are another way to fix "them." If I've learned anything in the last twelve years, it is that "I" can't fix "them" until "I" fix "me" first. Then I must change the systems and structures to *require* teamwork. The obstacle isn't simply a lack of teamwork. The obstacle is my leadership mentality, the actions that flow from it, and the systems and structures that prevent the teamwork.

Change the Information System to Get Teamwork

I worked with a major franchisor of luxury items, helping franchisees improve their customer service. Several franchise owners invited their customers to dinner to discover their views. Their customers' biggest concern was the lack of teamwork in the franchise. They reported everything from apathy toward other departments to animosity. The feedback surprised the franchisees.

The stores were divided into three functions: sales, service, and parts. Each of the functional units operated separately. Each had its own goals and measures of performance, which had nothing in common with the others. The franchise owners realized that if they wanted to improve teamwork, they needed to give the units something in common to work on.

The franchisees focused on customer satisfaction. Collectively, they set up a service that provided monthly measures of customer satisfaction. The franchisees were not surprised when their first report card indicated significantly less than great performance. The franchisees called the people in their stores together and showed them the numbers. Presenting the problem to the people, they asked, "What are we going to do to improve these numbers?"

Employees in each functioning group listed their key activities to improve customer satisfaction. When the people discovered that many of the activities were linked with other departments, they rewrote their own job descriptions and developed new measurements of their performance, which included their cross-functional team responsibilities. As a working team the entire franchise developed many new ideas that improved their collective service to their customers. Their customer satisfaction rating improved dramatically.

If You Want Teamwork, Change the Systems

The CEO of a Fortune 25 company faced a dilemma. The division that represented their biggest future opportunity was in serious trouble. Most of the other division presidents thought the company should divest the troubled division. Unfortunately, no division was doing well. By putting the spotlight on the troubled division the leaders of the other division took the heat off themselves.

Executive committee meetings were marvels of inefficiency. They wrangled, discussed, and harangued. Precious little was accomplished. All this was happening while the corporate ship was listing about thirty degrees. The presidents each went their own way and wanted as little as possible to do with each other.

The CEO saw clearly the need to change. The troubled division was a large part of the company's future. Its market was expanding by double digits, while the other divisions' markets were shrinking. It needed to improve its products, develop new ones, and expand rapidly at the same time. It needed a lot of help from the other divisions.

At the next meeting the CEO listed seven critical corporate-wide issues. He formed a task force composed of several executives for each issue. Each team was to bring back their recommendations to the entire group.

One of the task forces was assigned the development of a new executive compensation program which rewarded teamwork while acknowledging individual contributions. They recommended a corporate profitability hurdle, after which each division was rewarded on their individual performance. This system encouraged executives from other divisions to help the troubled division, since they couldn't earn their bonus until that division improved. These system changes created a dialogue and common focus that set the stage for teamwork.

The Opportunity Audit: Another Contextual Change

One of my clients had been struggling for years to get his executive team to work together. Like me, he'd tried everything—team building, rafting, group profit sharing. In a fit of desperation he called me.

I asked if he ever required his executives to work together. "Oh no," he replied. "They run separate divisions, which have very little to do with each other."

"Have they ever 'audited' each other?" I asked. "Visited each other's facility to find ways that they can learn from each other and improve their operations?"

"Never thought about it," he said.

"If you add a bonus based upon the number of implemented suggestions they give and receive from each other, sort of being both student and teacher, you'll likely get both sides to work together to implement ideas," I added. "And rather than trying to figure out the best bonus plan, why not ask the executives what they think a good plan would be?"

The president immediately got his executives together and they designed the "Improvement Audit" program. Three years later the program is going strong. Every division is visited twice a year by teams drawn from the other divisions. There's been a direct savings of more than 21 percent, and the president told me, "I've never seen such teamwork." Changing the audit and reward systems changed the mind-sets, which changed the behavior.

Motivation, communication, lack of commitment, and teamwork problems plague most organizations. These mind-set problems are usually created by systems problems. My leadership task in Leading the Journey is to remove the obstacles to great performance. The systems and structures obstacles are usually the "tall weeds."

QUESTION:
What systems are causing my people problems?

LEADERSHIP SOLUTION:
Change the systems to change the people.

PART VI

DEVELOPING OWNERSHIP

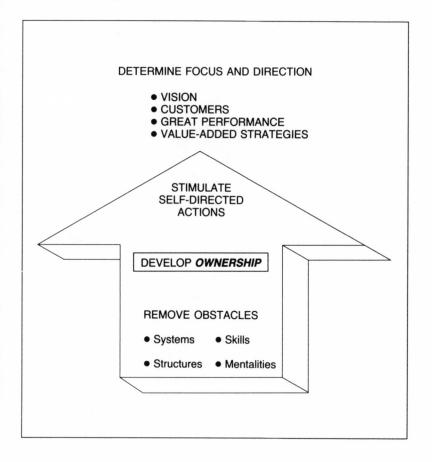

Introduction

Get Ready to Change Your Mind-set

The traditional leadership paradigm stresses the leader's responsibility for organizational results. I wrote a successful management textbook in the late 1970s. That book was organized around the five basic management functions: planning, organizing, commanding, coordinating, and controlling. Virtually every management textbook today uses a version of those same basic management functions. These are straight from Henri Fayol's book *Principles of Administration*, published in 1892. This obsolete leadership paradigm encourages managers to do things *to* the organization.

The Old Way: The Boss Is Responsible

Examples abound of the old mind-set "The boss is responsible." Do you remember the reply card in the hotel room, with the president's name and address on it? By having the information sent directly to him, the president was painting the picture for every employee that he, the boss, owned the responsibility for satisfying customers, not they, the people who served the customers.

Do you remember the rake story? That president could chase rakes all day and never get his company back on track. For every defective rake or typewriter or policy he'd find, there would be one hundred more he'd have to find.

The Old Way Stands in *the* Way

To my chagrin, I discovered I was perpetrating the old leadership paradigm. I had lots of company in my leadership style. An executive whom I'm coaching shared the following experience. It's not the first time I've heard it.

> Last July, we launched our change effort, which was faster-to-market and customer-focused. We kicked it off with a splash—a big-name speaker and customer panels. We hung four-color posters everywhere, set up action teams, and I spent time on the floor every day talking it up.
>
> For a couple of months it worked. Customer problems fell, teams met, and there was more conversation about speeding up development. But by September the complaints began to surface. "This takes too much time." "Too many others aren't cooperating. Why am I doing all this extra work?" By November we decided to give everyone a Christmas vacation, and suspended team activities.
>
> With the new year, I'm scheduling more time on the floor to talk personally to each person and fire them up again. But why do I have to keep feeding this process. Why isn't it self-generating?

When the Boss Owns the Problem, It Rarely Gets Solved: A Reprise

This story is repeated over and over again across the world. It has occurred personally to me too many times.

I had a cost problem in one of my plants. After much wasted effort, I recognized that I had to make cost reduction the people's problem, rather than my problem. I began by changing a part of the information system. Usually, I wrestled with the competitive issues and worried when we lost a customer or a bid for new work. I lost sleep over how we were going to make the budget, meet the payroll, buy new equipment, or invest in new product development. To shift that responsibility, I shared the hard economic realities of our business with the people, particularly the competitive situations we faced. I kept employees informed about upcoming bids, shared competitive pricing information, and every time we lost a customer, I told the people what happened and why I lost the customer. Initially, they were skeptical. Their doubts faded when I brought in several former customers and potential customers who had chosen another bid, to talk with the people about why we had lost the business. People began to get the message: "We've got to do something to protect our jobs."

After some "softening up," I asked, "In the best of all worlds, what is great performance? What obstacles prevent us from being great performers? Who owns these obstacles? What actions can we take?" Everyone participated in the process, some more enthusiastically than others.

I was surprised by the high expectations the group set for themselves. They were also willing to work to achieve their high standards. Volunteer teams went to work removing the obstacles that stood in their way. As one might expect, we found many of these obstacles to be inappropriate systems and structures.

As a result of team recommendations, we changed the compensation system to reward reduced costs; the information system to show each person how much cost he/she created; and the performance evaluation system to stimulate weekly discussions about reducing costs. All these systems were designed and administered by the employees. In short order, we had the lowest unit costs in the industry, and I was out of the business of personally selling the need for cost reduction.

The New Way: The Performer Is Responsible

People slip back into old patterns because the ownership for the new way rests with someone else, usually the boss. People don't see any real need to be different, so they revert back as soon as the pressure is off. Hence, to reinforce a new pattern of behavior, it is imperative to bring people into direct confrontation with the realities of the marketplace. I was wrong to shield the employees from the economic realities. Until great performance is everyone's responsibility, it will be no one's.

In today's intellectual capitalism world, the performers must be responsible for their own performance. The success or failure of the business must rest with the individuals who possess the critical capital. The leader's job is to determine the direction, remove the obstacles that prevent focus, and then get the intellectual capital holders to develop ownership for moving in that direction. From firsthand experience, I know how tough it is to achieve this mentality. I also know how necessary it is.

QUESTION:
Who's in the best position to be responsible?

LEADERSHIP SOLUTION:
Get the right people to own the right responsibility.

CHAPTER 29

The Two Levels
of Ownership:
Avoiding Victimitis

I Peddled and Practiced the Old Paradigm

I was a champion "the boss is responsible" practitioner. The buck clearly stopped at my desk, and in too many cases, it began there as well.

Several years ago I was busy growing the specialty chemical business. The ink portion of that business was the mainstay, chief revenue, and profit generator. We had good relationships with U.S. producers, but very little business in Europe. I decided that we needed/wanted that market. In my customary fashion, I laid out the strategy: frequent personal calls on the three key European pen manufacturers, buying the business with low prices, and speedy delivery. Sitting in my sun-drenched office in California, this was a strategy made in heaven.

Setting out to execute that strategy, I told the people in the two small European offices about it. I scheduled monthly trips to Europe to visit the manufacturers, and added additional manufacturing capacity to handle the new sales. With everything in place I went to work and landed two contracts. That's when the real fun began.

The European offices couldn't deliver. From day one they had problems. The specifications weren't clear; ink delivered was the wrong color or the wrong chemistry. They had manufacturing problems, delivery problems, and problems meeting the customers' quality levels.

In an effort to solve the problems, I lived on airplanes and 2 A.M. telephone calls. I tracked production daily. To gather every single scrap of information I could, I burned up the phone lines and held daily, one-hour, long-distance production meetings, with everyone in the European facilities huddled around a speakerphone. I even spent a week in Spain actually mixing a batch, delivering it, and helping the manufacturer install it to make sure it was right. Imagine my chagrin when "my" batch was rejected.

It took me seven months of nonstop effort to solve the problems. I blanched when I saw the bill for my grand strategy. During the first six months the flood tide of red ink threatened to drown us. A year later the red tide was still running strong.

As much as I complained about the hard work, I realized later how much I loved it. It was great being important enough to jump on a plane at a moment's notice and take off for a foreign country. While I cursed them, I secretly loved those 2 A.M. phone calls. I must be very important to get up in the middle of the night to handle important business. Reality, however, stalked me. When it was all over, I went into a blue funk. In my melancholy, I felt lost and missed the excitement.

I loved being the center of decision making. It felt good when people relied upon me and looked to me for answers. I felt I was important and had an important job to do. I enjoyed the satisfaction of resolving problems and completing a task, feeling as though I had "taken care" of important matters.

The Problem Is the Old Paradigm *Does Not Work*

If the old paradigm worked, I would still be using it, but it stopped working for me. The paradigm of planning, organizing, commanding, coordinating, and controlling resulted in my working harder and longer. Those 2 A.M. phone calls were followed by 3 A.M. phone calls. The circles under my eyes got darker and deeper.

Again I found that the more I solved other people's problems, the more problems they'd bring to me. I had worked myself into a full-time "solve other people's problems" job. When I asked myself, "Is this how I want to spend the rest of my life?" the answer was a resounding "No!"

My experience has taught me that the key to organizational success today is in *getting the people to want to own the responsibility for their own performance*.

The following anecdote illustrates the impotence of the old paradigm and the power in the new leadership paradigm with its different conclusions about ownership. This actually happened in a resort hotel in which I was staying.

As I stood on the first-floor landing overlooking the reception area, I observed that very early in the morning, when the reception area was deserted, the front desk manager entered from a side door. The receptionist, who couldn't see the front desk manager because the door was to the left and slightly behind her, was smoking a cigarette at the desk, arranging papers, working the computer, and apparently preparing for the day.

Simultaneously, the general manager, still talking with someone outside, backed in through the front door into the reception area. No sooner did the receptionist hear the general manager's voice and see him than she put out the cigarette and hid the ashtray. The general manager smiled as he passed by the receptionist, and went on to his office.

Later in the day the front desk manager wanted to talk with me about the incident.

"Is this a problem?" I asked. "Do you really want to be concerned? Maybe this isn't worth your time. Just ignore it and it will go away by itself."

"What? Are you crazy?" he responded. "I can't let this go on. She knows the rules allow no smoking on the job. It's posted everywhere, and I've told her at least a hundred times. No, I've got to do something about this. I'll go talk to her."

"First," I said, "think. In the best of all worlds, from the customer's perspective, what is great performance in this situation?"

"I don't want her to smoke on the job" was his quick reply. "It offends nonsmoking customers and we can't afford that. If we're going to be the resort of choice, we have to appeal to all customers. Besides, we have a commitment to delighting customers. How can you delight customers when you offend some of them by smoking? Look, the 'No

Smoking' rule is posted in the employee work area. No, she's clearly in the wrong. Maybe I should fire her and be done with it. Hire me a nonsmoker, that's the answer."

"Before you fire her, let us get it straight. You want her not to smoke because you want to delight customers. Right? And that way you can be the resort of choice. Right?"

"Absolutely," he said, shaking his head vigorously in affirmation. "Right on."

I continued, "Then, in the best of all worlds, you really want her to be so involved in delighting customers that she thinks only about helping customers, being a better host, and providing a great atmosphere, and not about smoking. Right?"

He nodded his head in agreement. We spent the next ten or fifteen minutes defining additional dimensions of great performance for the receptionist. At the end of the dialogue, the manager had a page full of notes.

As he rose to leave, obviously to talk to the receptionist, I asked, "Before you go, could you answer another question? What is the problem? I ask because how you define the problem will largely determine how you go about solving it. Define the situation as a smoking problem, and you've got an addiction problem on your hands. That definition leads to offering smoking-cessation classes and arranging break times and smoking areas. Is that a useful way to spend your time? Define the problem as a rule-infraction matter, and you are in the CIA business, sneaking around catching people doing something wrong. Is that what you want to do? Isn't this a performance problem? She isn't doing a great job. Isn't this a vision problem? She isn't living the vision."

The dawn of recognition crossed his face. "I see what you're saying. This is a bigger issue than just smoking. The issue is the heart of what we want to accomplish around here. I need to deal with the bigger issues, so we can be the resort of choice. I see what you mean now."

"Wait one more minute," I said. "Who owns the responsibility for this problem? Who's in the best position to fix it?"

"That's easy," he replied from his standing position. "I own it and I'm going to fix it by talking to the receptionist and reminding her of her responsibility to delight customers by not smoking."

"What makes you think that this talk will be any more productive than all the others you've had with her in the past? You've talked with her before, right? And you saw what happened. What's going to make this any different?"

"Well," he said, sitting back down, "I'm not sure. Any suggestions?"

"Let's first look at who owns the problem. Who can take responsibility for fixing the receptionist's performance problem?"

"Obviously, only the receptionist. She's got to be responsible for living the vision: for not smoking, for being a great hostess, and for doing all the things that delight customers that I have on this piece of paper."

"Right. And what are you doing or not doing that prevents her from delighting customers?"

"I wonder," he said thoughtfully. "I don't know. Maybe I haven't made it clear enough to her. Maybe I haven't been forceful enough in enforcing the rules and the vision. I just don't know. What should I do?"

"Probably the best place to begin is to find out where the receptionist's ideas are. You might do that with a series of questions. The first one would be 'What is great performance on your job?' Listen carefully for the items you've got on your list, including not smoking. Discuss with her and come to some conclusions. Then ask her, 'What obstacles prevent you from realizing great performance?' Focus the discussion on those items that either you or she can control or directly influence. Then ask her, 'Who owns the obstacles?' She should see right away that she owns most of them. Ask her what you do or don't do that enables her to remove the obstacles or prevents her from it. Let her tell you what you can do to help her be a great performer. Those items then become the obstacles you own. Then ask her the payoff question: 'What actions will the owners take to get rid of the obstacles?' Seed that discussion by volunteering to take several actions to remove the biggest obstacles you own. How does that sound?"

"Like a much more productive conversation. Thanks. I've got to run. I'm already late for a meeting. Next time you're in, let me buy you a drink and I'll tell you how I made out."

As he rushed from the table I called to him, "I'll see the results myself. Thanks for the great conversation."

Notice the old leadership paradigm at work: ". . . I own the responsibility . . . I'll fix it . . . Just fire her." Also notice the switch in mind-set that takes place when the ownership for the receptionist's performance gets clearly placed with the receptionist.

The New Paradigm: Two Different Owners

I have discovered that there are always two owners of responsibilities in every situation. The responsibility for performance is always owned by the performer.

In addition, in each situation, the leader owns the responsibility for empowering the individual's acceptance of his/her own responsibility. Leaders own the responsibility for designing the context within which this desire for ownership takes place. There are two levels of ownership in the smoking situation. The receptionist owns the responsibility for her performance. She is the only person who can own the responsibility for her performance, because she is the only person who can fix the problem of smoking and of neglecting the vision.

The leader, on the other hand, is doing something, or neglecting to do something, that allows the receptionist to ignore or neglect the vision. The leader owns the responsibility to find out what those somethings are and fix them. Often those somethings are systems that send the wrong messages, practices that tolerate continuation of wrong behavior, or actions that model incorrect behavior.

Keep the two levels of ownership separate. Keep the responsibility for performance with the performer, and the responsibility for empowering with the leader.

Empowerers Are Proactive in Empowering

Oftentimes executives look at me and say, "I agree with you. The people on the floor have to be responsible for quality, but I can't just sit around and wait to 'empower' quality. I've got to actively promote it or else it won't happen."

Right on! Empowerers don't sit around and wait, or else the world will pass them by. Empowerers proactively empower: asking questions, organizing data to confront people with reality, bringing customers and performers together to discuss standards of great performance and feedback on actual performance against those standards.

Empowerers Proactively Ask Questions

One client was a particularly creative executive. His forte was "smelling deals." His organization floundered in delivering, however, and he was tied down with details. I coached him to empower rather than perform. He checked every one of the more than two thousand invoices a week, because his people kept making errors. I coached him to engage his accounts receivable person and his salesperson in a dialogue to define the following: great performance for their mutual job of getting a correct invoice to the customer, the standards of great performance, the information feedback system necessary for them to know when they were great performers, and the rewards for being great performers. They spent several hours answering the questions, after which they put in place several systems that resulted in error-free invoices. My client no longer checks invoices, because they are perfect now. He empowered that perfection through his proactive question-asking.

Empowerers Proactively Insist on Meeting Tough Standards

Sometimes proactivity demands taking tough stands. Another client was in the grocery business. She was dissatisfied with the produce manager's performance. "Look at this display," she said, pointing to a vegetable cooler in disarray. "This is awful. I can't get him to keep it straight. He keeps asking for more people as the response. He already has more folks than most every other produce section in the chain. I've just got to get rid of him."

"Wait just a sec," I responded. "If you fire him, who's taking responsibility? And what do you think he'll learn from this? And what will the other people in the store learn?"

"They'll learn that I won't tolerate poor performance," she quickly responded.

"True, but will they learn what great performance is? And will they feel responsible for being great performers?"

"No," she replied haltingly. "What can I do to accomplish that? Obviously, if I could get him to be responsible for being a great performer, my life would be a lot easier."

"Let's engage him and his crew in a conversation about defining great performance and what it takes to execute it," I suggested. "But be tough about it. Make it clear that you will accept nothing less than the best. Make it clear that this store is going to be the best in the chain, period. Don't compromise your standards, and don't rush in to solve their problems. Keep the responsibility for performance with them."

She did it. They did it. He did it. Now the store is one of the best in the chain. She proactively empowered the produce manager and his crew to see and accept their responsibilities for their own great performance. Her insistence that "best" was the only acceptable solution helped the produce manager and his crew come to grips with, and accept, their responsibility.

Empowerers Proactively Confront People with Reality

Leaders often worry a lot, and they worry alone. That was formerly my custom when I was the head buffalo. I'd have information about the future and worry about whether the company would survive, or with information about what customers wanted, I'd worry whether we could meet the demands. I was busy owning all the wrong problems.

Rather than being the bearer of bad news, I designed the context to provide such data directly to the individuals who could do something about it. This design gave the intellectual capital holders the opportunity to hear firsthand what their customers defined as great performance. It also eliminated much of my worrying.

In one client situation, the salespeople consistently disputed the national customer survey data that showed average satisfaction scores of 3 out of 10. "Those aren't my customers," everyone argued. These disputes frustrated the national sales manager's effort to improve customer service. Together we designed a real-time, real-data system which collected and fed back quarterly data from each salesperson's and technician's customers. Within two quarters customer satisfaction scores, and sales, rose significantly. The sales manager saw that her job was to proactively confront people with the reality of their own performance, and then help them accomplish the great performance they all wanted.

Empowerers Proactively Support and Coach

Freddie was one of my great teachers. He taught me one of my most important proactive responsibilities as an empowerer. Freddie was a final assembler at my plant, assembling a critical component. After he finished, this component was hidden inside a much larger finished product which was critical to the equipment's performance. One mistake by Freddie and we would lose not only some very expensive equipment but many lives as well, as this equipment operated in a nuclear facility.

We carefully designed in many quality checks. Everyone knew the responsibility we all bore for the safety of all those people at the nuclear facility. Everyone took that responsibility seriously. The problem was that Freddie was an active alcoholic.

I stewed a long time about what to do. I knew and everyone else knew that Freddie often drank during work. Yet there was never enough evidence to do anything. He'd miss just enough work to get put on warning, but never enough to be fired. The others and I worried a lot about it. They turned to me and said, "Fix it."

In the old days, I would have gladly endeavored to fix it, believing, as I did then, that that was my leadership job. By this time, however, I'd grown fond of my new lead-goose role. So I thought at length about how to use this situation to transfer the ownership to Freddie's teammates.

Finally one morning, Freddie gave me the opportunity when he came in obviously unfit for work. Several of his teammates intercepted him and made him stay in the locker room to sober up. He spent most of the morning being nursed by them until, just around lunch, he showed up in the assembly room ready to go to work. I'd been waiting for him. I called a "stop work" emergency meeting of the assembly crew and asked, "What are we going to do? Can we always trust someone to 'smell' Freddie? Are we all willing to put our jobs on the line and the lives of all those other people? More important, are we doing Freddie any good? What are we going to do?"

Breaking the embarrassing silence, Freddie began angrily denouncing me in graphic language. He started to storm out when one of the most senior guys, also one of the biggest in the room, stood up and said, "Shut up and sit down, Freddie. We're not going to let you kill yourself and us, and who knows who else. We've got a problem and you're going to stay here and help us fix it." Then he turned to me and said, "You've got much more experience with this than we do. What do you think we should do?"

With that opening, I spent the next fifteen minutes discussing our options. They all centered around helping Freddie stop drinking. We formed a "Save Freddie" brigade. Freddie was the president. One of us agreed to accompany Freddie to an AA meeting twice a day. People agreed to make certain that he moved safely back and forth to work every day. Others arranged to cover weekends. Before anyone agreed to do anything, however, Freddie had to admit that he was an alcoholic and agree to "do whatever was necessary to stop drinking."

After a long, embarrassing silence, with every eye in the place on Freddie, he finally stood. He said the magic words: "I am an alcoholic and I promise you all that I will do whatever is necessary to stop drinking." In anticipation, I had located all the AA meetings in the area, and left shortly afterward to go with Freddie to his first meeting.

The story has a happy ending. Freddie did stop drinking. The last time I heard, he was a general foreman in a large machine shop in the area to which he moved because of his sinus condition. He's doing well, one day at a time.

Equally important, Freddie taught me another dimension of my leadership role. Being the cold shower of reality, drawing the line in the sand that I did by calling the emergency meeting, is not enough. Nor is insisting upon tough standards, which I did in reminding everyone of our responsibilities for all those lives. In addition to those actions, and asking questions as I did at the beginning of the meeting, a leader's proactive empowering responsibilities go beyond all of those. Freddie helped me learn that leaders also have to support the people in their needs and be ready to coach them, to help them, when they are ready to accept and execute their responsibilities. I created the conditions under which the assembly crew was forced to confront and accept their responsibilities. I stayed with them, providing information where the AA meetings were held. Playing an active role in the execution, I volunteered for Sunday time the first week to demonstrate my continuing commitment. Leaders don't just lob the ball into the person's court and walk away. That's not leadership. That's abdication.

Leaders continue to coach and support because they are genuinely interested in that individual's success.

Empowerers Are Still Significant Owners

Freddie also helped me learn that ownership and responsibility are not zero sum games. I can transfer ownership and get other people to assume responsibility without diminishing my own ownership and responsibility in the situation. I transferred ownership for Freddie's drinking problem to Freddie and his teammates. Yet I was also an owner for his drinking behavior, witness my going with him to an AA meeting and signing up for weekend duty. Despite the people taking responsibility for Freddie's on-the-job performance, I was still responsible as well. My boss held me accountable for producing perfect parts. Those people whose lives were at risk at the site looked to me to ensure their safety. We shared ownership and responsibility, and in the process both expanded our ability to be great performers.

Ownership is not a fixed pie. In fact, it is an expanding pie. The more I transfer ownership to others, the more ownership I possess myself. In Freddie's case, I had limited ability to influence Freddie's drinking and on-the-job performance. As long as his teammates protected him, I was largely powerless. In some organization sense I may have been responsible, but I couldn't effectively meet that responsibility. Once Freddie and his teammates owned their responsibilities, I actually expanded my ownership and responsibility. I could get things done that I couldn't get done before.

Freddie also helped me learn that expanding ownership is one way to avoid victimitis. Sharing ownership and responsibility is one effective leadership tool in this intellectual capitalism age.

Conversations Are the Grist for the Leader's Mill

Every situation, however personal, unusual, or even seemingly insignificant, can trigger productive conversations about great performance. The case of the smoking receptionist presents a seemingly insignificant situation that was pregnant with opportunity. Most leaders would have ignored it and focused on "bigger" issues, as I would have in my days of leading by the old paradigm. With a new perspective, we can see buried in the situation the golden seeds of opportunity.

After we talked, the front desk manager saw that he could use this opportunity to transfer ownership of great performance. He used this "insignificant" situation to trigger a conversation with the receptionist about her definition of great performance and what she was doing to be a great performer. As a result of this conversation, the receptionist saw the relationship between her performance, even at 6 A.M., and her own definition of great performance.

Conversations are the vehicles leaders use to develop ownership. Use all instances, even seemingly insignificant cases, to precipitate discussion and learning about great performance.

Understanding Is Easy—Doing Is Difficult

You are probably shaking your head affirmatively, saying, "Yeah, you're probably right. I'm clear now that I've got to get my people to set great performance standards. I'll go tell them tomorrow."

A word of caution is necessary at this point. After a presentation, I was riding back to the airport with John, a leader from the local utility. He was enthusiastic about my speech. "I'm really in favor of this empowerment thing," he said. "Always have been. Now you've given me a way to do it. I'm going back this afternoon and meet with my people and tell them my standards of great performance. That will get them going."

John was aiming for the right target but was going about it in such a way that he would likely not hit his mark. When John tells his people his standards of great performance, he's owning those standards. He would be putting the ownership in precisely the wrong place—with himself, not with them.

John needs to encourage his people to talk with their customers and let them, along with him as one important customer, establish the standards of great performance. In that way, the responsibility for executing those standards rests with the people who created them. Knowing that is easy; to do it consistently is more difficult.

Focus the Conversation on Great Performance

Don't get sidetracked into talking about side issues. The main issue in any organization is *performance—great performance*. Keep the conversations tightly focused on what it takes to produce great performance, and what you and the performer can do, separately and together, to assure that great performance.

The Leader's Main Job: FCLP

The leader's main task concerning this ownership issue can be summarized in four letters, FCLP.

> *F* is for focus.
> *C* is for conversation.
> *L* is for learning.
> *P* is for performance.

In every possible situation, Focus Conversations on Learning about Performance. We, as leaders, successfully Lead the Journey by developing ownership for the right responsibilities by the right people.

QUESTION:
Who really owns this responsibility, and how can I transfer ownership of it to its rightful owner?

LEADERSHIP SOLUTION:
Performers perform great performance, and empowerers proactively FCLP. Both must do their jobs well.

CHAPTER 30

You Can't Confer a Benefit on an Unwilling Recipient

The title of this chapter is an observation made by Cicero before Christ was born. It is still true today. I keep learning this lesson again and again.

People really want to be great performers. That desire comes from deep inside each and every one of us. The leader's job is to create the environment that surfaces this deep desire and gives it the opportunity to flower. The old leadership paradigm pours poison on this desire by forcing "benefits" on unwilling recipients. The intellectual capitalism paradigm fertilizes this desire for greatness, providing the recipients with the tools and conditions to exercise control. In Leading the Journey, we must determine direction, remove obstacles, and develop ownership, not confer benefits. That's the lead-goose mentality.

You Can Take the Horse to Water, but You Can't Make It Drink

A business associate of mine helped me learn about leadership in this intellectual capitalism era. She was distressed about her son. He had a drug problem and dropped out of high school. She desperately wanted him to go to college and then into business with her. She did everything she could to get him through school, and failed. She showered him with such "benefits" as a car, tuition at an expensive private school, tennis lessons, tutoring, and frequent conferences with the teachers to get them to give her son "one more chance." None of it worked.

Finally, when he turned twenty, she ran out of energy and patience. When he was released from drug treatment for the third time, she told him to find some other place to live and start supporting himself. She was no longer prepared to confer benefits on this unwilling recipient.

If You Want the Horse to Drink, Make Sure It's Thirsty

He moved in with some high school friends who were attending college in a city two-hundred miles away. He just "hung out." After a month, he started to get restless. His friends, involved in their college studies, were too busy to party with him every night. As they talked about what they wanted to do when they graduated, he realized they were moving on and leaving him behind.

Desperate for "something" to do, he enrolled in a local technical school and earned his GED (general equivalency diploma). He convinced the local college to allow him into summer school on probation. He did well in summer school and was admitted for the fall term on probation. His mother agreed to pay for his schooling, as long as he stayed sober. He is now in college and doing well.

She shared her insights with me. "I couldn't change him no matter how hard I tried. The more I did, the less he did." Sound familiar? She was busy conferring benefits on her unwilling recipient son. When she stopped conferring benefits, she created the conditions in which he discovered his own desire to learn. What she couldn't do for him, he did for himself.

She applied the same principle in her business. She focuses on creating the conditions in which people want to be great. They push her. Her story helped me in a number of ways, particularly when a difficult situation arose at Johnsonville.

Head Buffalo Lock the Barn Door
After the Horse Is Stolen

On the Friday before Memorial Day, we received a rush order for summer sausage. The customer wanted the product Tuesday morning, meaning that it had to be shipped Monday evening.

We didn't have enough inventory to fill the order, so a number of plant people worked over the holiday weekend to make the sausage. The sausage was finished on Monday afternoon. Unfortunately, the truck driver did not show up. Not knowing what else to do, the people locked up the product in the plant when they went home. When the plant opened on Tuesday, a special truck was dispatched to the customer at great additional cost. The customer was mad at getting the product late. It cost us our margins to special-ship the product. And the people were frustrated because they had worked overtime and not satisfied their customer.

When I heard about the problem, I asked Jack, the plant manager, what he did about the situation. He said, "I've given the truck driver, who's been an attendance problem in the past, a written warning. I've also set up a list of alternative trucker phone numbers to call in the event this ever happens again."

Lead Geese Make Certain Nothing Is Ever Stolen

I asked Jack what was really great performance, for his plant and for him personally, from his customer's perspective. He answered easily that great performance for the plant from his customer's perspective was getting the product we promised on time, no matter what.

Jack had more difficulty answering the second part of the question—about great performance for himself. "Making certain that this situation never happens again," he said. He's partially correct. We'll never miss shipping an order produced over a holiday weekend when the truck driver doesn't show up. However, what will happen if a piece of equipment breaks down, or if someone on the work crew doesn't show up? Jack couldn't possibly set up rules to handle the thousands of other situations that might arise. Neither Jack nor I nor anyone can manage exceptions in advance. The only people who can are the people who are present at the time the exception arises. Setting up rules is another "benefit" he was conferring on unwilling recipients.

Jack learned about his real leadership task in this intellectual capitalism age. Rather than setting up rules to handle exceptions, Jack saw his job as empowering everyone to know their great performance for their customers and be committed to delivering it, no matter what. Now people are focused on doing whatever it takes to satisfy their customers in spite of obstacles they must overcome—even truck drivers who don't show up. We stopped conferring benefits and started empowering people.

Leaders Demonstrate and Model

Leaders demonstrate actions that keep the responsibilities fixed in the "right" place. I had the opportunity to help another leader demonstrate his commitment to empowering rather than conferring.

Remember the high-tech manufacturing company with the bulging order book and delivery problems? Recall that though the factory was months behind, because they couldn't get the engineering drawings in time, the engineering section was receiving bonuses for no-schedule performance. The bonus system was the villain. Engineering met its deadline, and earned its bonus by issuing "white drawings," blank sheets with the correct drawing numbers on them. The bonus system was a benefit conferred by management and had become an obstacle to achieving great performance.

In this situation, the performance owners were the drafting department people. The empowerers were both the leaders who put this practice in the place and allowed it to continue, and the in-plant "customers" who didn't challenge the engineering design section on their nonperformance. Empowering the responsibility to be fixed with the performers, the leaders pointed out to the engineering group how this system sabotaged the entire company. People from other sections, the other group of empowerers, stopped accepting the white drawings. The engineering section people agreed to work with their "customers" to design a new system. This new system would more accurately represent great performance for them, which contributed to the company's overall success.

When the leaders stop conferring benefits, people assume responsibility for delivering great performance for their customers.

QUESTION:

Do your people want to own the right responsibility and be great performers?

LEADERSHIP SOLUTION:

The desire for owning the responsibility for great performance comes from within.

PART VII

STIMULATING SELF-DIRECTED ACTIONS

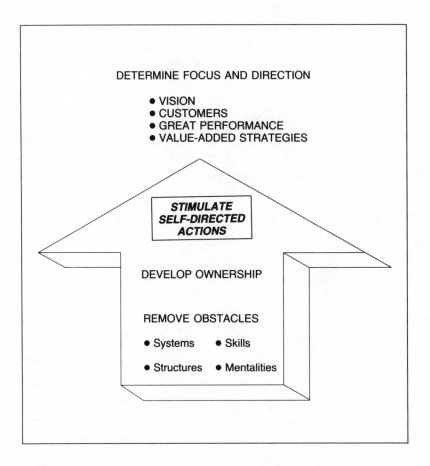

DETERMINE FOCUS AND DIRECTION

- VISION
- CUSTOMERS
- GREAT PERFORMANCE
- VALUE-ADDED STRATEGIES

STIMULATE SELF-DIRECTED ACTIONS

DEVELOP OWNERSHIP

REMOVE OBSTACLES

- Systems
- Skills
- Structures
- Mentalities

Introduction

After All Is Said and Done, There Is Far More Said than Done

If we weren't going somewhere, we'd call it "status-quo-ship." Leaders execute. But what do they execute?

Before I became the lead goose, I was a great paper shuffler, sitting in my office, processing papers, reading reports and commenting on them. I analyzed countless stacks of computer printouts, read tons of faxes, and processed E-mail by the megabyte. Just about everyone kept feeding my paper-shuffling addiction. I'd struggle onto the airplane with pounds of reading material. I envied people who could read a novel while traveling.

People would wait eagerly for my response. I'd get calls from executives asking, "Have you read the report I gave you yesterday? What do you think about it? Do you agree with my recommendations?" Heck, I had ten reports like his to read. My eyes were perpetually bleary from overuse.

Worse, nothing happened until I responded. Everyone waited for the official "blessing." My work derived from being the head buffalo, remember? When we lost a major customer because I couldn't read and respond fast enough to the sales manager's memo, I concluded, "This is out of control. I must find a better way."

I told my people to stop sending me all those reports and data, and instead to list the decisions they thought they should be making and could make without consulting me. When the list wasn't long enough, I challenged them to rethink it. I started sending back memos unread and asked the data processing department to take my name off many distribution lists.

My change disturbed some people at first. They had difficulty making the shift. With coaching, they finally got the message. Leadership isn't processing papers. It's about making things happen.

I learned another lesson about being the lead goose. The leader encourages people to take self-directed actions to achieve great performance and remove the obstacles that stand in their path. That's how leaders successfully Lead the Journey.

This part discusses the self-directed actions that lead geese encourage their flock to take.

QUESTION:
What actions am I prepared to take to remove the obstacles I own?

LEADERSHIP SOLUTION:
Get the "right" people owning the "right" responsibilities to take the "right" actions.

CHAPTER 31

Leaders Proact,
Not React

Great Leaders Prevent Problems, Not Solve Them

What are the "things" leaders make happen? I learned that my job was
to prevent problems, not solve them. This knowledge motivated me
to anticipate situations and implement long-term programs to prevent
problems.

How could I change the situation so I had fewer problems to solve?
The answer was simplicity itself. Stop rewarding people for bringing me
problems and start rewarding them for solving their own problems. To
accomplish that, I changed a number of systems and structures. Saying
what needs to be done is simple. Doing it is anything but simple.

Leaders Empower

Leaders take actions that empower people to be great performers. At
Johnsonville, while the responsibility for hiring the right people rests

with the work team, the performers, leaders have the responsibility to be certain that the team has the best selection, orientation, and training materials available. The team members work with their coaches/leaders to develop company-wide selection criteria and tools, orientation programs, and standardized training materials. The team members perform and the leaders empower.

The Same Old Actions Will Get Us the Same Old Results

We need substantially different actions to get us substantially different results. A definition of insanity is: doing the same thing over and over and expecting a different result.

I get angry when the management pundits tell us that it'll take years to produce significant change in large organizations. Saying that it will take a long time gives people the expectation that they don't have to change "just yet." There is no rush. Let's think about it next month. We are very busy now. Unless we change our leadership actions, their predictions are probably correct. I know that dramatic change in the largest organizations can/must take less than a year if it is to be effective at all. I have seen it happen. The following anecdote illustrates dramatic change which took place in *one day*.

The company manufactured radiation control equipment for use aboard nuclear submarines. It had a three-year order backlog, was fourteen months behind, and significant dollars over, on current orders. The company expected to lose $1 billion this year.

Three completely assembled units were finally tested and accepted by the customer. They had passed all quality control checks and were moved into the locked and secure storage shed outside the facility, awaiting pickup by the customer. Once the customer took possession of the units, more than $45 million of badly needed cash would be released.

During a routine check, it was discovered that wires had been cut and plugs displaced, so that under full nuclear power operation (which usually occurs during dives and underwater maneuvers), the equipment would fail, spewing nuclear material throughout the vessel and probably into the surrounding environment. The most favorable outcome of this failure would be destruction of the submarine, with the loss of all hands. The least favorable outcome would be a major nuclear incident causing significant environmental pollution, an underwater Chernobyl.

Many people had keys to the secured area. There was no real inventory control over the keys. Furthermore, every one of the executives believed that there was no way that the damage could have been done before the equipment was moved into the secured area.

The president called all 7,500 employees together. He showed them the sabotage. He then said, "We have a problem. If this had not been detected now, and it was noticed only by chance, all of us would not be employed here anymore. The customer would never trust another piece of equipment from us. What are we going to do to save our jobs?"

Right there in the covered launch yard, he asked each work group to meet and talk about the *great performance they needed to create* for the overall organization to produce perfect equipment, on time and under budget. With the help of outside facilitators, that process took several hours. The groups filled the yard with newsprint filled with notes.

Next he asked the groups to identify the *obstacles* that they either *controlled* or *directly influenced* that *prevented them from realizing great performance.* Again, after several hours, the yard was papered over with the products of the groups' discussions.

After six hours had been spent in the process, the president asked the groups to identify *who owned the obstacles.* He gave a short explanation about ownership, stressing the two levels—the performer for performance and the manager for empowering—using several personal examples. The groups spent another two hours to label each obstacle with two owners, the performer for performance and the manager for empowering.

At that point, the president asked the group the payoff question: *What actions will the owners take to eliminate the obstacles to great performance?* Although they had been at this process for more than nine hours, the discussion was lively and extended as individuals and groups negotiated "performance contracts." A number of times, the president had to refuse to accept primary responsibility for activities he felt more rightly belonged to the performers. He asked a number of times, "How can I empower you to do the job, support you in doing the job, facilitate your doing the job?" This period was the most difficult part of the day. While people had "heard" the words about empowerment and their own responsibility, they did not yet "believe" the words.

The result? More than 20,000 individual actions were generated from that twelve-hour meeting. A year later, the company is now on budget, on schedule, shipping perfect equipment—and no more sabotage. The FBI found the people who committed the crime and successfully prosecuted them.

See the actions that define great performance. Notice the actions that focus on obstacles. Observe the actions fixing responsibility. The president was able to turn his ship of state around in *one day* by taking the right actions.

Don't be misled. It is difficult to do what this president did. He had exceptionally strong support from his CEO. He had a superior team of coaches who helped him through the many rough spots. There was much backsliding and cynicism. It is not as easy as it reads on these pages. He worked at it, assiduously, for many months. But the change did happen, because he worked at it. That's the principal message.

Leaders Use Actions That Transfer Ownership

Actions must transfer ownership to the right people. Use the following steps to transfer/fix ownership:

1. Identify performers and empowerers. Almost always the performers will be the people actually doing the work, and the empowerers will be the leaders and specialists.
2. Involve the performers in defining direction, identifying obstacles, developing ownership, and taking self-directed actions.
3. Use the same approach to handle everyday situations to reinforce correct ownership of the performance responsibility, as in the examples of the smoking situation and the white drawings.

Here's how one of my clients did it. First he specified his vision of great performance: *to be the best perceived value in the market* by:

1. Delivering the best product quality as judged by the customer
2. Having people at the lowest possible level in the organization make quality decisions
3. Consistently improving productivity
4. Embedding this methodology so deeply that it becomes a permanent way of life

To achieve the vision, he laid out the following game plan:

1. The senior management at each facility will define great performance for the facility, as well as the obstacles, ownership, and actions.
2. Each department at the facility will identify great performance for them, as well as obstacles, ownership, and actions.
3. Then each person will define great performance for himself/herself, within the context of the definitions of great performance for the company, the facility, and the department. This is done at a workshop meeting led by the management of the facility/department.

Notice the emphasis on getting the "right" people to own the "right" responsibilities and take the "right" actions. The "right" actions are those that meet the following criteria:

1. *Deliverable:* some specific, concrete, and tangible action. A meeting. A plan. A program. Answers the question *"What will be done?"*
2. *Measurement:* an indicator that helps you know when you have accomplished what you set out to do. Answers the question *"How will we know when we have done it?"*
3. *Date:* It must have a date by when it will be done. Answers the question *"By when will it be done?"*
4. *Person responsible:* Names the person who is going to be responsible for getting it done. Answers the question *"Who will do it?"*

Leaders in the intellectual capitalism era proactively engage their people in assuming ownership for great performance and removing the obstacles that prevent that great performance. It's how we Lead the Journey.

QUESTION:
Am I proacting or reacting?

LEADERSHIP SOLUTION:
Get everyone to proact or we all will be gone.

CHAPTER 32

Get Rid of Nonessentials: Eliminate the Weeds

Lots of nonessential activities, like weeds, grow up in every organization. They did in mine. I learned to attack them vigorously and consistently, and enlist everyone else to join in the attack. I use weekly reports, task forces, bonuses, anything to deal with them. I keep asking the people, "What can I/we stop doing?" Stimulate self-directed actions that both achieve great performance and remove the obstacles to great performance. Eliminating nonessentials is one such set of self-directed actions.

While keeping the performance responsibility with its rightful owner, I also learned to take empowering action. The essence of the intellectual capitalism leadership paradigm is to empower others proactively while providing direction and focus, thereby successfully Leading the Journey.

Sales for Vanity, Profits for Sanity

Almost any business can look successful, at least in terms of the money at the top of the statement. Sales volume just seems to grow . . . and grow . . . and grow. How much of the money at the top of the statement, however, actually trickles down to the bottom line and into the profit pot? You'll be amazed and discouraged to discover how little of that top-of-the-statement money actually makes it through the sieve to the bottom line.

I used to deceive myself into thinking I was successful as long as sales volume kept growing. "I'm buying market share," I told myself. "It'll pay off in the long run." Then I read Lord Keynes's comment, "In the long run we are all dead," and wondered which would come first—my demise or the increased profits I'd been so busy purchasing. That comment triggered some thinking that led to my refocusing my efforts. Rather than the top of the statement, I sharply focused on the bottom line.

Get Back to Profitable Basics

Gaining weight, around my hips and around my organization, is amazingly easy. Success breeds the "wouldn't it be nice?" syndrome. I've seen lean and mean street fighters acquire plush offices, private jets, hordes of secretaries, and lose touch with what got them there in the first place.

Your continuing leadership task: Help everyone in your organization identify what's crucial and not crucial, and be dispassionate in dumping the noncontributors. Eliminate the "fat."

One of my clients ran a very successful business. He invented a category and owned it for several years. In the beginning, his company couldn't keep up with the demand. So the watchword was "Do whatever it takes to meet demand." Federal Express, telephone tie lines, extra secretaries—all became the norm.

Inevitably, times changed. Demand slacked off, and new competitors entered the marketplace. Sales increases slowed and margins fell. After margins crossed over into the red, the client called me.

I could easily see what was wrong. Fifteen minutes in the office convinced me that there were too many secretaries, too many offices, too many "essential" staff people. I knew from bitter experience that it wasn't my perception that mattered, however, but the perception of the people in the company.

We began by listing all the activities in the company, and asking, "What does this activity contribute to the bottom line? What would happen if we didn't do it anymore?"

The answers were startling. They had trouble finding activities that would cause a significant problem if left undone. They were surprised. I was not. They "found" ways to reduce costs by 37 percent.

Asking the right questions helped them get back to their essential basics. Relying upon the intellectual capitalism leadership approach helped assure successful execution.

Raid Your Own Business

Another way to eliminate nonessentials is to think about your business as a raider would. Challenge yourself and your people: "Does this activity contribute at least 20 percent to the bottom line—or growing fast enough that it will in a few years?" If the answer is no, then get rid of it.

I asked that question of a group of senior executives in an information systems unit of a large company. The unit had languished for years. Despite injections of more than three quarters of a billion dollars, they continued to bleed red ink. In frustration the CEO called me. "I've tried everything," he said. "Nothing works. I can't get these computer types to think like business people."

We held a meeting of all the division managers and their direct reports. Over 150 people were in the room when the CEO announced the "exercise." "We've just been bought by a corporate raider. He's put up $1.2 billion to buy us [which represented the current book value of the unit]. He financed the purchase with high-interest-rate junk bonds, and he needs cash flow to pay the interest. Our challenge is to restructure our business to generate that cash." The group had an afternoon and an evening to come up with their recommendations.

After much struggling and teeth gnashing, the group came back with their recommendations, which fell considerably short of the needed cash flows. The corporate CEO rejected the proposals, saying, "I plan to submit your recommendations to the board of directors. Does this represent your best work? Is this what you want to go before the board with your names attached?" The group went back to the drawing board.

Late that night, the light finally began to dawn on everyone. This was not an exercise. This was reality. Serious work then began to take place. The group reconfigured current operations, dropping several "sacred cows," slimming operations, redrawing responsibilities to eliminate many headquarters positions, and even consolidating divisions. Deep into the third day, the group reached the magic cash flow number.

"Thinking differently about our business was what made the difference," the CEO told me. "We would never have produced the ideas or the commitment to execution without this 'exercise.' "

Get More Efficient at the Basics

Getting rid of the "hangers-on" helps, but it's not enough. You also need to be more efficient at the essential activities. To inspire the people to improve, I kept asking, "How can we get better at doing what we do?"

Quality improvement was a big potential cost saver. We discovered that the cost of poor quality was adding almost 30 percent to our manufacturing costs alone. When the costs in the office were added, we were incurring a staggering 44 percent of our costs due to poor quality. That was a pretty tall weed to attack. Eradicating it was a profitable move.

When I shared the surprising data on the cost of poor quality, the people wanted to work on it. Since the people put the data together in the first place, they knew about the problem and became involved in figuring out how to improve quality. The people asked for and got training in using modern quality control tools. They set up frequent feedback (hourly/daily) on quality issues. They tracked their own quality measures and went out to customers to coordinate our measures with theirs. After a surprisingly short time, costs dropped significantly. I was amazed but not surprised. The intellectual capitalism leadership paradigm works. My leadership task is not to improve quality. It is to empower people to see that improving quality is essential to their great performance.

Simplify, Simplify, Simplify

Simplifying operations is another way to save costs. In an effort to solve problems, it's easy to get caught up in drafting procedures. The procedure lasts long after the problem has been solved, outlives its usefulness, and becomes part of a growing bureaucracy. I empower my people regularly to attack their own procedures. They do this in two structured ways.

First, we declare all systems null and void every year. On December 31 every procedure, process, form, and policy automatically disappears. Anyone who wants a system/process/form must argue for it *de nouveau*. We call it "zero-based administration." Interestingly, 75 percent of the administrative procedures eliminated never reappear.

Second, every week everyone writes a "5/15" report, no longer than one page, which takes fifteen minutes to write and five minutes to read. That report answers three questions: "What did I accomplish this week?" "What remains to be done next week?" "What needs to be fixed/changed/eliminated?" Anything that needs fixing/changing/eliminating must be handled before the end of the next week.

People constantly raise issues about procedures and systems that get in their way and prevent them from being great performers. The weekly airing of obstacles and the commitment to fix problems quickly, keeps the focus on simplifying activities to maximize results.

Measure the "Right" Stuff

Becoming efficient is only part of the fiscal control issue. Since what you measure gets produced, be certain to measure the "right" stuff.

The people track the following data every month. Use these figures, or others of your own choosing, regularly, and you will run your business rather than your business running you.

- Cash on hand and projected cash
- Sales calls made to targeted customers
- Customer moves through the sales cycle
- Customer service rating for each person

- Sales/orders
- Quality levels
- Weekly goal accomplishments

Eliminating nonessentials is one important set of self-directed actions you can take to Lead the Journey.

QUESTION:
How would a raider look at this business?

LEADERSHIP SOLUTION:
Get slim, get better, or get gone.

CHAPTER 33

You Get
What You Accept

"An army marches as fast as its slowest soldier" is an old military saying. This adage applies to an organization. The standard of performance is set by the poorest performer, not the best.

People look to the leader for clues and a model of great performance. The leader sets the standard for performance by what he/she will and won't accept. I learned what to accept and what not to accept.

My Expectations Influence What I Accept

In the past, before paradigm change, I thought that other people would not care about the business as much as I did. I wish I had a dollar for every time I said, "What can you expect? The business is not theirs." I let this attitude affect what I would accept from other people. I expected and accepted mediocrity.

I also accepted other people's problems. When the sausage wasn't coming out very well, I jumped in to solve the problem. I tasted it every morning to make sure it was right. I asked for reports on the quality of products. If managers had a conflict, I played Solomon. Because I accepted other people's problems and decisions, I got them, more and more every day. Finally, the situation was so bad that I did not have enough time in the day to get everything done. That's when I learned that others would do much more if I expected more and accepted less.

What I Accept Determines What Others Expect to Give Me

A story told about Henry Kissinger illustrates this principle. One of his aides was brilliant but did slipshod work. Mr. Kissinger counseled the aide on being more precise and doing more complete work, but the reports did not improve. Mr. Kissinger called his aide into his office to discuss a report the aide had sent to him several days previously. Mr. Kissinger asked, "Is this your best work?"

"Well, no," the aide replied. "I had a deadline and all this other work. It's good, but not my best."

"Then take it back and redo it," Kissinger said.

The scene was repeated several times until finally the aide answered, "Yes, this is my best work."

Kissinger replied, "Good, now I'll read it." From that day on, his aide's reports improved dramatically.

If I Stop Accepting What Others Give Me, What Work Will I Have to Do?

Renaldo, the general manager of a manufacturing plant, with six hundred employees and seventy managers, attended one of my workshops. He was frustrated because he was so busy that he didn't have time for the long-range projects on which he knew he should be working. He committed to a personal action plan before leaving the workshop. One item in his plan was to keep an activity log for the first several days back at work to see what he could delegate. When I saw Renaldo again, he gave me the following log of his first day back.

Observations of my typical day in terms of problems passed to me for corrections and/or solutions:

8 A.M. to noon

1. The treadmill in the exercise room is broken.
2. Tool crib issues are taking too much time.
3. I need an electrical motor repaired. No one is available to take it to repair shop.
4. A truck is in receiving with nine pallets to unload. I don't have a forklift.
5. Time clock near personnel is not working.
6. Our cross-training program is not working. People in areas they don't like!
7. We don't know what we are doing with the job scheduling system in rotary unions.
8. Have you scheduled quality advisers to a seminar?
9. Supplier won't ship until we pay him.
10. Has Dot been transferred yet and what is her classification?
11. Something is wrong with canteen coffee. Will you check to see if it's fresh?
12. Computer room roof is leaking. Repairs did not work.
13. I don't have a personal computer.
14. Betty's terminal needs to be hooked to mainframe.
15. No-smoking policy in lobby is unfair.
16. Rotary union focused factory did not ship a unit as promised.
17. Treadmill is broken. When are you going to fix it?
18. My estimator is out sick. Can I borrow J.P. from sales?
19. Clock in lobby has incorrect time on one face.
20. My office is too hot. Can you fix the air conditioner?
21. Can you fix the automatic door switch on the side dock? I don't like getting off my forklift to open it.
22. Betty Martin really screwed our forklift situation up. I can't find my team leader to get a key.
23. My coworker misses too much work. I have to do her work and mine.

24. Tool crib won't let us stock our own inserts.
25. I don't understand Wayne's training form. Will you fill it out for me?
26. Did you call Timken Bearing and arrange a plant tour?
27. The treadmill is broken. When are you going to fix it!

Renaldo meant to keep the log for a whole day. After four hours he had all the information he needed. His analysis went right to the heart of the issue. He said, "I love to solve problems and fix things. I've trained the people to bring their problems to me." Renaldo started training his people to solve their own problems by refusing to accept them. He learned to empower people, using the intellectual capitalism leadership paradigm, to solve their own issues. He said that he is now doing more of the work he always knew he should do but for which he never had time.

The Leader Sets the Standard

The CEO of a midsize California company spent a year working to improve the quality of his company's products. This was a critical issue for Stan and he devoted a lot of time and energy to it.

He invited famous speakers to talk about quality. He instituted quality awards. He wrote letters to employees. He walked around the plant talking to people about quality. He sent people out to benchmark competitors' products and visit customers.

Near the end of the year his people presented him with a problem. They'd produced a large batch of product that met the customer's specifications but was slightly below their own tougher standards. They asked him what they should do. Rejecting such a large batch meant missing their budget, and their bonuses.

Stan said "Ship it," thereby undoing everything for which he had worked. In fact, he more than undid it. In the past, it would have been shipped with no questions asked. People were now more aware of quality and that's why they asked him. Just when people were concerned about meeting specifications, he told them they didn't matter. He was worse off at the end of the year than he was at the beginning.

Not only did the people think quality didn't count, but they also thought less of Stan because his actions did not match his talk.

By accepting the question, Stan accepted responsibility for shipping lower quality. Here was a great opportunity to return the problem to the real owners, the performers, and he missed it.

The Standard Sets the Expectations

Vince Lombardi understood setting high standards by what he accepted. The story is told in Green Bay about Lombardi's first team meeting. The meeting was set for 8 A.M. Ray Nitchke got there at 7:59. Lombardi yelled at him, "Nitchke, you're late! That'll cost you one hundred dollars."

"But, Coach," Nitchke complained, "it's just eight o'clock. I'm right on time."

"On time at my meeting is ten minutes early," Lombardi said. People got the message that first day, and a team that had been chronic losers played for the world championship the following year.

You Get What You Accept from Your Customers Too

A small construction company on the East Coast was losing money on several of their large accounts. Their biggest problem was the way work was scheduled. The customers issued job orders randomly. Many of these orders were small and required immediate action. This practice caused crews to drive many miles between jobs. In fact, crews spent 30 percent of their time driving.

"Isn't there a better way to do the scheduling?" I asked. The owner replied that customers wouldn't cooperate. His shrinking profit margins finally convinced him that he couldn't afford to accept that answer anymore. He demonstrated how he could save his customers money and improve service if they could group orders. One customer finally agreed to test the idea. The results were impressive. In short order, the others agreed as well. His profits improved because his crews were more productive.

Finally, You Get What You Accept for Yourself Too

How many times have you said, "That person has great potential"? What's the difference between those who reach their potential and those who don't? I see people in every walk of life who do incredible things because they accept nothing less for themselves. Some, like Michael Jordan, have great talent. Others have modest talents but great hearts. They bring a discipline with them to every task they face. They are willing continuously to challenge themselves. They keep learning how to get better because they do not accept falling short of their potential.

I hate to write. Seems odd for an author to write that, but it's true. Writing is painful for me. In fact, writing is mostly rewriting for me. For instance, I've written this chapter eleven times. Yet I know the value of the discipline that writing brings to my thoughts. Sir Francis Bacon is correct. He's reputed to have said, "If you can't write it, you don't know it." It's hard, but I know I must do it to excel in my profession. If I'm going to write, I expect nothing less from myself than my very best effort.

As a leader, develop this mind-set for yourself. What you accept for yourself sets the tone for everyone else. Accepting nothing less than the best from everyone, including yourself, is the way to stimulate the right self-directed actions.

QUESTION:
Do you like what you see in the mirror?

LEADERSHIP SOLUTION:
Your organization is a reflection of what you accept.

CHAPTER 34

Master Polar Bear Club Management

Practice Polar Bear Club Management

I learned a valuable lesson years ago when I joined the Polar Bear Club. The membership fee for the Polar Bear Club is an annual dip into Lake Michigan, on January 1. Most years you have to walk across a hundred feet of ice to get to the open water. The anticipation of the cold water shock (thirty-three degrees) is worse than the experience. No one sticks a toe in to test the water. No one wades in slowly to get used to the temperature. They jump in, splash around, get it over with, and go home to celebrate.

When I need to deal with unpleasant, difficult situations, I switch to Polar Bear Club management.

Carpe Diem—Seize the Day

In the past, I was afraid of problems, so I avoided them, and believed that if I could keep problems below the surface, they would somehow go away. I thought that a problem wasn't a problem if no one talked about it. Unfortunately, the problems didn't go just because I kept them in the dark. They grew like a monstrous poison mushroom. What's worse, everyone in the organization copied my behavior. They avoided problems also, didn't allow issues to surface, and pretended that they didn't exist.

When I was forced to confront problems, my solutions were timid. I did only what was necessary to avoid risks. I did not know that to achieve success, I had to see everything as an opportunity.

A scene in the movie *Dead Poets Society* captures this theme vividly. Robin Williams teaches his class the Latin phrase *carpe diem*—seize the day. At first they understand it, but they don't have the heart to follow it.

At the end of the movie, they finally seize the day. They stand on their desks in defiance of the ruthless headmaster as Robin Williams leaves. Every one of them decides not to nibble around the edges of something that has to be done. They go straight to the heart of the matter. They are able to act because they know what great performance is for them. The same is true in business.

Robin Williams shows us an excellent example of a leader in the intellectual capitalism era. We see how a leader Leads the Journey by stimulating self-directed action. Williams doesn't shrink from taking unpleasant actions when faced with a difficult task.

Seize the Day with Great Performance for Customers

Turn problems into opportunities by focusing on great performance for you and your customers. Every day, every person confronts situations that can become problems or opportunities. Convert problem situations into opportunities by focusing everyone on great performance.

Many years ago, I failed to see an opportunity, and that failure cost me dearly. The people at Johnsonville made a batch of substandard product. We all tested it and decided that, while it was somewhat below standards, it wasn't "that bad" and could be reworked in small amounts into our regular product shipments.

A large potential customer, whom we had worked for years to try to sell, gave us a tentative order, depending upon the taste test. As luck would have it, she tasted some of the inferior product. She returned the balance of the shipment and refused to do business with us for many years. I should have dumped the faulty product immediately. I didn't, and it cost us. I learned a lesson I will never forget.

My First Loss Is My Best Loss

Johnson & Johnson is a first-class example of how to handle a problem. They didn't hesitate when they discovered that someone put cyanide in their Tylenol capsules. They pulled every Tylenol product off every shelf in the country. The cost was high, more than $100 million. They kept the product off the shelf until it could be sold with a tamperproof cap. Then they reintroduced the product. People appreciated the honest, forthright way they had dealt with the problem. Their quick actions not only restored people's confidence in Tylenol but *increased* it. J&J turned a huge problem into a public relations coup.

Johnson & Johnson sells medical products. They know that their customers' trust is their most important asset. Losing that was tantamount to losing the company. J&J knows that their customer is buying integrity from them, and they deliver it.

I had a poorly performing plant. It was a marginal performer for years. I told myself that I needed the plant because it provided product for an important area which I wanted to penetrate. So I put up with less than great performance for some time, rationalizing to myself that this was the price of admission into that market.

After approving one more check to cover their deficit, I finally had had it. "How do we get to a profitable position?" I asked the people responsible for serving that product market arena. "And if we can't, how can we get out?"

Two hours later, I felt foolish for having tolerated the losses for all those years. We had several other, better alternatives to operating this marginal plant. In the worst-case scenario, not having the plant and shipping product in from other areas would cost us less. In other words, we could stand the cost of not having the plant. "Let's make the changes. Let's just do it," the people concluded. "Let's stop talking about it and just do it." Their words were music to my ears.

When the people get the data and have the power, they make good decisions, at least as good as I, at the top of the organization, would have made. This is another example of the new intellectual capitalism paradigm at work. My leadership task is to establish direction, remove obstacles, develop ownership, and stimulate self-directed actions.

Establish Systems That Facilitate "Just Doing It"

Many executives say they want their people to be more risk-taking, but the people are reluctant. Yet employees tell me that they want to take more risks, but perceive that their executives discourage them. What a curious situation! Everyone wants to just do it, but no one dares.

Why don't people "just do it"? Because the systems and structures usually prevent them by building in long approval cycles and multiple approvals. If it takes several months of meeting and nine different signatures to get anything done, it's much easier to decide not to do anything.

In one company the people complained about being discouraged from risk-taking. They planned annual budgets beginning in July of the previous year. If some opportunity came up in August, twelve months after the budget had been planned (but with five months of the operating year left to go), the usual response to a request for additional risk capital was "There's no money left. Put it in next year's budget." By next year the opportunity might be gone.

To enable them to have more flexibility, they shortened the budget cycle to six months, rather than a year, and created an "opportunities" budget, which would give them the funds to capitalize on opportunities as they arose. This simple system change, removing one of the system obstacles, empowered the people to take more risks.

The performance management and reward systems also often disable the "just do it" mentality. The standards of great performance often don't include the expectation of "doing whatever it takes to delight customers." Without that expectation it's no wonder that people don't take risks. Closing the loop, the reward system must reward risk-taking. Removing these systems obstacles is an important leadership task.

In my organization I make certain that risk-taking is part of the standards of great performance for each individual and that taking risks is rewarded, even the risks that don't succeed. Ensure that systems empower the "just do it" mentality.

If Sleeping Dogs Lie Too Long, They Will Bite When Awakened

One of our largest customers asked us to prepackage our products for his retail stores. Neither I nor the people wanted to do it. We all had lots of reasons why we couldn't. It would take too much space, require new expensive machinery, and add to the cost of the product. Consumers didn't really want the new package. To appease him, the people packaged two of our products in a halfhearted attempt to keep him happy. We stalled him for almost a year.

One day I received an alarmed phone call from my vice-president of sales. Our customer, a large chain, had put our biggest competitor's prepackaged products in his stores. They had never carried our competitor's brand before, and our competitor had never prepackaged their products either. They did it just to get into that chain. They were willing to do whatever it took to do business with our customer, who was now also their customer. This was a serious challenge. We could be hurt badly if the customer started featuring their products in their advertising instead of ours.

Within three weeks, we found the plant space, prepackaged our products, and figured out a way to make a different package without a lot of additional equipment. We decided that if we had to do it, we'd be the best in the industry. Our prepackaged products were very successful.

That customer taught me several valuable lessons. I learned to take care of matters in a timely manner that are important to our customers. Something that we thought we didn't want to do became one of our biggest opportunities. We acquired the taste for facing up to our responsibilities and giving our customers what they wanted.

I also relearned the impact that my actions had on the behavior of others. My people were a mirror to me. When I avoided responsibility, so did they. When I faced up to the difficult challenges, they moved with courage. I had to model the behavior I wanted from others.

I also relearned the power of the paradigm. I saw again how to Lead the Journey with intellectual capitalism. When I establish a standard and clear goals, the people do whatever it takes to meet it.

"If it were done, when 'tis done, then 'twere well/ It were done quickly"—*Hamlet*

A large company faced a severe challenge. For many years their products were the industry standard. They produced outstanding earnings. Their success produced complacency. They took their eye off the customer. They woke up to face a well-financed competitor offering very fine products to their customers.

The vice-president of manufacturing, Henry, had thirty-three years with the company. He understood how the company worked and was very successful in their management system. He realized that he needed to dramatically change his management style from a directive to a more participative and empowering style if the company was going to recapture market share. He didn't want to change the management style he knew and cherished, but he knew he had no choice.

He worked with four plants to pilot his new participation-based management approach. He first worked with the pilot plant managers to revise how they managed their plants. After several months they made some progress, but it was slow. There was always a reason why the empowerment process couldn't move any faster. However, he saw enough progress to believe in the new empowerment system.

Almost six months went by and he was still struggling with his four pilots. He observed that the longer he took to make the change, the harder it was. So he resolved to move more quickly in the rollout to the rest of the plants.

He met with the rest of his management and told them that the new system would be installed in all their plants within the next ninety days. Many managers complained that he was moving too quickly. They urged him to slow down to make sure they got it "right." "We have no choice," he said. "The competitor isn't waiting for us to get it right."

Some plants made the transition to a more participative managerial style in less than thirty days. Many in sixty days. A few didn't get there at all, and the VP had to go back and work with them individually.

The results? The plants that made the transition in thirty days showed the best improvements. Most plants did better than the four prototype plants. Speed gave them focus. Henry learned in this hare and tortoise race, it is speed on the track that wins.

Focus on Great Performance Helps Leaders Be Great Performers

The focus on great performance helped all of the leaders in the previous examples know when and how to act. Action is the key. Many situations call for action even though the outcome is not clear. The picture of great performance is the leader's guide to action. The willingness to stand up and be counted is another useful leadership tool in Leading the Journey.

QUESTION:
Do you have any problems you are avoiding?

LEADERSHIP SOLUTION:
If you have to do it, do it with everything you have.

CHAPTER 35

Do What You Do Best—
Give Away the Rest
to Someone Else

Fixing Is the Wrong Work

I was the great "fixer." For a long time, I thought it was my job. I eventually realized the fixing wasn't the highest and best contribution I could make to my organization's success.

Effective leading in this intellectual capitalism era requires a different leadership behavior. Leading as a head buffalo doesn't work in this era. Lead geese are more successful. Stimulating self-directed actions to achieve great performance for customers and removing obstacles requires that I, as the leader, do what I do best and give away the rest. That rest belongs to someone else for whom it's his/her best. In that way I model the self-directed behavior I want others to adopt. That's how I successfully Lead the Journey.

Hard Work Is Not Its Own Reward

I recently attended a funeral for one of my business associates. He was forty-six years old, and ran a very successful, growing business. Late one night he went off the road. "He was coming home from one of his innumerable late night meetings at the office," his widow told me. "I wonder what the company will do now. They'll just have to learn to do without him, as I learned to do without him, so many years ago."

The experience caused me to stop and ponder the questions in my mind. "Why am I doing what I am doing? What do I truly want? Do I want to build a big business—or a big funeral? Am I doing all this to please myself, or am I just working all these hours to make my wife's next husband very happy?"

I'm Trapped in the Treadmill That's So Big I Don't Realize It's a Treadmill!

Most of us work very hard and long, being the head buffalo. Does the following sound familiar? The day, beginning with a breakfast meeting, is filled with rushing here and rushing there—telephone calls, meetings, conferences, one-on-ones. The daylight is gone before you get to that pile on your desk. You handle the items in the "red file" and head home, your briefcase bulging with "required" reading for tomorrow's activities. Even on the way home, you're so busy on your cellular phone that you hardly notice the scenery.

Weekends disappear in a blizzard of paperwork and phone calls. Your home fax vomits reams of paper all over the floor. You have trouble remembering the last family vacation you took without your ever-present cellular companion. Your handicap is out of sight.

Have I been reading your mail? Spying on you? Hardly. I'm too busy for that. It's just that I know how too many executives spend their time, because that's how I spent mine before my associate's funeral.

I Know I'm Busy, but Am I Busy with the "Right" Stuff?

When I went back to the office that afternoon, I looked at the pile of pink telephone slips, the overflowing in-basket, the blinking lights on the telephone, and asked myself, "Am I working on the right stuff?" All of that stuff couldn't be the right stuff.

Realizing that if they did without me for the morning, I knew they could limp along for a few more hours. I thought secretly, this might be good practice. I closed the door, then went through each item in the in-basket and each telephone slip and asked the following questions:

- Who's going to execute this action/decision?
- Who has the information necessary to make this decision/take this action?
- If it isn't the same person who's going to execute it, how can that executing person get the necessary information?
- Who should own this issue?

When I finished the process, I noticed that the pile of my responsibilities was the smallest of all. I was working very hard doing everybody else's job. I was busy, all right, working on the wrong stuff, busy making a big funeral, not a big business.

Back to Basics: What Is It That We Really Want to Create?

Once I found the problem in myself, the solution was simple. Change! You've read this story line before, as it comes up repeatedly in this book. Asking myself, "What do I really want to create?" I saw clearly that my owning so many of other people's responsibilities wasn't great performance. To transfer the ownership, like the early wagon-train leader, I circled the wagons.

Banish the Orphans: Help Them Find Their True Parents

When I shared my feelings with my direct reports, they looked both puzzled and relieved. I shared my determination not to wind up like my late business associate. I also told them I didn't think they should work excessively long hours either. Together we had to find ways to do our important work during normal working hours.

Asking them the same questions about ownership and great performance I'd asked myself, I found that when we finished, my pile of responsibilities was still the smallest of anyone's. The biggest pile was reserved for the direct reports of my direct reports. My direct reports understood the message and were determined to let go of what belonged to others. In fact, all the piles grew smaller.

The funeral marked the beginning of my insight into the intellectual capitalism paradigm and the beginning of my Leading the Journey, rather than directing or controlling it. Until I took the first self-directed actions, no one else had the nerve to do so. After I took the first step, always the most challenging, the people stepped up to the line to assume responsibility.

Slipping off the Wagon and Forgetting Is Easy

I would like to tell you that I have it all perfect now, that I've got it completely under control. The truth is my buffalo aren't flying yet and I continue to be the principal obstacle.

I recently replaced the COO of one of my larger units. He was a good man, but not for this job. I reorganized the unit into self-directed work teams. I'd accomplished this feat in other units and I knew it was possible.

Immediately, my office became the hub. The first week I was busy from 7 A.M. till 11 P.M. Problems surfaced, issues burned, and people couldn't live without me. Initially, I felt the situation was fun, and I liked being needed again. Feeling the power of the reins in my hands sent an adrenaline surge through my body. The saddle felt good and comfortable beneath me.

Then the old feelings started to come back as I struggled to do all of this "important" work. I had to write another chapter in this book, handle my current clients, talk with prospective ones, take my son to college, and . . . I realized that the saddle wasn't beneath me, it was on my back. The uneasy feeling was communicating its symptom message clearly: I had fallen off the wagon. I had forgotten my commitment to lead and not manage.

I circled the wagons again, asked the same old questions, made the same old piles, and helped others step up to the line and determine what responsibilities *they* needed to *own* to be great performers. Again I confronted them with the query of what *they* needed to *learn* in order to execute their responsibilities, and what *actions they* needed to take to remove the obstacles to their great performance.

The old story is forever new in its relevance and unfolds in varying experiences. Challenges lead to actions, which lead to learning, which uncovers more challenges. What is new becomes old. What we thought was the same has changed and is different. These endless challenges and changes make getting up in the morning worthwhile.

Leaders set the tone and model the self-directed actions, essential to achieving great performance for customers. They remove the obstacles to that great performance. One of the best actions to model is doing what you do best and giving away the rest to someone else for whom it's his or her best. In that way, leaders Lead the Journey.

QUESTION:

What is my highest and best contribution to the organization?

LEADERSHIP SOLUTION:

Old roads lead to old destinations. New roads lead to new destinations.

CHAPTER 36

Get the Right Players in the Right Positions

It's hard to win the Super Bowl playing with a team composed of ten-year-old Cub Scouts. The heart of Leading the Journey is people taking self-directed actions that either deliver great performance for their customers or remove the obstacles to taking the right self-directed actions. Each person must be doing the work at which he/she is the best. Therefore, I learned how to get the right people to do the right work.

Identify the Right Work: The Key Leverage Positions

When the animals in George Orwell's classic *Animal Farm* took over the farm, they wrote a law that said, "All animals are created equal." Later on, when the pigs took over, they amended that law to read, "All animals are created equal, but some animals are more equal than others." Orwell's pigs are right. On your journey, all jobs and all people are important, but some are more important than others.

When I reorganized my company to eliminate many layers of management, everyone knew we still needed skilled business people. One of our shipping people said it best: "You don't expect people in the shipping department to run the company, do you?"

Begin by Asking the Thinking-Strategically Questions

- What skills, attitudes, and behaviors of people are required to deliver great performance?
- What positions give me the maximum leverage to infuse these skills, attitudes, and behaviors throughout the organization?

When I first took over the ink company, it was losing $400,000 a year. We needed to improve both customer service and internal efficiency. There were two key leverage positions to accomplish these improvements: the vice-president of manufacturing and the vice-president of sales. Together we developed job profiles. I'd significantly rewrite these now in light of all I've learned. Here's what I wrote then, many years ago:

Vice-president of Manufacturing:
1. Create the most efficient manufacturing process without significant additional capital investment.
2. Meet every customer shipping date on time.
3. Have the highest quality product and production process in the industry.
4. Create conditions where production people feel appreciated, rewarded, and productive.

Vice-president of Sales:
1. Grow the business 30 percent compounded annually over the next three years.
2. Enter at least three new markets and establish a minimum of 20 percent market share.
3. Dominate current markets, winning at least 50 percent share.
4. Operate a productive third-party distribution channel where we have the best distributor in each area.
5. Ensure satisfied customers.

These items represented what we thought each job had to produce in terms of specific, concrete, tangible results for the company to achieve its goals.

Define the $6-Million Bionic Person to Do the Job

Then we jointly defined the few critical skills that would produce the behavior we wanted.

Vice-president of Manufacturing:
1. Experienced in chemical processes
2. Deadline- and customer-oriented
3. People person
4. Able to work under pressure and not transmit that pressure
5. Open to new ideas

Vice-president of Sales:
1. People-oriented—strong people skills
2. Achievement-oriented—wants to accomplish goals
3. Understands both customer's and our business, doesn't make unrealistic promises
4. Creatively structure deals to meet customer's needs and sell our products

We used these profiles to create performance contracts with both incumbents aimed at improving efficiency and customer service. Within weeks I noticed substantial improvement throughout the company modeled and driven by these two key people.

Keep your definitions simple, though. You may come up with twelve important dimensions, only three of which are critical. Look for the critical dimensions first, then the "it would be nice if . . ." ones.

You Can't Coach Tall—Get the Best Person

Once you've got the profile, find the person who best fits it. Choice is the key to good selection. The wider the pool, the better the choice will be. Find lots of people from which to choose.

Choose carefully. Don't compromise. Here are some techniques I've found that work for me:

1. Preparation is vital. Review your profile before you talk to anyone.
2. Ask open-ended questions, such as:
   - What would you redesign about your last job, and why?
   - How would your references answer the following question . . . ?
3. Take good notes. You'll likely forget otherwise—count on it.
4. Ask tough questions like:
   - What are your weaknesses and how do they show up in performance?
   - What would you do differently now, in light of what you've learned?
5. Hold multiple interviews and get independent judgments from each interviewer.
6. Involve everyone who's going to be involved with that person: customers, suppliers, peers, employees.

Choose the Least Imperfect Person

When all is said and done, I've discovered that there are no perfect candidates. No one fits the profile perfectly. Selection is a process of trade-offs. So I've learned to ask myself, "Can I live with the person's deficiency? How serious is the deficiency? Can I correct the deficiency in some way—hire a complementary person or organize around it?" I've learned to choose the least flawed person, or at least the person whose flaws I can most easily live with.

Organize Around Weaknesses

Recognizing that perfect people don't exist helped me recognize that no perfect organization scheme exists. Organization structure eliminates people's weaknesses. So organize around people's weaknesses. As people grow and develop new strengths, and weaknesses emerge, reshuffle the boxes. That's why organizing is really a process of constantly reorganizing.

I'm a good idea person, who loves to dream the dream and invent the new way. I am terrible with detail. In fact, I almost lost my learning-center business because I "forgot" to pay the withholding taxes. Therefore, I organize around my weaknesses, choosing people to work with me who are very detail-oriented. They do what they do best, handle the details, which frees me up to do what I do best, invent and create.

I Never Heard of Anyone Lying on His Deathbed Who Said, "I Fired That Person Too Soon"

Sometimes great people get placed in the wrong jobs, or the jobs in which they were great performers changed and they didn't change with it. For whatever the reason, leaders step forward and remove the nonperformer.

Firing anyone is tough. You have to stand eyeball-to-eyeball with that person and tell him/her that he/she isn't making it. I don't know of anyone who finds firing someone easy.

I hesitated to fire nonperformers. I knew that keeping them wasn't fair to the other people who were performing well. Moreover, keeping the nonperformer wasn't fair to him/her, because these same people might perform very well in a different setting. Refusing to deal with the poor performer was condemning him/her to a lifetime of mediocrity.

I was afraid of ruining someone's life. I believed it was my responsibility to "take care" of people. I was trapped by guilt, the guilt of having put them there in the first place, of not supporting them enough, or not giving them enough opportunities.

Head buffalo suffer with a lot of these inappropriate guilt feelings; at least they disabled me. When I learned to become the lead goose, I learned to Lead the Journey, not direct or control it. Modeling the "step-up-to-the-line behavior" in confronting underperforming people is one of the self-directed actions we leaders need to take, so that others throughout the organization will be stimulated to do the same.

If Someone Has to Go, Make Sure It's Their Fault, Not Yours

I knew something had to be done. One of my senior executives was adversely affecting other people's performance. The people were frustrated, and I was making myself crazy trying to fix the problem.

Finally deciding to act, I called the senior executive into my office, told him he had failed, and I would have to let him go. He said angrily, "The things I did were always fine in the past. Why aren't they good enough now? Why didn't you tell me sooner?"

I had told him, or at least I thought I had told him. He hadn't heard, or hadn't believed I was serious. I talked about the problems for years but never did anything about it. The experience was painful, especially since I felt I had contributed to his failure.

We had a poor performance measurement system for managers. They didn't know how they were doing. I resolved that day to make people's performance so clear to them that if they failed it was their responsibility, not mine. They would, in effect, fire themselves.

I asked people individually to define their great performance for their customers. We discussed their definition and matched it up with mine and those of their other significant customers. Once we agreed on what was to be created, and how it was to be measured, we built personal action plans to deliver the agreed-upon great performance.

We talked about great performance at every weekly staff meeting. All had established standards of great performance with their customers and got regular feedback from them. When individuals didn't perform, their customers told them directly. When people slipped behind, there was lots of help from colleagues to get them on track. When anyone consistently doesn't deliver great performance, it was also obvious to everyone. I'm not usually involved at all. In fact, in situations of consistent nonperformance the person usually leaves voluntarily before any action on my part is necessary.

Now Is Better than Later

I can always find many good reasons to postpone a termination action. But the reasons to take action are always better. For example, there's Bernie, a route driver for Johnsonville many years ago, from whom I learned a valuable lesson.

Bernie was not a good truck driver. He had had several minor accidents. Some carelessness on Bernie's part was always involved. I should have known Bernie wasn't going to improve, because he claimed that none of those accidents were his fault. After the third accident, Bernie should have been grounded. Instead, he was given a warning and sent to driving school. He barely passed the course and was sent back on his route.

Several months later I learned that Bernie was in the hospital. He had pulled his truck into a grocery store next to a railroad track to deliver sausage. When he finished, he backed out of the parking lot over the tracks and was hit by a train. Fortunately, the train was going slowly and Bernie was not seriously injured. The truck was a total loss.

Bernie was released from the hospital the following day. The next time I saw him in the plant, after inquiring about his health, I asked him, "After all your training, how could you back your truck up into the oncoming train?"

Bernie's reply was classic. "It's not my fault," he said. "The train hit me."

That remark told me how misplaced my faith was that training would help Bernie be a better driver. He never saw any need to improve. We made ourselves responsible for Bernie's improvement in an effort to "save" Bernie.

Be a Sorter, Not a Savior

The difference between being a sorter and a savior is ownership. Sorters make the performers responsible for their own performance. Saviors make themselves responsible for the performance of others. When I was trying to save Bernie, I owned the problem of Bernie's performance. I didn't establish clear performance standards, feedback, and consequences for nonperformance with Bernie, all of which should have been done the first day Bernie started driving a truck.

I allowed Bernie to avoid facing up to his incompetence as a truck driver. My refusal to make Bernie responsible for his own performance almost led to his death. I spent many years trying to save people. I finally learned that my job was to sort them, not save them. Great performance is a valuable separator.

QUESTION:
Who is the bionic, $6-million person to do this job?

LEADERSHIP SOLUTION:
**You can't coach tall. Great players make the
coach look great.**

PART VIII

LEARNING TO BE THE LEAD GOOSE

Introduction

Learning Is the Door to Tomorrow

It's tough being a leader today. Rapid change is everywhere. Politics, technology, markets. The pace is dizzying, and there's no respite in sight. It seems that these are the most trying of times. Things weren't nearly as bad in the past as they are now.

The premium is on learning fast enough to cope and to stay ahead of the pack. Learning is the key. Faster is the pace.

When I started Leading the Journey, I thought I knew a lot. After all, I had lots of education and experience. That ought to be enough, right? Wrong. I've done more learning in the past twelve years than in all of my previous years. Moreover, I've learned that I've only just begun because there's so much I don't know.

Changing My Leadership Behavior Begins with a Paradigm Shift

I've changed a lot of things in my life. Important things. But the toughest change of all has been changing my leadership paradigm. You can't turn leadership behavior on and off like a light bulb. It isn't that simple. My leadership didn't change until my leadership paradigm changed. I had to see myself as the lead goose, rather than the head buffalo.

What Is It That I Think I Know That Just Isn't So?

I learned how to be proactive in getting help in my education. I tape-recorded my meetings, then asked for feedback. I learned to listen to myself. I asked myself, "What is it that I think I know that just isn't germane now?"

That great management philosopher Yogi Berra said, "You can observe a lot by just watching." I experienced the truth of his words as I learned from everyone. I became a student of everyone and a follower of no one. I picked out the one or two people who modeled the behavior I wanted most to assimilate, studied them, and learned how and what they did. Then I adapted their skills to my own situation. I didn't have to reinvent the wheel, just reinvent the application of the wheel.

Because learning is so important to leading in today's intellectual capitalism age, I've included an entire section on it. Learning to be the lead goose is essential to getting the buffalo to fly.

QUESTION:
Am I equal to the constant challenge of learning to be a different leader?

LEADERSHIP SOLUTION:
Think. Practice. Reflect.

CHAPTER 37

Leading
Is Learning

Learn to Leave My Comfort Zone Behind

I learned to love new things, to think in new ways. It was uncomfortable. It still is uncomfortable. I learned to see beyond the discomfort and recognize the need to stretch and challenge myself. I learned to be my own competitor. The origin of the word "competitor" tells the story. The word originated in the Olympics. It means, literally, "same [*com*] feet [*ped*]." In the Olympic training, competitors were the people against whom the athletes trained. They were the people who ran alongside and challenged the athlete to greater heights of performance. I learned to be my own competitor, to be my own challenger to greater heights of performance.

It isn't easy trying new things. There was a lot of fear on my part when I started this journey. It's unsettling for others to witness a radical change in the boss's behavior. For example, they'd come to expect me to tell them how much inventory to carry. They didn't know what to do when I insisted that it was their responsibility.

It's uncomfortable to learn, because learning involves doing things differently, leaving your comfort zone behind.

311

Learn to Give It Up

It isn't easy to give up one bauble in hopes of getting a bigger one later. Monkeys get trapped that way much like us humans. When the trappers want to catch a monkey alive, they put a bright bauble into a bottle with a neck just large enough for the monkey to slip its open hand into the bottle. The monkey is attracted by the bright bauble and reaches inside to take it. With its hand wrapped around the bauble, the fist will not come out. Struggle as it will, the monkey will not relinquish the bauble and therefore cannot free its hand. Eventually, the trappers come along and capture the monkey—trapped by its unwillingness to give up the bauble.

Most of us overestimate the value of what we currently have, and have to give up, and underestimate the value of what we may gain. A relative of mine was the regional sales manager for a large company in Seattle. He was offered a promotion at the corporate office to become vice-president of sales and marketing for the entire corporation, with a 50 percent salary increase. He called me wondering if he should take the position.

"I don't know. There are so many downsides. I've got this lovely corner office now with two large windows overlooking the Sound," he said. "It's so relaxing to look out and see the white boats sailing on the blue water. My new office has one tiny window overlooking the concrete wall of the factory. Furthermore, we had a great year last year, so we bought ourselves all new furniture. I got the desk of my dreams. It's beautiful teak. And the chair is just right for me. My office at headquarters is so small none of the furniture fits in. I don't know if I should take the job."

Observe him overvaluing the "important" factors in the current situation of his desk, chair, office size, and view, and undervalue the "unimportant" aspects of the future job like a major promotion and a 50 percent salary increase.

I reminded him that you can't get to second with your foot still on first. In the end, he really wanted the promotion, so he moved, but not without a lot of stewing and post-buyers' regret. He did very well, once he learned to give up the present so he could move on into the future.

Learning New Leadership Patterns Isn't What You Know, It's What You Do

I learned a lot about learning on my journey. Mostly, I learned that I learned a lot more by doing than I did by reading or listening to lectures. Doing presents me with the opportunity to learn.

Get on with the doing. The more you do, the more you have the opportunity to learn. Widen the scope of doing. Go up in hot-air balloons. Go down in submarines. Take the risk to speak up and stand out.

Learn from everything, even the worst disaster. Everything has the potential for learning. The worst mistake may be the best learning opportunity.

One of my clients was a quiet, self-effacing fifty-six-year-old man who'd lived in the shadow of his dominant father for years. I helped him learn how to deal more effectively with his father by engaging in a series of actions from which he could learn. He spoke at industry meetings, gave speeches at local colleges, and engaged suppliers in hard bargaining, all experiences designed to build up his skill in dealing with difficult and personally threatening situations. After a year of these experiences, he was ready to deal with his dad. He arranged to have dinner with his dad to discuss a new corporate structure, which replaced his dad as chairman. His dad resisted, but he persisted in his presentation, calling upon the skills he had developed over the past year. The issue was left unresolved, but he knew he'd won when his mother called and praised him for standing up for himself.

Knowledge is nothing without action. Nothing changes until you *do* something. What you *do* will directly determine what you learn.

Anything Worth Doing Is Worth Doing Poorly— At Least in the Beginning

When you are learning something new, you are not very good at it. The temptation to want perfection the first time we do something keeps us from trying new things and prevents us from building skills and expertise. We tend to want everything to be "just so" before we launch a new activity. Children learning to ride a bike don't spend weeks planning. They get on and fall off a few times. Their desire to learn is greater than their fear of falling. Nothing ever works exactly according to plan. Life and business are not like that. Doing it just right is not what's important. Starting is. You can't start getting better until you start.

Since the greater risk is in doing nothing, you can minimize the risk by starting. When I started Leading the Journey, I worried about getting things just right and was afraid of making mistakes. Remembering that "he who makes no mistakes ends up making nothing," I recognized that mistakes are a part of learning. High performance these days is practicing being excellent while on the move.

The following excuses are frequently given as reasons for not doing anything:

1. We've been moving too fast. We have to slow down and get this right.
2. We could never afford to take that kind of risk.
3. If we make a big push on this, people will think it's just one more program.
4. Many of our people will never accept this. They will not want to change. We have been hearing about what "they" will or will not do for years. We have never been able to find one "they" in any company. "They" always seem to be in the next room, the next level, the next division, the next building, the bathroom . . .
5. Thirty percent of our people are illiterate. (Are the other 70 percent doing what they should be doing? Couldn't some of them help the 30 percent?)
6. But we're a big company. But we're a small company. But we have a union. But we don't have a union. But we're a public company. But we're a private company. But the wind is blowing from the east and it's Tuesday . . .

One can always find reasons not to do something. The only reason to continually learn is to provide great performance for your customers. That is the right thing to do.

Learning to be a different kind of leader is hard. It's the hardest

piece of learning I've ever done—and the most important. My advice
is get on with it! It's already almost too late.

QUESTION:
Can I learn enough, fast enough?

LEADERSHIP SOLUTION:
Get on with the learning—now!

CHAPTER 38

Great Teacher #1: Mistakes

Situations are filled with teachers, ready to show us important learnings. To improve as leaders, we must keep learning. The experience of making mistakes provided me with an important opportunity for new learning.

Ever worry about being wrong? About making a mistake? Ever have egg on your face? Ugh! I have and I hated it more than anything. I suppose I thought being wrong was failure. I discovered that failure wasn't fatal. Now I know that whenever I avoid mistakes, I lose a lot of opportunities to learn. If I were never wrong, then I would have nothing to learn or change, and no reason to progress.

Mistakes Are Not Sins

The origin of the word "sin" and its current interpretation graphically illustrate the heavy negative connotation we attach to making mistakes. Sin originally was an archery term which meant missing the mark.

If you missed the mark, or sinned, you just tried again. Today, the word "sin" means "to violate God's law," according to the Oxford dictionary. With this meaning, people are reluctant to "sin" or make a mistake. That makes it awfully important to always be right on the mark.

Mistakes Are Great Feedback Mechanisms

Mistakes tell us that whatever we're doing is not working. They tell us something is wrong. Most of the time we look for "something" other than ourselves. The lengths to which I've gone to avoid making a mistake or own up to one I made illustrate my propensity to avoid feedback. Let me tell you about some of the mistakes I've made and how I learned from the experience.

In one situation, I chose the wrong person for a key job. I chose her and I stuck by her. Other people told me she wasn't performing, that she was letting them down and prevented them from doing their job. I listened, and defended my choice.

Six months went by. The downward slide continued. Still I stood firm. "Give her time," I said. "She'll catch on. With her credentials, she'll be a big asset to us all." Finally, a delegation of senior executives visited me and demanded that their profit-sharing bonus be separated from hers. They showed me data that her performance would wipe out their bonus and reduce the bonuses for many other people.

I was stunned, not by their data, for I saw the same information they saw. I was stunned by my own refusal to acknowledge my mistake for so long. I had deliberately ignored all of the early, middle, and late warning signs of her inappropriate placement. A several-hundred-thousand dollar mistake was made worse by my nine-month cover-up.

"Why was I so slow in acknowledging my mistake?" I asked myself. The answer wasn't very pretty. I was impressed with her academic credentials. I couldn't believe that someone so qualified could not perform the job I had in mind for her. In retrospect I saw my mistake clearly. She had advanced analytical and planning skills, but my small and struggling business needed action, which was not her long suit.

My own bias distorted my evaluation of her qualifications. Then my pride prevented me from admitting the mistake and doing something constructive about it in a timely manner.

I learned two important leadership lessons from this mistake. First, focus on the skills required to do the job that needs to be done. Background is secondary and relevant only as it supports performance in *this job*.

Most of all, I learned to "own up." Avoidance and denial were the biggest mistake of all. I covered up my mistake and cost myself not only many dollars but considerable credibility with my people. They saw my unwillingness to admit I'd made a mistake they knew I had made.

Mistakes Tell Us Where the Oil Isn't

Jean Paul Getty is reputed to have told the following story which aptly illustrates the value of mistakes, recounted here as I heard it from the platform:

> Jean Paul Getty set out to drill for oil in Oklahoma. His partner was an old prospector who owned the drilling rig. They drilled for over a week in one place. When the drill ran out, and there was no oil, Getty got mad. He stomped around the little hovel in which they were living on the dusty prairie. In frustration, he grabbed the old prospector, who seemed unperturbed by this failure, and said, "You old coot. We spent a whole week out here eating dust and all we got to show for it is a dry hole. What are you going to do about it?"
>
> The old prospector sat down and put his feet on the table and said, "Well, I guess there's no oil here. So we'll pick up the rig tomorrow and go drill somewhere else."
>
> Getty recalled that when he stood covered by the black gold spewing from the ground, he finally understood the wisdom in the old prospector's words. "Knowing where the oil isn't is almost as valuable as knowing where the oil is," he said.

Mistakes tell us where the oil isn't. So we can learn not to drill there anymore. That's valuable information for a leader in setting direction for Leading the Journey.

Am I Working on the Right Stuff? Is There Oil Here?

I continue to question the stuff that flows across my desk. No matter how diligently I work at it, I can still make the mistake of adopting other people's problems. I continue drilling dry hole after dry hole in the same location.

I had another placement situation when I chose the wrong person for the job. Only this time it was years, not months, that I wrestled with what action to take. He was coordinator of one of my major units. I kept him long after the data indicated I should take action. My organization is very decentralized with high employee involvement. He talked a good game about his dedication to continuing and deepening that involvement and decentralization. Deep down I didn't believe it. I chose to ignore my intuition and accept his words, even though I saw signs of creeping centralization and control.

Why did I ignore the warning signs? I was concerned about butting into his domain. I was concerned about my "owing" his responsibilities. After all, I reasoned with myself, just because someone does it different from me isn't reason enough to step in and usurp his responsibility. My concern for working on the right stuff immobilized me.

What leadership lesson did I learn from this mistake? I gained some insight into the proper definition of my leadership role. It's easy to confuse leadership in an intellectual capitalism world with abdication. As his customer I needed to play a more active role in defining what great performance I wanted from him. As the leader I also needed to be more proactive in defining the direction for the organization so he could more precisely define his great performance.

Am I Doing the Right Stuff for the Right Reasons?

In the situation mentioned above I worried often over whether I was intervening for the wrong reason. I kept asking myself, "Am I stepping in because he isn't doing a good job or because I want to try out my newest and latest ideas?" If I were motivated to move him aside because I wanted to try out my ideas, that would be the wrong reason to act. My moral dilemma further paralyzed me.

This wasn't the first time that ethical/moral question had arisen. That question is never far from the surface. When I decide to intervene in a situation, the question plagues me, "Am I intervening because I want to exercise my ego or because the situation demands my expertise?"

That question forces me to think about my potential contribution to the situation. If my knowledge and insight are crucial to the outcome, then the "Do I intervene?" answer is affirmative. If not, then I butt out. I do not rely exclusively on myself to answer the "Do we intervene?" question. I ask others whose opinions I value and trust. They help me do a reality check.

Falling down and Getting up Is As Much a Part of Skiing as Schussing and Cutting

I learned to ski in middle age. My ego was particularly threatened when I watched seven-year-olds ski effortlessly down the hill while I spent most of my time watching them from a prone position. One of the many times I quit in disgust, my instructor said, "Learning how to fall down and get up again is as much a part of skiing as cutting and schussing. You can't learn the latter without first learning the former." Wise words, I learned as I schussed down the hill.

Several years ago a CEO I know wrote eleven principles to guide his multibillion-dollar company. Rule number seven was "I expect everyone to make ten mistakes a day, but I expect originality in those mistakes." His message was clear. Making mistakes was no crime. Not learning from them was. As the pace of change picked up he later revised those principles. He wrote, "They're gaining on us. We need to make more mistakes so we can learn more, faster."

Mistakes Trigger Learning

On my journey I've learned to keep using mistakes to stimulate my learning. Mistakes are road signs along the journey which read, "Learning opportunity ahead."

Mistakes are the servomechanisms of life. I used to fight or fear them. When I learned to use them to trigger my own learning, both I and my company made progress.

I even formed a "Mistake of the Month Club" to stimulate discussions about mistakes made and learning from them. I offered a "Shot in the Foot Award" for the person who made the biggest mistake from which he/she learned the most. It was a coffee cup cast in the form of a foot with a hole in it. I was determined to have individuals see mistakes as an opportunity to learn and try again, not as an act against God's law. I am committed and encourage others to commit to seek great performance and not necessarily perfection.

QUESTION:
Am I making enough mistakes and learning enough from them?

LEADERSHIP SOLUTION:
Mistakes are learning opportunities—seize them.

CHAPTER 39

Great Teacher #2:
Fear

As the animal moves through its hostile environment, it senses danger. Immediately, adrenaline is released into the body. The heart beats faster. The eyes widen to see more clearly. All systems rush to a "DEFCON 4" heightened state of readiness. The principal driving force for this increased level of performance? Fear.

In the human animal fear produces all of these physiological responses. So does excitement. Even though fear and excitement trigger very similar physiological phenomena, we perceive fear negatively and excitement positively. When we permit the negative emotional feelings of fear to overcome us, we miss out on great learning opportunities which excitement presents us.

Deeply held beliefs about change are the basis for fear. We can learn to neutralize fear, and stimulate the positive effects of excitement, by redefining beliefs. Learn to seize these moments of excitement as you Lead the Journey.

We Learn Fear at Our Mother's Knee

Well-meaning and loving parents taught us to be afraid. They used fear to teach us what to avoid and what to do. Can't you hear your parents telling you, "Don't run into the street." "Don't talk to strangers." "Mind your manners."

We learned early and often to be afraid. We were particularly taught to be afraid of anything new or different. The Rogers and Hammerstein words from *South Pacific* say it well: "You've got to be taught before it's too late. You've got to be taught before you're seven or eight. To hate all the things your relatives hate. You've got to be carefully taught."

Do you wonder why someone's face tightens up when you talk about doing things differently? It all goes back to their early training. They learned to be afraid of change at their mother's knee.

Why Am I Afraid?

When I recently reorganized one of my units, I found myself not sleeping very well. I'd get up in the middle of the night in a cold sweat with some vague sense of foreboding. After my physician thoroughly eliminated the possibilities of heart problems and ulcers, I decided that my symptoms must have something to do with the reorganization.

I asked myself, "Why am I afraid?" The answers came in a rush, and were not surprising. "Did I do the right thing?" "Can I really manage this business this way, or will I be dragged into the day-to-day problems?" "Will the people really support this change, or will there be a palace revolution?" "Am I meddling just for the sake of meddling?" And the big one: "Will it really work?"

Fear was waking me in the middle of the night. Fear of making a mistake. Fear of looking foolish. Fear of losing respect.

This was not a new experience for me. I've had it before many times: the night before I went skiing, the night before a particularly important presentation, the night before I had that important date. Fear was a familiar visitor in my tent.

The "They" Cover-up

I see fear daily in the people with whom I work. I get told regularly, "I'm in favor of change. I think this is a great idea. But 'they' will be opposed to it." I've come to believe that "they" are a manifestation of the individual's fear. "They" are a legitimate reason not to do something different.

The "Nothing but the Facts, Ma'am" Cover-up

I worked with the management of a small semiconductor company. The president was enthusiastic about doing things in a different way. The company hadn't introduced a new product in three years. Its market share and margins had been falling for five years. Its profit was so low this current year that they were in violation of several bank covenants. He saw the urgent necessity to do something different.

Many members of his management team, however, urged caution. "We need to know more about this new system. Has it worked anyplace else like our company? We know it's worked in a sausage factory, but we don't make sausage. We know it's worked in a software firm, but we don't have computer types around here. Has any semiconductor company, with our level of sales, in our labor market, made it work? If not, how can we be certain that it can work in our company? Anyway, we're not certain our people can master this new way. After all, we have so much to do already, the organization will just break down if we add more stress to it."

Listen to fear running rampant. Whose fear? The management's fear of something new and different. The not-so-secret agenda: slow down or derail the president's effort by raising all kinds of objections. Fear appears in many disguises, with many different faces, and speaks with many different voices.

The "Factual Vomit" Cover-up

Oftentimes people overwhelm you with data when they are afraid. It's a safe way to oppose something and still appear to be supportive of it. I ran into this defense in a recent client meeting.

I encountered difficulty with the COO. He was a very smart individual who was fundamentally opposed to leading in a noncontrolling manner. He liked being the head buffalo. It worked for him and he saw little reason to change his ways. He knew he couldn't directly oppose the president, who was in favor of the new leadership paradigm.

When participating in the discussion, the COO would always give extensive input. He occupied better than 60 percent of the total air-time. His comments always were chock-full of details and facts. He'd repeat conversations in detail, authoritatively recite cost and sales numbers, and quote from customer letters. By the time he finished, summarizing what he'd said was difficult, because he'd said so much.

In fact, I noticed that he almost never answered a question directly. Once I decided to time him, so I asked him, "What do you think about the great performance standards your people set?" He spent fourteen minutes and never answered the question. I tried again, "On a scale of one to five, with one being great and five being terrible, how would you evaluate their answers?" I got nine minutes of facts and figures but no numbered evaluation.

This man apparently felt he was fighting for his life. He didn't know what would be left for him to do if the company shifted to the intellectual capitalism leadership paradigm. He was concerned about his job, afraid of this new and different process, and the worst part, he was afraid to talk about his fear. Therefore, he verbally vomited over everyone hoping to distract and cover up.

Of What Am I Afraid?

My fears were almost always the same: the fear of looking foolish lying spread-eagle on the ski slope; the fear of looking foolish after forgetting a point during a presentation; the fear of looking foolish when picking "her" up and standing there tongue tied when her father asked a question. You can see that my fear of looking foolish is the fear of not knowing what to do in a new and different situation.

Something more is involved, though. Why should looking foolish be so bad? It happens to all of us. And besides, who's going to see you on the ski slopes? And who cares? Who's really going to know when you forget to make a point in a presentation? Does her dad really expect you to be calm, confident, and self-assured?

That "something" is deeper. Remember the phrase "I was so embarrassed I could have died." Have you felt it? Perhaps that's the real fear. If we really screw up bad enough, maybe . . . ? Or worse than death, maybe no one will pay attention to me anymore. The programming goes deep because it started early and gets reinforced often.

In an organizational setting, like the semiconductor company, the fear of organizational "death" is involved. The subtle litany in the brain goes something like this: "What will happen to me if we turn over major decisions to the people? Will I lose my job? If I have a job, what will I be doing? Will I be able to do it? What will people think of me in my new role? Will I lose my status? My perks? My salary?" The blood rushes. The adrenaline pumps. The eyes widen. And the heels dig in. "They will never be able to handle this," the cover-up words spill out, fooling no one.

What's the Worst Thing That Could Happen to Me—and What Can I Do About It if It Does?

When fear gripped my heart, I learned to ask the question that heads this section. This question focuses the fear and makes it more manageable. Not surprisingly, I most often discover that the worst that can happen isn't nearly as terrible as I initially feared, and I can do much to cope successfully with it if it does.

In my recent reorganization, I asked myself the "What's the worst thing that can happen?" question. I found that the worst thing that could happen would be a palace revolution. The people could rise up and say, "You fool. You made another stupid mistake. Things were going along fine until you messed it up." If that happened, I knew that I could turn that potential disaster into an advantage by asking the people, "How would you handle the situation now?" and getting them to own the responsibility for making a success out of the current situation.

In the semiconductor business I asked the "What is the worst thing that could happen?" question. I discovered that many managers were afraid of looking foolish because they couldn't execute the new coaching responsibilities, or they would be fired and never be given the opportunity to do them at all. I helped the managers define the education and training they needed to become competent in executing their new responsibilities. I also helped the president put together a severance package which treated terminated people with dignity.

Examining the worst possible scenario and seeing that there are creative ways to deal with it successfully helps to reduce the fear of the new and the different.

Actions Destroy Fear

Knowing you can do it isn't enough, however. You actually have to do it. When you fall off the bicycle, the best way to conquer your fear is to get right back on again.

When I began to reorganize, I called all the people together and shared my concerns and fears about whether I was doing the "right" thing, along with my vision for what the "right" thing would be. Sharing my fear helped to both disarm any opposition and to avoid cover-up behavior. The vision of a better tomorrow helped people respond very favorably. One group even applauded when I announced the change. Several other groups said, "It's about time." So, many of my fears were groundless. I learned that's also typical. I worry more than I need.

Use Fear to Increase Performance

Fear is a wonderful stimulant. It quickens the mind, sharpens the senses, heightens performance. I've learned to focus the stimulant on doing better, rather than worrying about doing worse.

When fear runs through my system, I ask myself, "What can I do to remove the potential causes of failure?" "What can I do to ensure success?" I've evolved rituals to answer these questions constructively.

When I have a speech to give, I'm up early, rehearsing the first few lines of each major point in the shower. I show up early to check out the microphone and the room for sound. I walk back and forth across the stage to get a feel for where things are onstage, load my slides and run through them to check both their proper positioning and to take another opportunity to rehearse. I review my notes, working to word-associate the names of key people so I can remember to personalize the facts and give credit publically to those who earned it. While the person is giving my introduction, I rehearse my first few lines. Throughout the process, fear and excitement are coursing through my veins, causing heightened awareness for performance.

When I have to make a difficult decision, such as the reorganization decision, I follow a similar ritual. I mentally identify who's likely to feel or want what, and how my proposal will or won't meet their needs. I rehearse what I will say when they respond. I mentally reexamine the alternatives. I reexamine my own rationale for making the decision and ask myself why it is valid. I plan how I'll keep myself alert to the first twinges of fear and what I'll do to dispel it when it comes, as it always does.

Leaders face fear all the time. It's a permanent part of the leader's job. Use fear as a stimulant, not a limitation, for performance. Understanding and accepting these realities will help you learn faster, and Lead the Journey more effectively.

QUESTION:
What's the worst thing that can happen and how can I handle it?

LEADERSHIP SOLUTION:
Use your fear to mobilize your resources and stimulate your performance.

CHAPTER 40

Great Teacher #3:
Anger

The ears burn. The eyes narrow. The frenetic pace of finger tapping increases. The teeth grind. I am angry. I feel it. I know it. Why do I get angry with that person, that topic, that situation? The answer to those questions tells me about myself, my best contributions to my organizations, and what I need to learn to Lead the Journey.

One of my greatest teachers is my own anger, because it helps me learn more about myself as a leader. What I get angry about is what I need to learn more about. As tough as that insight is to swallow and digest, it is very valuable to my learning.

What About You Reminds Me of What I Don't Like About Me?

Some time ago I had a partner named Ben who was a good salesman. He sold franchises for my learning center business. The education and business side was my responsibility, and the selling and marketing side was his. It was a good partnership, I thought, at least until I discovered more about it.

Very soon after we formed the partnership and launched our expansion efforts, I found myself being angry at almost everything Ben did. I criticized his choice of franchisees, doubted his expense bills, and worried about his ability to deal with superintendents of schools. Of course, I never raised these issues with Ben directly. Doing so wouldn't be partnerly. I just let my blood pressure rise and my teeth grind down a little.

One day at a seminar I heard the presenter report on Abraham Maslow's theory that "what you don't like in someone else is a reflection of what you dislike about yourself." The light bulb went on in my mind. What was it about Ben that reminded me about myself? The answers weren't very complimentary. Ben was loud, frequently bragging about something he'd done. He liked to show off and be the center of attention. Ben was a lot like me. By looking through the prism of what I didn't like about Ben I saw more clearly things I needed to improve about my own leadership behavior.

Because I didn't like the leadership picture of me I saw, I committed myself to change. I determined to turn down the volume, reduce bragging and name-dropping. I endeavored to reduce the use of the word "I" and substitute the word "we." I committed to focus on other people's contribution and downplay my own.

In an effort to kill two birds with one stone, or more precisely, tone down two loud braggarts at the same time, I enlisted Ben to help me accomplish my changes. I asked him to watch me for loud bragging and self-centered kinds of behaviors. I arranged a signal for him to tip me off when I was slipping into the unwanted behaviors. I shared with him that I wanted to change because I believed that loud braggarts wouldn't be successful in our business. I hoped that having Ben work with me on changing me would also help him change.

I wish I could report a success story here. Unfortunately, I can't. I worked on my change plan, and I think I succeeded to some degree, although not as much as I needed. I found that practicing the new behavior consistently was much more difficult than I imagined. I tended to slip back all too frequently. But Ben was still Ben. He didn't change at all, and I found myself still in a perpetual state of anger with him.

Elicit the Right Help in Changing— Some Help Is No Help at All

I gained several leadership insights from this experience. Changing leadership behavior without lots of the right kind of help is very difficult. Ben was the wrong person to help. He wasn't around enough to give me consistent feedback, and he wasn't observant enough to catch me doing my "act." Since he didn't think the behavior style was so bad to begin with, he was not committed to my improvement. He did not subscribe to my premise that this behavior style would be dysfunctional in the business. My effort to work on both him and me together resulted in neither of us getting the help we needed.

As I changed my leadership behavior, I became angrier at Ben for his lack of change. The less I bragged, the more I resented his bragging. Have you ever noticed how a new convert is the most dedicated to conversion? The person who has just given up smoking is the most intolerant of smokers.

Focus on Performance to Overcome Anger

Ben was a valuable contributor to our company. I couldn't let my anger rob us of his contribution. I had to learn how to live with him and control my anger. Once again, questions came to the rescue. I asked myself, "What is the performance I want from Ben, and am I getting it?" When I focused on performance, it helped me deal with my anger. With this focus, I was able to separate the personal emotional issues from the performance ones.

Anger Sends the Message "It's Time to Confront the Situation"

Recognizing that I was unable to change Ben made me even angrier. First I thought I was angry at Ben. "Why can't he see the need to change?" I kept asking myself. The answers that came when I was in that state of mind were simple. They all revolved around Ben and his stupidity, his insensitivity, his rigidity. To blame Ben was easy, and that absolved me. I'd be great, if only he would be different.

Eventually, I realized that the "blame Ben" answer wasn't working. I consulted the "man in the mirror" and saw that my anger was a reflection of my unwillingness to confront Ben. I preferred the private suffering to taking public action. My anger was calling on me to act.

I've had many Bens in my life. Only recently have I learned to listen to the message my anger is sending me and, as a leader, confront the issues rather than stay secretly mad about them. Sometimes I discovered that my perceptions were wrong. Most of the time I discovered that open confrontation and discussion of the issues resulted in swift improvement.

Anger tells a leader that he/she is shirking responsibilities. He/she is avoiding facing up to key performance issues. Anger is the red warning light that says, "Engine needs service."

Anger Tells Us We're the Wrong Person in the Wrong Place

Some situations trigger anger. I sit in meetings and hear myself thinking, "What am I doing here? Why am I putting up with this junk? How much longer can I take this?" Yet, when I look around, everyone else seems to be enjoying the game. What's wrong? Why am I so angry when no one else is? I learned to ask, "What is causing my anger in this situation?"

I think it's my impatience. I see, or I think I see, what needs to be done and I want to move on to the action phase. While others seem not to be ready yet, I sit and stew, and stew, and stew in frustration.

One situation that illustrates this issue involved a hiring decision. I saw three candidates and selected the first one as my choice. "Why waste time seeing more?" I asked. "Maybe there is someone better in the next batch," several people responded. "Yeah, and maybe there's a man in the moon," I thought to myself. "Okay, let's keep looking for a little while longer," I agreed.

Five weeks and four more candidates later, my frustration had reached the boiling point. At the weekly meeting I exploded, "Have we turned enough corners to satisfy ourselves that the perfect person isn't waiting around the next one." "Absolutely" was the answer. "Now let's talk about who's the best candidate." We chose candidate number five, one of the ones I interviewed after I wanted to stop. That person has done and continues to do an outstanding job. She was the right one, and I would have missed her had I not continued looking.

What did I learn about my leadership role? My anger said more about me personally and about my most productive role in the situation than it said about the process of selection. The process of selection was a good one. My anger would short-circuit the process and result in a less than best choice.

I forced myself to ask more relevant questions. Did I belong there in the first place? Was participation in this selection process really part of my job? Was this great performance for me? Was participation in this process my highest and best contribution to great performance for the organization? When the anger subsided, I realized the answer to all of those questions was a resounding "No!" My anger told me, again, that as a leader I was owning the wrong responsibilities and not contributing to great performance either for myself or for the organization.

Anger Is Fear in Another Disguise

At its root, I discovered, anger is fear in another disguise. Why was I angry at Ben? I was *afraid* that he would ruin my business. Why was I angry during the selection process? I was *afraid* that I would waste too much time and not get to the "important" items I felt I had to do. I was also *afraid* that without me the best person wouldn't get chosen. The fear, a.k.a. anger, showed me my lack of faith in both the process and the people. Anger was revealing my fears and raising them to an action level.

I'm Mad as Hell and Won't Take It Anymore

Most important, I learned that anger is a trigger to action. Sometimes, until leaders get mad enough to act, nothing really happens.

I recently spent some time with the president of a midsize construction-related company. He wanted his organization to be different. He defined great performance as doubled market share, tripled margins, and perfect quality delivered to the customer. He then wanted to step back and "let the management council decide."

I made the mistake of taking the assignment. I met three times with the management council. Three days later they were still debating the standards of great performance—for example, whether doubling the market share or increasing by 80 percent should be the goal. I finally met with the president again. It was clear to me now that this was an intellectual exercise for him. He wanted to see if it was possible to get his team to buy in. He personally didn't know whether 80 percent or 100 percent was the right goal. Moreover, he would accept the current situation exactly as it was.

The president's level of anger at the current situation hadn't yet reached the action level. I gave back his retainer. He wasn't ready to use my services.

QUESTION:
What is my anger telling me that I need to learn about myself and what I'm doing?

LEADERSHIP SOLUTION:
Listen to your anger and learn from it.

CHAPTER 41

Great Teacher #4: Stubbornness

Stand up for What You Believe

My parents taught me to be firm. I can still hear my father saying, "Stand up for what you believe." I knew I had to be firm in my beliefs. A famous author wrote, "It's a funny thing about life; if you refuse to accept anything but the best, you very often get it." He also wrote, "Most progress is made by unreasonable men." Early on, I determined to be an unreasonable man who accepted nothing less than the best, in myself and others.

My unreasonable firmness and stubbornness give me power and tenacity for a cause. Therein lies both my strength and my weakness. Firmness works for me when I have the right cause. Therefore, my task was to identify the right cause, and learn when to abandon the wrong ones.

Stubborn for the Wrong Cause: *MY* Ideas to the Exclusion of All Others

For too long I stubbornly believed that I had the answers and unyield-ingly insisted that people follow my way. The head buffalo stubbornly believed that he was right. Here's one situation where I held out for my ideas and caused a big problem.

One office was a good, but not great, performer. While I knew that it could do better, I had other fires raging which urgently demanded my attention. The situation might have gone on for a long time, except that one day we were fired by a longtime customer of that office. It was crisis time.

We held a big meeting. I was right in there telling the herd what to do. The group had all kinds of rationales for why they lost the account. They insisted that it wasn't their fault, how we were better off without that "headache," and how they were going to replace the volume with other, better customers. I listened for a while and then said, "Look, we can't afford to lose this customer. We must get them back. What are we going to do to get them back?"

Then I told the group what to do. They went to work following the guidelines I laid out. They made a number of significant changes. Several times the office staff tried to wiggle off the hook. I wouldn't let them. Within a few months we got back the customer. I smiled to myself: score one for stubbornness.

As usual with my head-buffalo stories this one does not have a happy ending. The changes were not permanent, and within six months we had another problem, followed by still others. The buffalo were struggling. My dogged insistence on having it my way produced short-term results and long-term problems. My stubbornness did not serve my interests.

Stubborn for the Wrong Cause.
My Way or the Highway Most Often Results
in the Highway for Everyone

This message came home to me as I struggled with another performance problem. I just knew I had the right answer and obstinately insisted on it despite the protestations of the local management. Finally in a fit of anger, I said those magic words: "Look, I don't mean to be unreasonable but, in the final analysis, it's my way or the highway." The local manager chose the highway, leaving me with the privilege of doing it my way. My way not only did not work, it was an absolute failure. The local manager was right. I closed the office, suffered large losses, and learned a very valuable leadership lesson. Stubbornly sticking to "my way" often means "the highway" for me.

Don't Get Personal—It's Too Expensive

A speakers' bureau booked me to give a speech with a newly organized professional training group. They had big plans and a little budget. As with many entrepreneurial ventures, this one failed before my scheduled speech. The president of the failed group called me asking for a return of her deposit, since she was canceling the program. The deposit was paid to the speakers' bureau. Furthermore, the contract was between the speakers' bureau, not me, and the training group.

The bureau's representative felt he did everything possible to help the president succeed, yet was rejected at every turn. He did his job. He felt that her ineptness had cost him a lot of time and energy, not to mention money. He wanted to keep the fee.

My policy is to keep only those fees I earn. Thus, I wanted to refund the advance. The longer the conversation went on, the clearer it became that the bureau representative was personally involved in punishing the training group president. The agency's policy was to refund advances, except in unusual circumstances. The representative felt that this was an "unusual" circumstance.

I've learned as a leader that often I wrap personal issues in an organizational disguise. I stubbornly dig in on the organizational issues when I am really bothered by the personal issues. Stubbornness often signals to me that I may be disguising my real concerns.

Stubborn for the Right Cause—Delighting Customers

Over time I've learned some of the right causes about which to be firm, tenacious, and persistent. Heading the list of the "right" causes is delighting customers. A situation involving one of my daughters' business illustrates this point.

One of her bigger customers was a problem. In what is traditionally a cash business, he paid monthly, and recently stretched it out to six or seven weeks. The biggest problem, however, was his practice of questioning every item on every bill—usually only after she called to collect on the overdue account. He returned an average of 30 percent of his orders, saying they were either defective (she has yet to find a defect) or the wrong part. This "churning" cost her in two ways. She was stuck with unsalable inventory because some of the material was special-ordered for him, and the costs in handling the material twice and processing the double paperwork reduced her margins.

We talked about the situation. She assured me that it wasn't a "personal" thing with her. "It's strictly a business matter, Dad. He's 5 percent of my business, so I need him. But the way he handles his account robs me of my margins. What should I do?"

She decided to change the basis of the conversation. Now she was in the adversarial "pay me for what you owe me" mode. This was a no-win situation, which would inevitably lead to losing the customer. Rather, I suggested that she sit down with him and work out a more productive relationship built around the question "How can I help you be more successful and how can you help me be more successful?"

She talked to the store owner. After some stewing, since he wasn't sure she really meant it and she wasn't certain that he'd follow through, they reached an accommodation. The driver reviews the bill with the store owner when the material is delivered. The store owner gives the driver a six-week postdated check for the agreed-upon amount. In return for a 5 percent discount, from the newly raised base price, he agreed to make no returns except for truly defective parts. Thus far, the agreement is working. Another victory for determinedly standing up for the customer.

Leaders stubbornly stand up for delighting customers. Keep asking the LTJ questions "What do your customers want?" "How can you validate that that's actually what they want?" "What are you going to do to deliver great performance to delight your customer?"

Stubborn for Another Right Cause—Getting the Right People to Own the Right Responsibility

I'm also absolutely stubborn about locating the ownership in the right place. Compromise on that issue significantly reduces the likelihood of great performance.

While working with one company, I allowed the president to avoid responsibility for Leading the Journey. He begged off, saying that his presence would dampen other people's participation. I charged forward meeting with his direct reports, who also begged off from leading the next step, using the same excuse as the president. Since I was caught up in the process, I failed to notice the pattern, and kept moving. To shorten a long, sad story, four months into the process, I realized that changes weren't happening as fast or as completely as we needed. I misplaced the responsibility for Leading the Journey. I had not insisted that those who had to be responsible for making the Journey work, take responsibility for it. I went back and redid a lot of work in order to patch up the process and get the president and senior managers owning the responsibilities for execution. I righted the wrong, but it cost me months.

In that situation, I wasn't stubborn enough. However, I learned. Consequently, I recently turned down a consulting assignment because the president refused to lead the process with his people.

Stubborn for Another Right Cause— Great Performance

There's another cause that's worthy of a leader's stubbornness: great performance. In too many instances, people are willing to "settle" for average, okay, or good performance. They want to avoid the stress and strain and unknown of "great" performance. I won't let them off the hook in my organization. I've learned to ask a set of Leading the Journey questions:

- What is the world-class standard for this kind of work in our industry?
- What is the world-class standard for this kind of work in any industry?
- What is the best-of-all-worlds performance that our customers demand?

QUESTION:
Am I stubborn for me or my customers?

LEADERSHIP SOLUTION:
Stand for customers, ownership, and great performance—not ego.

CHAPTER 42

Great Teacher #5:
Divorce

For Everything There Is a Season

Nothing in the business world is forever. Things change. Circumstances change. The product that was a star last year is a dog this year. People change. The person who was the best performer given yesterday's requirement is unsuitable given today's requirements.

Change happens as a normal part of the cycles of life: product life cycles, person life cycles, organization life cycles. The Bible says, "For everything there is a season," which means for everything there is an ending. We can't change the fact that there are endings, but we can change how we handle these endings.

In truth, I didn't do a good job of handling the inevitable endings in my business life. Terminations always felt like a divorce, and that seemed to me to be a failure of my leadership. When I learned to see these divorces as completions, I learned to use it as a leadership tool. My perspective enabled me to set standards for the organization to specify acceptable behavior.

Beware the Ego Trap

I was the biggest problem in handling inevitable divorce. My ego often got in the way, and my emotions led me down blind alleys.

In one situation, I had a long-term employee problem. My book-keeper, who was there at the birth of the organization, worked hard. She was dedicated and loyal. At first she worked part-time, because that's all the business could afford, then full-time as it grew. She became accountant, then chief accountant, then controller. Then chief financial officer. She held the title, but behind that big desk sat a bookkeeper in heart and mind. The business had outgrown her.

I built around her by hiring talented people as her direct reports. She was more than willing to work with these people, who knew much more than she did. Everyone in the company dealt directly with the specialists. Because I felt I owed her for her hard work during the difficult early days, I couldn't move her. I talked with myself at length about it, but could never bring myself to take any corrective action. My ego was fully involved. As usual I was owning the wrong responsibility. I was busy playing rescuer. Left to me, the situation might have burned a hole in my stomach, and my pocket-book, forever.

Beware Sleeping with Corpses

In another situation, I found myself committed to a business relationship with a certain customer in the wire mill business. We supplied the ink coloring for their wire coatings. They were a relatively small account, but they were our first customer in their segment. They took a chance with us when no one else would, and became a reference site which helped us secure additional business.

I struck the deal with the father who started this family-owned business. We played golf together and enjoyed a friendly business relationship. After several years, the father turned over the business to his MBA-trained son, who was friendly but less personal. He drove hard to lower costs and he pushed us hard to lower our prices. He kept insisting upon "special deals." He became our most expensive customer to sell and service. Our cost records indicated that we were actually losing money to maintain his account.

The people who sold and serviced his account came to me and wanted to either raise his prices substantially or drop him as a customer. Their bonuses were based on margins, and his account was costing them earnings. I argued against doing it. "How can you fire one of your oldest and best customers, the guy who got you started in the business in the first place? Where's your loyalty, your heart?" I asked the people. Chagrined and embarrassed, they left with their heads hung low in frustration.

Of course, this customer deserved to be fired. The times and people had changed. The people I dealt with, who dealt so fairly with me, were gone. Without seeing the way things are now, I was hanging on to the way things used to be. There was a need for an ending to a relationship that had long since died. Only my emotions prevented me from seeing the season had ended. Like the king of ancient Spain who slept with the corpse of his dead wife for years, I had allowed my emotions to blind my good judgment.

You Can Fire Anyone—Even a Family Member

I struggled with this divorce issue in both my business and my family. One of my sons is an alcoholic. Living at home, he was enjoying all the protections and comforts which shielded him from the consequences of his abusive drinking. We did everything we could as parents to help him. We talked with him. We urged treatment. We paid for additional schooling. We physically took him to treatment, paying thousands of dollars to fix his problem. We did it all and it didn't work. He continued to drink, sometimes staying out for days at a time, and flunked out of school. He was a serious problem, but he was our child and we had to handle it.

Finally, after he returned from a four-day bout of drinking, we had finally reached a new conclusion. We couldn't control his drinking, but we could set standards for our own home. After he sobered up, we sat down with him and put him on final warning. We told him that he could no longer live there and drink. The next time he didn't come home, we were throwing out all of his belongings. The only way back into the house then would be through a treatment program in which he chose to participate and from which he "graduated" with at least forty-five days of sobriety.

He tested us three days later, when he did not come home. We swallowed hard, cried a lot, and put out his belongings. Five days later he called us from a residential program where he had enrolled. At this writing, two and one-half years of sobriety later, he is a working, fully employed contributor to society.

The first step in handling a divorce is to gather up the courage to act. In AA terms, this is called "hitting bottom." I've learned some ways to "raise the bottom" so the fall isn't quite so far.

Back to Basics

I've learned that one of the best ways to deal with divorce is to get back in touch with the basic principles and philosophies that guide my life. All too often, the emotional heat from a potential divorce melts my resolve There are several basic principles to which I return to get me out of the emotional and ego trap posed by a pending divorce.

Get the Divorcee to Be Responsible for the Divorce

In the case of the misplaced bookkeeper it is clear in retrospect that I was owning the responsibility for her performance. I thought that I owed it to her to protect her. I felt that she couldn't handle the situation on her own. How wrong I was.

One day she asked to have lunch with me, a very unusual request given the informal nature of the organization. At that lunch she confessed that she was absolutely miserable and felt useless. She was embarrassed by her lack of contribution. She wanted to look elsewhere for a job. I was stunned. And relieved.

Here was my opportunity and I seized the moment. "What do you think you really can, and want to, do?" I asked her. That triggered a lengthy discussion. She wasn't certain about her talents or interests. I suggested that she take some career counseling and talk with her customers in the company to get their views on her potential contribution. I confessed that I too didn't believe that she was doing the CFO job. I suggested that there may be some other tasks she could do in the organization, then deferred to her to think some more about it and gather some additional data. Both of us walked away believing that forty-dollar lunch was the best investment we'd ever made.

Within a week she came back to me with her decision. She decided to return to school full-time (at the age of forty-four) and seek a BBA and an MBA in accounting. She had saved up the money and refused my offer of financial assistance. "You've already given me an abundance of support," she said.

She returned to school, got her degrees, and is now working as a CPA for one of the big accounting firms. She's very pleased about her career and talks frequently with me and the others in the organization. She has even volunteered her time to help us update some of our cost systems.

She helped me learn an important leadership lesson. Keep the responsibility for performance with the performer. I gave her the opportunity to be responsible for her own future. She chose to leave us because she could see better opportunity for herself, and greater personal fulfillment elsewhere. I didn't have to fire her. She fired herself, and loved it, and me, for giving her the opportunity! This divorce was easy because both parties recognized that the cycle was complete.

Great Performance Discussions Raise the Bottom

I've learned that to initiate a divorce I don't have to wait until the individual is failing. Continuing conversations about great performance are often triggers for positive divorce.

In one situation, we had an above-average performer as a site manager. She was very popular with her teammates, and her location did a creditable financial job. Nothing would have happened had this been a "normal" business. In fact, she probably would have been rewarded for above-average performance. But we are not run like a typical company.

Every six months everyone defines great performance for himself/

herself over the coming six-month period. These definitions are worked out in conjunction with internal and external customers. In the course of this activity, several significant discrepancies appeared between her definitions of great performance and those of her teammates and end-user customers. How the site manager saw her job was very different from her teammates' view. They wanted more coaching and coordination help from her. Her end-user customers wanted more technical guidance and support from her. She saw her job as a much more passive role than her customers did.

Efforts to work out these discrepancies failed. The site manager decided that since she couldn't or wouldn't meet the expectations of her customers she resigned her position and returned to being a member of her product/market team. She told me, "I feel bad about losing the position. But I'd rather have a job I can do my way and know that I'm being successful than take some other job and get into conflicts."

I learned two important leadership lessons from this experience. First, customers play a key role in surfacing issues that may lead to a divorce. All too often, I rush in to be the carrier of bad news about performance. While I don't like doing it, I somehow think it's my responsibility. I've discovered that customers are a much more credible source of performance information. Getting customers to say, "I want this. I don't accept that," is an excellent way to introduce reality and authority into performance discussions.

Second, the stream of continuing conversations about great performance serves as an early-warning signal to potential causes of divorce. Because the performers are involved in the discussions, they see these signals first and are in the best position to act on them. These great performance discussions serve as a feet-forward device to warn of potential endings ahead. They also keep the responsibility for acting where it belongs—between the performer and the customer. Only when these parties cannot agree does the leader need to step in.

Managing Backward from the Future Encourages Constructive Endings

Thinking strategically also helps to pinpoint divorces in the making. In handling the customer problem mentioned before, managing backward from the future is exactly what we eventually decided to do. It became apparent to me that the group was right and I was wrong. I really couldn't afford to be blinded by sentimentality for what once was. We really didn't want and couldn't afford this customer.

I urged the group to engage the customer in a thinking-strategically exercise. As practice, I asked the group to create a best-of-all-worlds great performance scenario, from both our perspective and the customer's. They saw the significant differences between them. They talked about some ways, from our perspective, that they might narrow the gap. But all of this was practice for confronting the customer. If he refused to participate, then we felt free to refuse to sell to him.

The group met with the customer and went through the process. He saw a very different future relationship than the group wanted. It was easy to agree to divorce once the widely discrepant desires were on the table. They parted friends.

Several years later he sought them out and wanted to resurrect the relationship. They once again went through the thinking-strategically process with him and identified what both sides needed to do to make the relationship work. Today he's still a small customer in our business. But we've established a more personal relationship, which the group finds more satisfying. In fact, the group that works with him helped him do the thinking-strategically process with his senior managers.

Use the Divorce to Send the "This Is What We Believe" Message

I learned in the customer case discussed just above that *how* you handle the divorce is as important as the completion itself. My thinking-strategically approach sent a message: "We are seriously interested in being your partner." That message reverberated throughout the segment and we won several important jobs because we established our credibility as a partner. Our actions spoke so clearly that they drowned out the other competitors' words.

Moreover, I learned that my willingness to confront poor performance sends the message that we care about ourselves and our standards. My offer to support the misplaced bookkeeper also sent the "I care about you" message.

Notice how divorce can contribute to the intellectual capitalism leadership task:

- Establishing direction (business partnership in the segment)
- Eliminating obstacles (getting myself and my ego out of the way)
- Developing ownership (the group did the customer discussion, not I)
- Taking self-directed actions that send the clear message about standards of acceptable and nonacceptable behavior

QUESTION:
How can I use this divorce to stimulate important learning about what it takes to be successful?

LEADERSHIP SOLUTION:
Endings can be beginnings—when they are handled correctly.

CHAPTER 43

The Eternal Circle: Doing, Learning, Changing

Business Is a Metaphor for Life

Business reflects, and is a reflection of, life. How we handle business is how we handle life. Business *is* life. When things went well for me in business, they went well for me in life. When things turned down for me in business, you can guess what happened in my personal life.

I learned to see business as a metaphor from which I could learn. As I learned to think strategically, beginning with the end in mind, I saw the application in my family.

We recently adopted a grandson, who had a tough life before he came to us. We wanted to give him a better opportunity. Yet I had learned from business that you can't "give" people things and have them value the things they get. They only value the things they earn.

I sat down with our grandson and talked with him about what he wanted. Initially, the conversations were about "toys," highly visible toys like Nintendo and Corvettes. When he didn't have any idea how you got those things, I took him to the store, showed him the prices, and asked him how much money he'd have to earn to buy them. He was particularly impressed with a $50,000 Corvette. He was amazed to see how much things cost and was not able to comprehend how to acquire them.

Soon the conversations switched to how to make the money needed to buy the toys he wanted. This led to discussions about education and college, and an opportunity to talk about what it costs to go to college. Subsequently, we discussed what it takes to be admitted to a good college.

All of this was eye-opening. Thinking strategically helped him start to understand some of the realities of what it took to get what he wanted. He began to build commitment to do whatever it takes to get what he wants.

The process I used with our grandson is similar to the process I use in my company. In Leading the Journey, I constantly urge people to dream the dream, step out of their box to see beyond the horizon of the current situation. To establish direction, I push them to confront the realities of what it will take to achieve what they want, thereby identifying obstacles. I've found, with grandsons and groundskeepers alike, that this process builds ownership and stimulates self-directed action.

This is the essence of the LTJ process I've outlined in this book. Learning to be more effective in executing the four leadership tasks is the best way to create real motivation and commitment both at home and in the office.

The Business of Business Is Learning

Each business situation is a classroom opportunity to learn about ourselves, and about what works and doesn't work. The great teachers in this classroom of business are mistakes, divorce, fear, anger, and stubbornness. In every business setting, these great teachers are present and ready to teach me. Sometimes I am not ready to learn. The lessons are there to see, but I am too often blind. My challenge: Be ready to learn from every situation.

The dominant theme in my life now is learning. Learning more and faster is the only true competitive advantage. I work to instill that love of learning throughout my organization, and my life.

We have several systems that foster that love of learning. We set aside a sum of money for each person to spend any way they wish on their learning. We pay for scuba diving lessons as well as calculus instruction. Learning is learning. Learning the discipline to master scuba diving carries over into mastering the discipline of making better sausage and writing better computer code.

Everyone sets personal development plans, discusses them with their teammates, and publishes them for everyone to see. To participate in the bonus plan, each person must accomplish his/her development plans.

To learn more, faster, is essential to success in the present and the future. People in organizations obsessed with learning will succeed.

Business Is Not a Spectator Sport

I've said it before in many different ways, but it bears repeating again. Leading requires learning. Learning requires doing. So get on with the doing. Then study how you did it. Tony Gwynn, one of the best hitters in the National League, illustrates my point. He never misses an opportunity to practice batting. He videotapes himself and studies the replays to identify how he can improve. He constantly swings, studies, and swings some more, and has a lifetime batting average of .300. His star status is no accident. He earned it.

As a thirsty person seeks out a water fountain, I've learned to seek out experiences. I deliberately put myself in new situations. I'd never dealt with a Japanese company before. When we received an inquiry from a Japanese company, I joined the team making the trip to learn how to do business with Japanese business people. I'd never been behind the former Iron Curtain before. When a business opportunity came up there, I volunteered to take it on so I could learn about doing business in that part of the world.

I actively seek out nonprofit and volunteer activities. It's valuable to see, firsthand, how different people wrestle with the challenge of leading an organization with authority based on knowledge, rather than organizational position. Many of the ideas now at work in my organization came originally from these volunteer and nonprofit organizations.

I feel the urgency to continue learning to lead as the world around me changes at a frenetic pace. I see former hugely successful companies go down in flames. Many talented and competent CEOs, lost in old paradigms, play out their death spiral on the daily news. I still worry about my company's ability to continue to succeed. Anxiety never quite goes away. The only antidote is learning, continually growing my storehouse of knowledge and leadership talents. What is true today I know will not be true tomorrow. Only by learning can I assure myself a place on the stage tomorrow.

Anything Worth Doing Is Worth Doing Now

I worked with one organization that faced a monumental problem, largely of its own making. This company was frequently found among the short list of high-performing organizations. The CEO recognized two years ago that their primary markets were maturing. He embarked on a huge investment in a revolutionary technology. To raise the $2-billion-plus needed to fund the research, he sold off many profitable parts of his company. He wasn't certain that his research staff could meet the beta test delivery date. That's when he called me.

I met with his top research directors. They flew in from the three separate research sites working on the project, one in the Far East, one in Latin America, and one in the United States. The meeting revealed a big surprise for everyone, particularly for the CEO. Unknown to the CEO, each of the three research labs was independently pursuing tasks with little coordination with the others. They had no overall research plan, no milestones established to monitor progress toward a commonly agreed-upon goal. All three were drilling tunnels into the same mountain without any knowledge of where the other two were drilling. If they met, it would be purely by chance.

The CEO was dismayed. "How did this happen? What can I do now?" he asked me. I urged radical and immediate action. "Get all of the senior staff together—the top three levels from all locations," I suggested. "Lock them in a room and don't let them out until they have a plan you can accept, a set of milestones they, and you, can measure with continuing communication fixed among themselves to work out mutual problems."

"I'll do it," he said.